P9-DNB-230

Restructuring the New York City Government

Restructuring the New York City Government: The Reemergence of Municipal Reform

Proceedings of
The Academy of
Political Science

89-485

Volume 37
Number 3

ISSN 0065–0684

Edited by Frank J. Mauro
and Gerald Benjamin

New York, 1989

Contents

THE NEW REFORM AGENDA

Preface

Questions of municipal reform were central to political science during the late nineteenth century, the founding era of the profession, and therefore to the Academy of Political Science in its early years. A review of the first volumes of the *Political Science Quarterly* reveals an interest in every aspect of the progressive agenda for the reconstruction of municipal government in America. In fact, more than a fifth of all the articles published in the 1890s were on reform themes.

Because the Academy was located in New York City, because many of its founding members lived and worked there, and because of the great national importance of New York, special attention was given in the *Political Science Quarterly* and later in the *Proceedings* to the city's governance. Articles on general themes concerning municipal government almost invariably presented examples drawn from New York City experience. But New York City government was also a specific focus. A notable early example is an article by Frank Goodnow in the Fall 1902 issue of the *Political Science Quarterly* concerning the 1901 charter changes, still regarded by experts as the best brief explanation of the effects of "the revolt of the boroughs" in the newly consolidated city. Later, during the great battle for municipal home rule at the 1915 New York State Constitutional Convention, the first issue of the *Proceedings* entirely devoted to the "Government of the City of New York" was published.

In ensuing decades, although occasional articles were published on city government, the Academy largely focused on national and international concerns. A rekindling of interest in municipal reform was signaled by the publication in 1960 of an issue of the *Proceedings* edited by Thomas Peardon on "The Urban Problems." Racial unrest in the mid-1960s intensified concerns about large cities, reflected by the appearance in 1968 of a *Proceedings* on "Urban Riots," edited by Robert H. Connery.

The following year Robert H. Connery and Demetrios Caraley edited the second issue of the *Proceedings* focused on the governance of New York City, "Governing the City: Issues and Options for New York." Additionally, since the mid-1960s, urban politics and policy have been given regular attention in the *Political Science Quarterly*, with some specific attention to New York's political history and practices, to its fiscal crisis in the mid-1970s, and to the politics of race in the city.

The Academy's renewed interest in its home city during the 1960s and 1970s was also reflected in *Proceedings* on the New York Constitutional Convention of 1967 and the record of the Rockefeller administration in state government. Each of these publications, though not directly about city governance, included as a central concern New York City's relationship with the state. Also in recent *Proceedings* the tradition of interest in municipal reform has continued, but now with a focus on specific policy concerns—education and children's issues, for example—and on new approaches to addressing urban problems, such as public-private partnerships and privatization.

In this volume we return more explicitly to structural issues in local governance, reflecting renewed attention throughout the country to these issues among both policymakers and academics. In the course of the research done for the revision of the city charter, the New York City Charter Revision Commission investigated both matters on the traditional reform agenda and more contemporary concerns in urban governance. Traditional issues included mechanisms for effective representation, the design of the local legislature, the degree to which governing power should be centralized or decentralized, the sharing of power among citywide institutions, and mechanisms for land-use decision making. Newer concerns included the effects of federal voting-rights requirements, infrastructure maintenance, strategic planning, conflicts of interest, and campaign finance reform. After reviewing this research, the Academy agreed to edit and publish a number of the papers that were originally prepared for the commission together with several others about the commission's work that were written especially for this collection.

The essays by Briffault, Viteritti, Mauro, Gelfand and Allbritton, Muzzio and Tompkins, Pecorella, Benjamin, Alexander, Bigelow, and Silverman were all revised and, in most cases, substantially condensed versions of papers originally prepared for the commission. Lane's essay was originally prepared for and published by the American Association of Law Schools's *Urban, State and Local Law Newsletter*. The essays by Mauro and Benjamin, Givens, Bailey, and Regan were prepared for this issue of the *Proceedings*.

Frank J. Mauro, director of research for the commission, and Gerald Benjamin, professor of political science at the State University of New York at New Paltz and a principal research advisor to the commission, took on the tremendous task of selecting and editing the material for publication. The Academy is grateful to them for their excellent work, which was accomplished with great diligence and dedication, while, with other staff members, they were doing background research and preparing the charter commission's ballot submissions. We are grateful, as well, for the assistance of the commissions and their chairs, Richard Ravitch and Frederick A. O. Schwarz, Jr.

The intellectual historian Michael H. Frisch reviewed the history of progressive thought in the summer 1982 issue of the *Political Science Quarterly*. He noted that, in the early days of the Academy, political science engaged "the most fundamental questions about the nature and legitimacy of political institutions," but, more recently, "American academic culture is substantially without the sense of obligation to engage and transform the political reality it studies" (p. 315). Insofar as this volume helps return attention to these fundamental governance questions, it both affirms the original purposes of this Academy and helps refocus, in a positive way, the efforts of the interested academic community.

Nonetheless, the views expressed in this volume are those of the authors and not necessarily those of the Academy, the Charter Revision Commission, or any other organizations with which they are associated. The Academy of Political Science, founded in 1880, serves as a forum for the development and dissemination of opinion on public-policy questions. A nonpartisan, not-for-profit organization, it does not make recommendations on political and social issues.

A special note of thanks is due to Pfizer, Inc., and the Charles H. Revson Foundation whose financial contributions helped the Academy to publish this book.

We are also indebted to William V. Farr for his editorial direction of the project and to Stephen H. Weinstein and Adam Karpati for their editorial assistance.

FRANK J. MACCHIAROLA
President

Contributors

HERBERT E. ALEXANDER is professor of political science and director, Citizens Research Foundation, University of Southern California. He is the author of *Financing Politics: Money, Elections and Political Reform*.

TERRY E. ALLBRITTON, formerly executive director, Louisiana Commission on the Bicentennial of the U.S. Constitution, is associate professor of clinical law, Tulane Law School. He is the author of *State and Local Government Debt Financing*.

ROBERT W. BAILEY is assistant professor of political science, Columbia University. He has served on the staffs of the Emergency Financial Control Board for New York City and the city's commissioner of consumer affairs. He is the author of *The Crisis Regime: The MAC, the EFCB and the Political Impact of the New York City Financial Crisis*.

GERALD BENJAMIN, professor of political science, State University of New York at New Paltz, is a principal research advisor to the New York City Charter Revision Commission. He is coeditor, with Charles Brecher, of *The Two New Yorks: State and City in a Changing Federal System*.

PAGE E. BIGELOW is director of the Gulick Center for Citizenship and Ethics, Institute of Public Administration. She serves on the staff of the State-City Commission on Integrity in Government (Sovern commission) and the New York State Commission on Government Integrity (Feerick commission).

RICHARD BRIFFAULT is associate professor of law, Columbia University School of Law.

M. DAVID GELFAND, formerly visiting Fulbright Senior Lecturer, Chuo University and Foreign Service Training Institute, Tokyo, Japan, is professor of law, Tulane Law School. He is the author of *Federal Constitutional Law and American Local Government*.

RICHARD A. GIVENS is of counsel to the New York law firm of Botein Hays & Sklar and chair of the Task Force on Simplification of the Law, New York State Bar Association. He has served as regional director of the Federal Trade Commission and as an assistant United States attorney in New York.

ERIC LANE is executive director and counsel, New York City Charter Revision Commission, and professor of law, Hofstra University School of Law.

FRANK J. MACCHIAROLA, formerly chancellor of the New York City school system, is president and executive director of the Academy of Political Science and professor of business at Columbia University. He has served as a member of two New York City charter commissions.

FRANK J. MAURO is research director, New York City Charter Revision Commission. Formerly secretary of the Ways and Means Committee, New York State Assembly, he teaches in the Graduate Program in Public Policy and Administration, Columbia University.

DOUGLAS MUZZIO is associate professor of political science, Baruch College, City University of New York. He is the author of *Watergate Games: Strategies, Choices, Outcomes*.

ROBERT F. PECORELLA is associate professor of government and politics, St. John's University.

EDWARD V. REGAN is the New York State comptroller. He has been a city councilman-at-large in Buffalo and served two terms as county executive of Erie County.

RONALD H. SILVERMAN is Kalikow Professor of Law, Hofstra University School of Law.

TIM TOMPKINS is special assistant to the counsel, New York City Charter Revision Commission.

JOSEPH P. VITERITTI is associate research professor, New York University Graduate School of Public Administration. He is the author of *Across the River: Politics and Education in the City*, *Bureaucracy and Social Justice*, and *Police, Politics and Pluralism in New York City*.

New York City Charter Revision Commission, 1986

Richard Ravitch
Chair
Harriet R. Michel
Vice Chair
Nathan Leventhal
Secretary

Aida Alvarez
Amalia V. Betanzos
Fred W. Friendly
Judah Gribetz
Frank J. Macchiarola
Therese M. Molloy

Patrick J. Murphy
Archibald R. Murray
Joseph A. O'Hare, S.J.
W. Bernard Richland
David G. Trager
Robert F. Wagner, Sr.

Eric Lane
Counsel/Executive Director

New York City Charter Revision Commission, 1988

Frederick A. O. Schwarz, Jr.
Chair
Harriet R. Michel
Vice Chair
Nathan Leventhal
Secretary

Aida Alvarez
Amalia V. Betanzos
Fred W. Friendly
Simon P. Gourdine
Judah Gribetz
Therese M. Molloy

Patrick J. Murphy
Archibald R. Murray
Mario J. Paredes
W. Bernard Richland
Most Rev. Joseph M. Sullivan
David G. Trager

Eric Lane
Counsel/Executive Director

The Reemergence of Municipal Reform

GERALD BENJAMIN
FRANK J. MAURO

During the 1980s the structure of the New York City government's representative institutions was successfully challenged on two occasions in federal court. Both cases, *Andrews* v. *Koch* and *Morris* v. *Board of Estimate*, were heard by the same judge, Edward R. Neaher of the United States District Court for the Eastern District of New York in Brooklyn. And in each instance the city responded by creating charter revision commissions, pursuant to a state law that authorizes such bodies to propose directly to the voters, for their approval, changes in the city's charter — its fundamental governing document.

On 17 November 1981, Judge Neaher in *Andrews* decided that the charter provision allowing for two at-large council members from each of the city's five boroughs, elected by a limited nomination, limited voting system, violated the one-person, one-vote standard of the United States Constitution, since the boroughs varied widely in size — the smallest borough, Staten Island, had 350,000 residents, while Brooklyn, the largest, had 2.2 million.[1] In April 1982, in response to the United States Circuit Court of Appeals affirmation of Judge Neaher's decision in the *Andrews* case, Mayor Edward I. Koch appointed a charter revision commission chaired by Michael I. Sovern, president of Columbia University. At the time, it appeared that this commission might also have to consider changes in the structure of the Board of Estimate, since on 2 December 1981, less than a month after Judge Neaher's decision, the New York Civil Liberties Union filed a test case challenging the constitutionality of that board on similar grounds. This unique body, with significant power in budget, land use, franchising, and procurement matters, had been composed since 1902 of New York City's three citywide elected officials (the mayor, the comptroller, and the City Council president) and its five borough presidents. Since 1958 each of the borough presidents has had equal voting power on the board.

The mayor's decision to respond to *Andrews* by appointing a charter commission was not viewed, at the time, as particularly noteworthy. It was, however, a significant step by New York City in utilizing the home rule charter-making authority available to it under general state law. For more than half a century, New

York State's home-rule provisions allowed cities to establish charter commissions to draft new or revised charters for presentation to the voters. But only once during this period did New York City utilize this ongoing grant of authority. And that one previous locally initiated charter revision, Mayor Robert F. Wagner's appointment of the Cahill commission in 1961, followed two years of activity by a state commission created to review New York City's governmental structure and operations and recommend changes.

Wagner's action was made possible by a general change in state law, enacted for this specific purpose, allowing mayors acting alone to appoint charter commissions. That very state law provided the basis for Mayor Koch's action in 1982. Koch's action represented the city's first use of its authority to create a body to alter its basic governing document without authorizing or related state action. The idea of establishing a charter commission under the Municipal Home Rule Law as a way of developing an acceptable solution to the *Andrews* decision was struck upon by Jeffrey Friedlander of the corporation counsel's office.

In appointing the Sovern commission, Mayor Koch was not consciously trying to blaze new frontiers in the city's exercise of its home-rule authority, even though in retrospect it can be seen as a clear break with traditional practice in New York. Rather, he was looking for a way to respond expeditiously and responsibly to *Andrews*, since he had, on the advice of his corporation counsel, Frederick A. O. Schwarz, Jr., concluded that the city should not appeal that decision. Schwarz believed that an appeal was meritless and that it would be harmful to the city not to get the matter resolved as quickly as possible. His views of the merits of the case were clearly validated when the Supreme Court in the summer of 1983 decided by a 9-0 vote to deny an application for certiorari by one of the borough at-large members of the council.

The Sovern commission ultimately decided against a comprehensive review of the structure of city government because, in its view, this had been done less than a decade earlier by a state charter commission for New York City, chaired by State Senator Roy Goodman, and substantial changes had been adopted by the voters in November 1975 on this commission's recommendation. The Sovern commission decided instead to focus on just three matters — the at-large council seats, the city's redistricting process, and the size of community districts. Redistricting was addressed because of a year-long imbroglio over the discriminatory effects of a 1981 City Council reapportionment. This led Mayor Koch to ask the Sovern commission to consider having an impartial, nonpartisan citizens commission take over the decennial redistricting of the council. Finally, the commission reassessed a provision of the 1975 charter that set a minimum size of 100,000 for the city's community districts. The 1980 census found that nineteen of the fifty-nine community districts that had been created only five years earlier did not meet this population standard, and a substantial redrawing of the community district map would have been necessary if this charter requirement was not altered. At the November 1983 election, the voters approved commission recommendations for the elimination of the at-large council seats, the establishment of an independent districting commission to redraw council district lines (in accordance with specific criteria) after each decennial census, and the elimination of the minimum size requirement for community districts.

During the course of the Sovern commission's deliberations, Judge Neaher rendered his initial decision in *Morris* v. *Board of Estimate*. In November 1982, he concluded that this board was not a legislative body to which members were elected directly and was therefore not covered by the one-person, one-vote standard. This decision was reversed, and the case remanded, by the Circuit Court of Appeals in March 1983, with instructions that the District Court examine two questions. The first was to determine the degree of malapportionment on the Board of Estimate. At issue were whether and to what extent the six votes cast by the board's three citywide members offset the inequality resulting from each of the borough presidents representing jurisdictions with vastly different populations. The second issue focused on whether any deviations from the one-person, one-vote standard that were ultimately found to exist could be justified on grounds previously accepted by the United States Supreme Court.

In August 1984, Judge Neaher determined that the citywide representatives should not be considered in evaluating the deviations in size among the boroughs and that the board was therefore substantially malapportioned. He did, however, give the city additional time to find a rationale for the status quo. Finally, in November 1986, he ruled against the city and directed that this unconstitutional situation be redressed by the city "with all deliberate speed." In this case, as contrasted with *Andrews*, Corporation Counsel Schwarz did not believe that an appeal would be without merit. The result was a decision by the city to proceed on two fronts simultaneously — to press its case in court while developing a solution should its appeals fail.[2]

The day after Judge Neaher's 1986 decision in the *Morris* case, Mayor Edward I. Koch made clear the city's intention to appeal. But he also announced that he would again appoint a charter revision commission to recommend appropriate changes in the structure of city government to the city's voters. Within a week the mayor named Richard Ravitch, a prominent business leader with extensive experience in government, to chair the commission. Ravitch in turn selected Eric Lane, a law professor at Hofstra University and the counsel to the Democratic minority in the state Senate, to be the commission's counsel and executive director. By the end of the year fifteen men and women, broadly representative of the social, racial, ethnic, and geographic diversity of the city, had been selected to serve as commissioners. (See page xiii.) While all the members were appointed by the mayor, five were selected from a list of nominees provided by the council and five were named from a list of nominees submitted by the Board of Estimate.

While it was defining its agenda, the commission recruited a staff and retained consultants. Work began, not only on the substance of issues but also on creating an awareness in the city of the commission's work. One of the characteristics that distinguished this commission from its predecessors was the continuous effort to educate the public. Every charter commission ultimately faces the need to explain its proposals to the voters, but this commission undertook to broaden participation and understanding from the beginning.

Under the direction of Gretchen Dykstra, the commission's director of communications, a comprehensive communications strategy was undertaken. Public hearings and meetings were used to gather the views of interested groups and individuals throughout the city and to give visibility to the commission's work. Publications were prepared in a number of media and in several languages and distributed widely both to those especially interested in the charter revision process and to the general public. Communications staff members immediately began to develop contacts with citywide and local radio, television, and newspaper reporters. Additionally, field workers established continuing contacts with neighborhood groups and community boards in all the boroughs, seeking opinions, and encouraging involvement. With the help of corporate and foundation grants, posters were prepared and a subway advertising campaign was undertaken to heighten the visibility of the process and public knowledge of its importance.

The overall objective was to ensure the greatest possible understanding when the charter commission presented a new governance plan to the voters, as it was scheduled to do in less than two years. In a brief essay, first published in the *Urban, State and Local Law Newsletter* in the summer of 1988 and reprinted substantially unchanged in this volume, Eric Lane explores some of the difficulties of the charter revision process, the political challenges that arose as it went forward, and the opportunities that were presented to achieve that most elusive of goals, "good government."

While the charter commission met, the appeals process in the *Morris* case proceeded. On 8 October 1987, the United States Court of Appeals for the Second Circuit unanimously upheld the District Court. But then, somewhat surprisingly, on 4 April 1988—just a week after the commission had begun considering an alternative structure for city government presented by its chair—the United States Supreme Court decided to review the case. Concerned about the controversy that might be generated by proposals to alter the city's political institutions fundamentally at a time when it was not clear that such substantial changes were absolutely required, the Charter Revision Commission decided to defer final action on all matters having to do with the structure and powers of elective offices until the Supreme Court issued its decision in *Morris*. Supporting this decision and unwilling to request that the court expedite its review, Mayor Koch expressed his intention to reappoint the commission after election day in 1988, when its term would expire under state law.

The Ravitch commission continued its work, however, on many other aspects of the governmental reform agenda. Major focal points of this effort included: reforming campaign finance, establishing new conflicts-of-interest standards and procedures, improving internal controls in the city government, establishing a new tax appeals process, strengthening efforts to register and inform voters, altering the process for filling vacancies in elective offices, enhancing incentives for better infrastructure maintenance, and reforming the city's administrative procedures.

Some changes adopted by the commission in 1988, such as those concerning conflicts of interest, involved the removal of entire chapters from the charter and the addition of new ones. Others entailed new language in existing provisions. One example of the form of these changes is included as an appendix to Gerald Benjamin's essay on filling vacancies in elective offices.

Because of their diversity and complexity, considerable thought was given to how to present the proposed charter changes to the voters on election day. It was clear that whatever form the ballot questions took, citizens could not be expected to educate themselves on these complex matters in the few minutes that each of them would be able to spend in the voting booth. Indeed, the commission's entire public-education effort, described above, was an attempt to prepare New Yorkers for the ultimate act of voting on these questions.

History provided the commission with reasonable guidance in deciding on its ballot questions. Charter commissions had previously presented proposals to the voters at four general elections—1936, 1961, 1975, and 1983. In each of the first two instances, a general question on the comprehensive charter changes being offered was presented, along with a separate question on the innovative methods proposed in each of these years for the election of council members. In 1936, the Thacher commission recommended the use of the "single transferable vote" method of proportional representation for the election of the entire council and in 1961, the Cahill commission proposed the limited-nomination, limited-voting system for boroughwide, at-large City Council seats that was ultimately repealed by the voters in 1983 following the *Andrews* decision.

The state law creating the Thacher commission in 1934 specifically required that its work be presented for ratification to the voters in the form of the following single question: "Shall the charter proposed by the New York City charter revision commission be adopted?" This law also provided, however, that any proposal for the creation of a system of proportional representation be separately submitted to the voters. The general state law pursuant to which cities are authorized to create charter commissions has for the past sixty-five years included similar language calling for a single question covering all revisions other than proposals for proportional representation. This general law, however, has since 1939 allowed city charter commissions to present their work to the electorate in either one or a number of questions.

But in 1975 and in 1983 a less comprehensive set of changes was presented by charter commissions to the electorate as a series of separate questions, ten in the former year and three in the latter one. Because of a political compromise within the 1975 commission, it became the only one in New York City history to use the statutory option of competing ballot questions. Six of the ten questions it offered were endorsed by the commission; the four others, some of them competing, were presented to the voters without endorsement. Only the first six passed. The 1983 commission presented each of its three separate agenda items as individual questions.

The Ravitch commission at first decided to offer two ballot questions, one covering campaign finance, the most visible issue it had taken up, and the other a package of nine good-government reforms. After some criticism was received regarding the complexity of the "package question," the commission decided to offer its proposals in five parts rather than two. All of these questions were overwhelmingly approved on 6 November 1988, with voter participation relatively high, when compared to the experience with referenda in New York City in similar election years.

Following the 1988 election, Richard Ravitch declined reappointment as commission chairman to explore the possibility of mounting a mayoral campaign in 1989. In his place, Mayor Koch appointed Frederick A. O. Schwarz, Jr., a former corporation counsel and a partner in a leading Wall Street law firm. He also appointed three other new members, while reappointing eleven members of the 1987–88 commission. Chairman Schwarz retained Eric Lane as his counsel and executive director, and generally preserved continuity in the commission staff. (See page xiii.)

In early 1989, at Schwarz's urging, the commission agreed to proceed on a schedule that would allow it to move expeditiously if and when the Supreme Court affirmed the *Morris* decision. It decided to continue the functional approach of its predecessor and scheduled full-day hearings on budgeting, contracting, franchising, and land use. The commission also decided to pay substantial attention to the concept of oversight, a particular interest of its new chair. Oversight served as a vehicle for focusing on a variety of issues: the number of independently elected officials; the relationship between the legislative and executive branches; the interactions of the city's other separately elected officials (the comptroller, the council president, and the borough presidents) with the mayor and his agencies; and the division of legislative authority between the Board of Estimate and the city's legislature, the City Council.

On 22 March 1989, the Supreme Court unanimously upheld the Circuit Court of Appeals decision in the *Morris* case, despite reversing Judge Neaher's conclusion that the board's citywide members should be excluded in determining compliance with the one-person, one-vote standard. Justice White's majority opinion and the concurring opinions of Justices Brennan and Blackmun are reprinted in this volume. Soon after, with it now definitively established that the system of representation used for the Board of Estimate was unconstitutional, the Schwarz commission intensified its activities, announcing its intention to proceed on a schedule that would allow it to put an alternative city governance structure before the voters on election day in 1989, simultaneous with elections for all major city offices.

Soon after, with it now definitively established that the system of representation used for the Board of Estimate was unconstitutional, the Schwarz commission intensified its activities, announcing its intention to proceed on a schedule that would allow it to put its proposals before the voters in November 1989, simultaneous with the elections for city offices.

In an effort to bring together the more than two years of work which preceded the court's final decision, the commission then held more than thirty additional hearings and meetings. These included two sets of public hearing in all five boroughs and three rounds of intensive mark-up sessions, the first on concepts and the latter two on specific charter language.

In its most far-reaching decision, the commission voted to abolish the Board of Estimate and to reallocate its functions, rather than attempting to restructure the board or change its voting system. Additionally, the commission decided to retain New York City's strong-mayor system, while transferring some of the mayor's authority, primarily in the preparation of the budget and the selection of sites for city facilities, to the borough presidents. It also endeavored to balance the executive's power with a significantly strengthened City Council and to enhance the representativeness of that body by increasing the number of council districts from thirty-five to fifty-one. The comptroller, still powerful, was more than ever before limited to fiscal functions, and despite some controversy, the commission decided to retain the office of City Council president with a variety of new advocacy and oversight powers in order to maintain the number of meaningful citywide electoral opportunities and to help sustain a healthy political tension in the city.

The Charter Commission's Agenda

In contrast to the approach of the Sovern commission, the Ravitch and Schwarz commissions decided to go beyond the immediate reason for their creation and to exploit their formal authority under state law to undertake a comprehensive review of the entire structure and operation of city government. Both commissions were keenly aware of the fact that extensive debate had occurred historically in New York City and elsewhere over such matters, and that many different approaches had been tried. An understanding of options for the city therefore required a review of this experience, with an eye toward both general lessons and specific applications in the nation's biggest, most complex city.

Consequently, the record of the development of urban governance in the United States was carefully reviewed, and more limited consideration was given to models from other countries. Special attention was paid to the progressive-era reform proposals that transformed American local government in the twentieth century. Among the key recommendations of this now classic reform agenda were strong executives, fewer jurisdictionwide elected officials, smaller councils, at-large representation, professional management, and nonpartisan elections.

Many of these reforms later became the targets of reform themselves. For example, the at-large election of council members was advanced in the early twentieth century to reduce parochialism and strike at the ward-based power of working-class party leaders. Although it still has its fervent advocates, at-large election is now recognized as having the clear effect of reducing the representation of geographically concentrated minority populations. In addition, a new wave of support for districts, and in municipalities with districts for smaller districts, has resulted from a desire to increase representation and ease of access to elective office.

The issue of reducing the size of New York City's council districts, on average which included more than 200,000 people, became an important focal point for the Charter Revision Commission. The essay by Douglas Muzzio and Tim Tompkins in this volume reflects an attempt to assist the commission in balancing concerns about the size of individual districts with the need to provide better representation for the city's minorities, on the one hand, and the overall size of the local legislature on the other.

As the essays in this volume attest, an understanding of the specific experience of New York City, the nature of its politics, and the sources of its institutional arrangements was central to the commission's research activities. Joseph P. Viteritti's essay illustrates that three themes have dominated debates over governmental structure in New York since the creation of the consolidated city. One of these themes, addressed in greater detail in Richard Briffault's discussion of the legal doctrine of home rule, concerns the degree to which the city may rule itself. A second traditional issue is the degree to which power should be located in central-city or borough-based institutions. And a third question concerns how powers are shared within the central city government.

As Briffault notes, the leeway for local action under New York law may be greater than is commonly acknowledged. But in general, as New York City has become less affluent and powerful relative to the rest of the state, it has grown less interested in autonomy than in assistance from Albany.[3] With regard to the other two themes, the historical trends have been toward centralization of city government and strengthening the executive powers of the mayor. Some steps away from these directions and toward decentralization, not to the borough but to the community level, were undertaken as a result of the work of the Goodman commission in the mid-1970s. The mixed results of that effort were explored in detail for the commission by Robert Pecorella, and he summarizes them here. Pecorella's work for the commission and the testimony of many past and present participants in New York City's unique experiment with community government and administrative decentralization served as the basis of the Schwarz commission's recommendations on this subject.

In addition to the traditional focus on governmental institutions and processes, the charter commission sought through its research to understand how the key functions of city government were actually performed, so as to assist it in the identification and analysis of alternative means for performing these functions. Taking this approach, Ronald H. Silverman's two-volume work for the commission, "Land Governance and the New York City Charter," a summary of which appears in this volume, reviewed in detail the historical development of the city's approach to its scarcest resource, critiqued current practices, and offered a range of options for charter change.

In fact, the functional research approach revealed the interaction of the city's political and governmental institutions and defined issues for the charter commission that might not otherwise have been perceived or addressed. The examination by Gerald Benjamin of the processes for filling vacancies in elective offices, for example, revealed that they had in effect been converted to appointed positions with de facto appointing power in the hands of county Democratic party leaders. This trend had a substantial limiting effect on competitiveness.

But perhaps the most dramatic way that the commission's research altered its agenda arose from the Voting Rights Act problems with the Board of Estimate that were identified by M. David Gelfand and Terry E. Albritton in a legal memorandum for the commission, published here in updated and revised form. In a companion piece, Frank J. Mauro outlines how this issue developed and how the values that inhere in the Voting Rights Act came to be incorporated in later commission deliberations. Ultimately, the commission decided that it was not possible to devise a board with three citywide members casting a majority of the votes, and five members elected at large from the existing boroughs, which would meet both one-person, one-vote and voting-rights requirements. In addition, the use of weighted voting on such a body was found to have unacceptable policy consequences, including the virtual disenfranchisement of Staten Island and the elevation of the borough president of Brooklyn to near equality with the citywide members of the board.

Efforts at charter change did not, of course, go forward in a vacuum. Members of the commission and its staff brought to the task a commitment to and intimacy with city government, a range of specialized training, experience in government at various levels, and an array of connections with professionals in government within and outside New York. This resulted in a familiarity with a variety of issues and concerns that had current political relevance in New York City and which were receiving significant attention in broader professional and policy-issue networks. These issues include reform of administrative procedures, campaign-finance reform, oversight of the executive branch, legislative-executive relations in budgeting, internal controls, the adaptation of strategic planning techniques to the public sector, infrastructure maintenance, and reform of the capital budget process. They constituted an important part of a "new reform agenda" that is changing the structure and operations of state and local government in the 1980s. Many of the items on this agenda proved germane to the charter commission's work and became the subjects of staff and consultant research. For example, Richard A. Givens, who did the initial research for the commission on administrative procedures, discusses the charter provision that was adopted on this subject in his essay and sets the commission's work in the context of the relevant state and national experience.

The charter commission's activities were also shaped and changed by immediate events in the larger political environment. National, state, and citywide news about undue influence by major campaign contributors, misappropriation of public resources for political purposes, and other excesses in financing election campaigns led to an interest in reform in this area. A national expert in the campaign-finance field, Herbert E. Alexander, prepared an options paper for the commission on this subject, shortened for publication here, summarizing efforts and achievements at the national level, in New York and other states, and in a number of cities and counties across the country, and making suggestions for action.

The campaign-finance issue also raised the question of the reach of the charter commission's authority within the framework of New York's statutory and constitutional provisions for home rule as interpreted by the state's highest court, the Court of Appeals. The extent of local authority is a hoary and perennial issue in state-local relations everywhere in the United States. In his research for the commission, also shortened for inclusion in this volume, Richard Briffault found ample authority for the commission to proceed but, perhaps more interestingly for readers outside New York, formulated from the decisions of the state's courts a new standard that might be applied when weighing state interests against local ones in a particular area of action.

The commission's work on campaign finance clarified the city's authority to reform the financing of city elections. This led Mayor Koch, who had previously been unsuccessful in efforts to secure state enactment of legislation providing for partial public financing of campaigns and a series of related campaign-finance reforms, to propose a local law along these same lines. With some changes, the City Council adopted this program, and the charter revision commission later reinforced the actions of the mayor and City Council by establishing the new Campaign Finance Board in the charter and ensuring the initial funding necessary to enhance the program's viability.

Concern about ethical standards for public officials, raised by the campaign-finance issue, was reinforced by a major municipal corruption scandal dramatized by the suicide of Queens Borough President Donald Manes, one of the Board of Estimate's most influential members. The commission replaced the ethics provisions of the charter with an entirely new set of standards, institutions, and procedures to deal with conflicts of interest. This action was based, in part, on research for the commission by Page E. Bigelow, summarized in her essay in this volume.

There are at least two other examples of current events affecting the charter commission's agenda. In both cases, these events intensified interest in issues of lesser visibility. Mayor Koch's minor stroke in August 1987 caused the commission to pay increased attention to the adequacy of charter provisions for temporary mayoral inability and succession. This heightened the interest that was already present because of commission member Judah Gribetz's work on the succession issue at the state level. Additionally, the April 1988 closing of the Williamsburg Bridge dramatized the need for the city to bolster it's efforts in infrastructure maintenance. This event was followed by a suggestion presented to the commission by State Comptroller Edward V. Regan, discussed in his essay in this volume, for providing a charter basis to encourage improved infrastructure maintenance.

The initiative in this policy area was also an example of the aforementioned role of previous experience and issue networks in helping to set the agenda for charter change. Comptroller Regan's idea was sympathetically received by Commission Chairman Ravitch, who had been the principal architect of the Metropolitan Transportation Authority's major capital reinvestment program. In addition, commission staff members had long been a part of the national infrastructure network of state and local officials from across the country that emerged in the early

1980s, and was nurtured by national professional organizations, particularly the Council of State Planning Agencies.

Ideas were sought not only from current city and state office holders but also from those who had served in the past and from a broad array of interested groups, civic organizations, and community activists. A series of early hearings were held to determine concerns from all quarters about the structure of city government, its functioning, and the distribution of power within it. These hearings were transcribed and an inventory of issues and ideas for possible charter changes was compiled for reference and to guide further research.

Proposals by good-government groups to improve the city's voter-registration and voter-information efforts reflected national concern about low turnout and sought to draw upon the experience of other states and localities. Ultimately, these resulted in the charter commission's creation of a Voter Assistance Commission, charged with encouraging voter registration and voting. Additionally, as a result of the 1988 charter changes, the city is now required to publish a nonpartisan, impartial voters' guide whenever city elections are held.

Municipal Reform: Old and New

New York City's recent charter-revision efforts reveal that the impulse to improve government through changing structures, so characteristic of the American experience, is very much alive and well. Even the agenda of reform, though in part new, is deeply rooted in the classic municipal-reform tradition. Today, as in the past, those examining urban institutions confront choices having to do with the strength of the executive, the size and powers of the City Council, the design of legislative districts, alternative electoral systems, and a host of related issues.

There are less obvious similarities as well. Contemporary reformers continue to use business as a model, but as Robert W. Bailey's essay on strategic planning reveals, this is now more for processes designed to make government more efficient, effective, and accountable than for structural ideas. Additionally, despite the opportunities for wider participation noted above, the public remains relatively unexcited by structural issues in city government. Moreover, academics continue to debate whether substantial effects flow from most institutional and process changes. Despite these realities, politicians sense that charter change affects in important ways who has power in the city and to what ends power is used. Consequently, office holders and potential office holders pay careful attention to the charter-revision process. They seek to make their views known not only to the commissioners but also to other interested parties and to key opinion shapers — particularly those in the media. They also seek to mobilize visible constituencies in behalf of their positions.

There are at least two fundamental differences, however, between classical and contemporary municipal reform. The first is in the hierarchy of reform values. Democracy is now the primary goal; achieving efficiency is secondary. The other is in the political dynamics: the sources of demands for reform, the key arenas in which battles are fought, the number and relative weight of the effective actors, and the process by which fundamental structural change is pursued.

In contrast with earlier reform efforts, which clearly made achieving democracy a secondary value in local governance, the current reform agenda is driven by demands to open up the political system. In the 1960s and 1970s this took the form of efforts to make city government more accessible by decentralizing both power and service delivery. In the 1980s, perhaps as a result of the opportunities offered by the Voting Rights Act, the emphasis has been upon seizing greater power in the central-city government itself.

Whatever the form of the immediate structural goals, modern reformers are much more self-conscious about the "big trade-off" between democracy and efficiency. Reformers remain convinced of the need for a competitive political system but do not organize themselves to capture power, as did the Citizens Union in New York City in the early twentieth century. Rather, they seek to create structural conditions under which competition is encouraged to emerge; simultaneously, practices that dampen competition are discouraged. In the late-twentieth-century context, this means seeking to constrain the effects of big money and organized interests in local politics and to lower barriers for entry of new groups and citizens into the political process.

Classic reform sought to close down the urban polity, to limit it to the most educated and professionally best qualified—a governing elite. It reacted to the influx of new populations in cities by finding ways to limit their access to power. Thus its argument was that there was no Democratic or Republican way to run a city, that municipal governance could be depoliticized, and that it should be. In short, classic reform was exclusive, not inclusive.

In contrast, the current reform agenda accepts and embraces the political nature of big city government. It seeks to be inclusive. It does not solely seek to redistribute power among those who are already power holders. Rather, it has as one of its fundamental objectives the admission of new actors into the system — that is, basic alteration of the local political balance. Thus a central thrust of new reform is to open up the governing process — to include those previously excluded from elective office, public employment, and government contracting opportunities; to make information more readily available; in sum, to admit the mass public fully into daily public business.

Because of the priority it gives to democracy as a value, new urban reform is far less confident than classic reform that the best possible municipal government may be achieved by making government more like business and by putting the "best people" in public office. The emphasis now is not on changing the kind of people who serve but on building systems that are fair and effective and giving recognition to whoever is chosen through the electoral process. Thus, for example, new reform seeks probity in public office not as classic reform did, by structuring the electoral system to produce different winners with different values, but by creating stricter rules of conduct for officials once they are elected.

Though deeply committed to democracy, contemporary reform in New York

City, like classical reform, remains basically wary of political parties as instruments of democracy. Classic reformers disliked parties because they were corrupt and inclusive — that is, their power was based on mobilizing the newly arrived immigrant masses. New reformers value the functions of parties, particularly the benefits of party competition, but despair of their real-world shortcomings as organizations — their ties to governmental corruption and the insufficiency of their responsiveness to the minority populations that have now become a majority in the city.

Unlike their predecessors, new reformers realize that the political functions of parties — coalition building, integrating new groups into the political and social system, candidate recruitment, and leadership development — have to be performed by some means in the city. They believe, however, that the healthy functions of parties are premised on the presence of a competitive interparty environment and that it is unrealistic to assume that these functions can be effectively and consistently performed in localities, like New York City, which are totally dominated by one party. In the absence of competitive, and therefore accountable, parties, they seek to accomplish the traditional functions of parties through changed governmental structures and altered electoral rules.

Partly as a result of general changes in public expectations regarding the openness of government decision making but also as a consequence of some government decision makers' own commitment to democracy, new reform goes forward in a goldfish bowl. The openness of the charter-change process in the late 1980s was unprecedented in city history. And, of course, decisions were taken with the understanding that they had to be presented for popular approval at the polls.

Thus, the process is far less bounded than in the past, when access was restricted to a small number of political and civic leaders. In a seeming paradox, public interest is not widespread, but urban reform has become more participatory. There is the potential for far more individuals and groups to be effective actors in it. Relatively small groups, and individuals operating on their own, can influence outcomes through the force of their ideas.

In an era of enormously enhanced technical capacity to communicate widely, there are several consequences of these process differences. One is that both the tenor of information in the media and its flow through the media to those who are interested and involved are enormously important in affecting events. A second is that charter-change proposals appear to have greater fragility. More proposals are now seriously considered and debated, but the process moves rapidly and more are quickly discarded as well. Finally, as noted above, far more resources than previously must be spent by those at the center of the reform effort — charter commissioners and key staff — on the process of listening and communicating.

As in the past, efforts for restructuring city governance still arise from both outside and within city government. Traditionally, the state government has been extensively involved in the structuring and restructuring of New York City's government. From the early nineteenth century onward charter commissions have been state creatures, created by state law. Until 1914, in fact, when the Optional Home

Rule Law was adopted, the state legislature could grant charters "with or without the wishes of the local populace."[4] Indeed, until 1923 any effort by the legislature to allow a locality to adopt its own charter would have been regarded as an unconstitutional delegation of legislative authority by New York State courts. Only after the adoption of the Constitutional Home Rule Amendment in 1924 was local charter making possible. In fact, until the last decade, state involvement has been substantial in changing the New York City charter, even when the initiative was local.

But outside pressures are now far less likely than was the case for much of this century to derive from Republican efforts at the state level to gain added power in the Democratic stronghold of New York City. The last charter commission created by an entirely Republican-controlled state government was the Goodman commission, in 1972. Continuous Democratic control of the governorship and the state Assembly since 1974 has ensured that structural change would not be imposed on New York City by upstate Republicans and their city allies purely for partisan advantage. As the recent Staten Island secession bill indicates, however, changes may still be imposed as a consequence of the internal dynamics of majority party conferences in both houses of the state legislature in Albany.

Local government structures are now the national government's business as well as the states', and have been for a quarter of a century. The establishment of the one-person, one-vote standard by the courts in 1962 and the enactment of a strong federal Voting Rights Act by the Congress in 1965, along with the willingness of formerly excluded groups to press for these rights with the U.S. Justice Department and through the judicial process, have worked a revolutionary change in federalism and in the politics of municipal reform. Consequently, external pressures for charter change are now far less likely to be initiated at the state level by those already in power than by new actors seeking access to the system through use of the federal courts. The *Morris* case is only the most recent example of this.

Within the city, the role of the mayor has emerged as substantial during the 1980s in the initiation of charter change. Although mayors must consult widely in appointing charter commissions to make sure that the ensuing effort has sufficient legitimacy, they may do so on their own. A local charter commission may also be established under the home-rule provisions of New York State law by action of the City Council or as a result of popular initiative and referendum. But only mayoral appointment has been used when charter commissions have been locally initiated in New York City.

Also within the city, local scandals continue to be a key element in providing the opportunity for charter change and shaping its agenda. It is often argued that whole systems ought not be altered in response to the peculations of specific office holders. In this as in earlier eras, however, highly publicized instances of corruption made the current institutional arrangements suspect, revealed structural weaknesses, and in general energized advocates of reform. The city administration's procurement reforms of the late 1980s, which were built upon and expanded by the charter commission, are a prime example of this phenomenon.

Finally, the analogy is often drawn between charter change and constitutional change. Those who approach a charter as a local constitution seek to apply "constitutional values." They advocate a short document, a fundamental outline, a framework for government. In contrast, some who reject this analogy advocate a much more detailed document defining the structures and processes of city government and the limits upon it. Still others simply see this detail as an unavoidable necessity.

In New York City in the national bicentennial period many members of the charter commission were attracted to the constitutional analogy in describing their undertaking. Though some of their decision making dealt with fundamental institutional arrangements, much was legislative in character. The details of the charter chapters on conflicts of interest and equal employment opportunity, topics of significance in the late 1980s, are notable examples.

The goal of the charter commission was never to pare down the charter to bare essentials, the published views of the National Municipal League concerning what ought to be in charters notwithstanding. Rather, it was to use this rare opportunity to address in detail, for the immediate future, serious structural and process issues in city governance. Based on the historical record, the expectation was that if the new charter was adopted it would be framing governmental decision making for decades, not for centuries. If the constitutional analogy ever had force in classic urban reform, judging from recent New York City experience, it has lost that force in the contemporary era.

NOTES

1. *Andrews* v. *Koch* 528 Fed. Supp. 246 (E.D. N.Y. 1981).
2. A time line history of this case may be found in *New York Times*, 20 Nov. 1986.
3. See Gerald Benjamin, "The Political Relationship," in *The Two New Yorks: State-City Relations in a Changing Federal System*, ed. Gerald Benjamin and Charles Brecher (New York: Russell Sage Foundation, 1988), 114–16.
4. Chap. 444 Laws of 1914. Quotation is from Judge Aron Steuer in *DiPrima* v. *Wagner* 14 A.D. 2d. 36 (1961).

The Tradition of Municipal Reform: Charter Revision in Historical Context

JOSEPH P. VITERITTI

Three paramount themes have recurred over the institutional history of New York City. The first concerns local autonomy. Throughout New York's history the city has sought to rule itself, while the state government seated in Albany has consistently imposed serious compromises to municipal self-governance. The second issue concerns the devolution of authority from the central institutions of the city government to those at the borough and community levels. The boroughs asserted themselves almost immediately after the consolidated city was created and then saw their roles diminished over time. A community role was preserved in early charters. But the movement toward community government really became prominent in the 1960s and was the focal point of the Goodman charter commission reforms in 1975. The efficacy of community-based institutions remains a seriously debated policy issue today with regard to both charter reform and educational governance. The third issue of concern, which is at the center of discussion for the present charter commission, is the distribution of authority among the major citywide actors and institutions. These include the mayor, the comptroller, the council president, the borough presidents, the City Council, and the Board of Estimate. As a result of the decision of the United States Supreme Court in *Morris* v. *Board of Estimate*, the Board of Estimate is likely to be abolished. And history has shown, as this essay will demonstrate, that it is not possible to alter the power of any major institution in the city without substantially affecting the power of all the others.

Early Years

The original government of New York City, established as New Amsterdam by the Dutch Governor Peter Stuyvesant in 1656, was modeled after the free cities of Holland. Like the Dutch burghers, New Amsterdam included a chief executive called the *burgomaster* and a *schepens*, or common body. When the city passed into the control of the English in 1665, the English Governor Richard Nicolls granted New York City a new charter. This document created the first municipal corporation in colonial America, making it a model for other cities. The New York City charter of 1665 went through several revisions — in 1686 under Governor Thomas Dongan, in 1708 under Governor Edward Cornbury, and again in 1730 under Governor John Montgomerie. The resulting municipal corporation had a mayor and a recorder appointed by the governor and aldermen elected by the qualified voters of six city wards. All sat together in a common council.

While there was no real separation of powers between the mayor and aldermen in colonial New York, there was an inherent tension built into the system, since the mayor was an appointee of the governor and the aldermen were locally elected. As in other colonial cities, the mayor, the recorder, and the aldermen were also vested with judicial powers, subject to the colonial court of common law. The Montgomerie charter also provided for the election of assessors, collectors of colonial taxes, and constables to serve as peace officers in each of the six wards. Since the city had no general taxing powers of its own, the scope and functions of the municipality remained limited. However, New York had several advantages as a colonial city because it received significant property, ferry, dock, and wharf rights. Eventually, the colonial government granted the city the power to impose taxes for special purposes. As early as 1676, for example, the corporation applied for and received authorization to levy a tax to finance the rebuilding of one of its docks. Thus, notwithstanding its colonial status, the seventeenth-century city enjoyed a good deal of autonomy from British rule.

After the American Revolution the mayor of New York, like the chief executives of most other colonial cities, was selected by the state governor. This practice exemplifed both the tendency of postcolonial municipalities to imitate the English model and anticipated the power that state governments would wield over American cities. New York City soon began to expand its range of functions and services as a working municipality. In the early-nineteenth century, the city initiated construction of the Croton Aqueduct. By midcentury, New York had established independent police and fire departments, constructed its own park system, paved streets, and laid out a network of sewers. The ability of the city to govern its own affairs, carried over from colonial times, continued through the first quarter of the nineteenth century.[1]

In 1821, the state finally granted the city corporation authority to choose its own mayor. This power of selection was given to the City Council, which would choose the mayor from its own membership. In 1834, New York became one of the last large municipalities in the United States to elect its mayor by popular vote. After this separation between the legislative and executive branches, New York City moved rapidly to develop the mayoralty into a coordinate branch of government. The charter of 1849 provided for the creation of independent executive departments by taking appointment power away from the council and establishing a system of popular election. In 1853, New York took another significant step and allowed the mayor to appoint department heads, subject to the approval of the City Council. He was not, however, empowered to remove these officials; consequently, many appointees often outlasted the mayor in office, and the council used its approval power to ensure that the new appointment procedure did not undermine the effectiveness of the spoils system.

As an outgrowth of state domination of local affairs, party politics, and local corruption, much of the mayor's new appointment power came to be shared with the state government, which by the midnineteenth century had become an intrusive presence in local affairs. Few cities had developed the art of political corruption to the level of sophistication it had reached in New York, and no division of city government possessed a system of patronage, graft, and political payoffs more elaborate than that found in the New York City legislature. Frederick Shaw wrote in his classic history of that body: "With the bestowal of the first trolley franchise in 1851 the Board of Aldermen embarked on a career of spoilation. The body in which Boss Tweed served his apprenticeship the following year was known as the forty thieves."[2]

In 1857 the state legislature assumed the right to appoint the heads of most administrative departments in the city, thus granting upstate Republicans a share of the political patronage that was formerly the sole province of city Democrats. Seven years later, the legislature created the Board of Estimate and Apportionment to assess the expenses of the new Metropolitan Police District, which encompassed New York City and its neighboring counties. The board was composed of the police commissioners, who were appointed by the governor, and the comptrollers of the cities of New York and Brooklyn, who were locally elected. It was a clear illustration of the kind of state domination that existed over local affairs at the the time and anticipated a locally selected Board of Estimate and Apportionment that would compromise the financial prerogatives of city legislators.

In 1870, at the urging of Boss Tweed, the state finally returned the power of administrative appointment to the city, where it was again assumed by the mayor, subject to approval by the council. In the same year the Metropolitan Police Department was abolished, along with the state-dominated Board of Estimate and Apportionment. But the charter granted by the state legislature in 1873 created a new Board of Estimate and Apportionment to manage the finances of the city. The new board included the mayor, the president of the Department of Taxes and Assessment, the comptroller, and the president of the Board of Aldermen. Since the selection of only the latter official was still in the hands of the council, the structure of this board represented the continuing decline of the body's budgetary power in New York City. This pattern grew more pronounced in 1884 when the president of the Board of Aldermen, along with the comptroller, again became popularly elected.

The significance of the changes that took place in New York City government in the latter part of the nineteenth century cannot be overemphasized. It was extraordinary to take control of public finances away from a popularly elected legislature. In New York City, this was accomplished in several stages. As early as 1849, the legislature lost its power to appoint the city's chief financial officer, the comptroller. Perhaps even more unusual was the measure that denied the legislature the right to choose its own president. Then the greatest blow to traditional legislative prerogatives came with the creation of the Board of Estimate and Apportionment. All these steps were part of the ongoing reform effort that came to dominate New York politics at the turn of the century. The ultimate outcome was a strong mayoralty at the expense of the legislature.

While New York City provided the country with one of the most dramatic illustrations of municipal corruption, it was also a major hotbed of reform. The New York Civil Service Reform League had been a key actor in the national campaign for a merit system. The Bureau of Municipal Research in New York City was a crucial force in the effort to bring sound management practices to local government. New York State passed its own Civil Service Reform Act in 1883 to coincide with the passage of the federal law. Pleas for reform in New York City can largely be credited to these legislative achievements at both the federal and the state levels.

In Brooklyn, the campaign to bring sound government to the municipality accelerated when Seth Low was elected mayor in 1882. Low effectively combined and put into practice the principles of centralized power and responsible government. The Brooklyn charter of 1880 had already given the mayor the authority to appoint department heads without council approval. The 1882 charter empowered him to replace all executive department heads within twenty days of his election. Brooklyn was the first municipality in which the chief executive was granted such broad appointment and removal power. Seth Low took advantage of this situation by holding each commissioner responsible for the performance of his department. He publicly announced that "the acceptance of any appointment at my hands will be evidence to the community that the gentleman accepting it has personally given me his assurance that he will without delay give me his resignation whenever I ask for it."[3] Low made it clear that his appointees were his representatives, and for that reason he would assume responsibility for their actions. He was the first municipal chief executive to hold weekly cabinet meetings with his commissioners.

What began in Brooklyn in 1882 and became known as the "single head" law emerged as a national model for responsible local government based on the idea of a strong executive. In 1893 the corporation counsel, a mayoral appointee, was added to the membership of the Board of Estimate and Apportionment in New York City. This development gave the mayor control over three out of five votes on the board, the others belonging to the popularly elected comptroller and president of the Board of Aldermen. In 1894, the state legislature passed a law modeled after the Brooklyn charter that empowered the mayor of New York to replace department heads within the first six months of his tenure. In 1901 the mayor of the now consolidated city was finally granted absolute power of appointment and removal without any time limitation.

As Greater New York approached the prospect of consolidation in 1897, it was clear that power over administrative appointments had been effectively moved from the state to the city and that the chief beneficiary was the mayor. Despite the emerging home-rule movement, regular state interference in local affairs continued to the extent that many of the public functions assumed by the city were performed in its capacity as an agent of the state. State legislators often failed to draw the line, and a very fine line it was, between state matters and those of an entirely local nature. The state government still decided on such important city matters as the construction of a subway system, the building of the Great East River Bridge, and education policy. Combined with the mayor's discretion over administrative affairs and the Board of Estimate's control of the budget, state dominance over many legislative matters relegated the City Council to a trivial role. As Shaw sarcastically explained it: "By 1898 when New York merged with neighboring communities, the Aldermen did little more than grant permits for peanut stands and confirm the tax computed by the Comptroller."[4]

The Consolidated City

The great achievement of 1897 was the consolidation of Greater New York through the annexation of Brooklyn, Western Queens, and Staten Island. As a result, the evolving pattern of government continued in New York and Brooklyn, characterized by a strong mayoralty. In fact, the government that came into existence in 1898 gave its chief executive more institutional power than the mayor in any other major American city ever had and perhaps ever will. The new government also continued the Board of Estimate and Apportionment, dominated by the mayor, with power over the budget. The authority of New York's first mayor reached into so many apsects of city government that no real separation of powers existed. Indeed, given the magnitude of the mayor's power, it could hardly be claimed that New York City had an effective system of checks and balances. The city took the reformist model of a strong mayoralty to an extreme, the assumption being that accountability could be achieved by concentrating responsibility.

The original New York City plan gave the mayor a four-year term of office. His role in the local legislative process was fully established by the fact that it took five-sixths of the vote of both houses of the legislature to override his veto. His dominance over the budget process was ensured by his power to appoint three of the five seats on the Board of Estimate and Apportionment. The mayor also appointed the city chamberlain, who served as the treasurer. The mayor's position with regard to public works and planning was defined by his appointment of a majority of the members of the Board of Public Improvements. In keeping with his position as chief executive, the mayor also appointed most administrative officials, though many of these commissioners and board members served for fixed terms, thereby reducing his actual power over them to some extent.

A common misconception about New York City is that the Board of Estimate was created at the time of consolidation to provide borough-level representation in the municipal government. As noted earlier, the Board of Estimate and Apportionment actually predates consolidation and was continued in the original charter of the consolidated city as an instrument of mayoral domination. The constitution of the board after the 1898 charter allowed the boroughs no representation of their own. The board consisted of the mayor, the president of the Department of Taxes and Assessments, the corporation counsel, the comptroller, and the president of the council. Significantly, only the latter two officials were elected independently of the mayor, although the two mayoral appointees enjoyed terms that exceeded the mayor's. The board was responsible for preparing the city budget, which would then be submitted for approval to the Municipal Assembly. The latter body had no power to add to the budget, and the Board of Estimate gave final approval to all expenditures. The Board of Estimate also had the authority to approve franchises, debts, taxes, and assessments. This approval power was extraordinary, since only franchising is commonly controlled by the executive branch; the others are usually considered the prerogative of the legislature.

Before consolidation, New York City had a unicameral Board of Aldermen composed of thirty-five members chosen from state senatorial districts. The new charter established a bicameral legislature, called the Municipal Assembly, which consisted of a council and the Board of Aldermen. The council had twenty-nine members, chosen from ten districts. Five of these districts were in New York County, three in Brooklyn, and one each in Richmond (Staten Island) and Queens. (At the time Manhattan and the Bronx were both still part of New York County.) Each district in Manhattan and Brooklyn elected three council members, and districts in Queens and Richmond elected two apiece.[5] Thus, New York County, with its larger poplation, enjoyed a dominant share of membership in the council, as a result of both the number of councilmanic districts and the number of councilmen per district. Council terms were extended to four years, and every former mayor of Greater New York was granted a seat on the council, provided that he continued to live in the city. In addition to its legislative duties, the council appointed the city clerk.

The lower house of the legislature was called the Board of Aldermen. It contained sixty members, elected from state assembly districts for two-year terms. While the president of the council was chosen by popular vote, the president of the Board of Aldermen was chosen by its own members. The geometrical growth in the size of New York's Municipal Assembly was inversely related to the level of its prestige. The large membership of this two-house legislature that had been stripped of much of its power made it exceedingly difficult to attract highly qualified people to serve in it. And its structure was so cumbersome that it was nearly impossible to accomplish anything. Moreover, most important legislative matters continued to be decided in the state legislature. The City Council president, now popularly elected, served on the Board of Estimate and Apportionment, sat on several other local boards, and was designated to succeed the mayor in case of a vacancy.

Starting in 1884, the comptroller was popularly elected. After 1898, he headed the Department of Finance and was responsible for the receipt of revenues in the form of taxes, assessments, and arrears. He oversaw all city contracts and served on the Board of Estimate and Apportionment. However, his power over financial affairs was checked to some extent because the mayor appointed a city chamberlain within the Department of Finance who served as the city treasurer. The borough presidents, elected on an at-large basis in their respective boroughs, held little power in the government created in 1898. Their major function was to chair local boards, which were designed to represent community interests regarding local improvements. They also sat on the citywide Board of Public Improvements but were permitted to vote only on measures concerning their own boroughs.

Twenty-two local boards, corresponding to state senatorial districts, were created in 1898. They were composed of the members of the Municipal Assembly from the district and the presidents of the boroughs. These boards, which established a precedent for the notion of community government in New York City, considered proposals for local improvements before submitting them to either the Board of Public Improvements or the Municipal Assembly. The Board of Public Improvements approved all major public-works projects in the city. It was composed of the mayor, a president appointed by the mayor, the corporation counsel, six departmental commissioners appointed by the mayor, and the five borough presidents. Since the latter were permitted to vote only on measures concerning their own boroughs, there was no opportunity for logrolling or coalition building among the borough presidents. The only other official on the board who was not a mayoral appointee was the comptroller. For all practical purposes, the Board of Public Improvements, like most other arenas in city government, was dominated by the mayor.

The Revolt of the Boroughs

In 1901, so the oft-told story goes, a coalition of Republicans and Brooklyn Democrats, displeased with the control of municipal government by Manhattan Democrats, joined forces to demand a new city charter that would better reflect the interests of the outer boroughs. Of course, there were other circumstances that led to Governor Theodore Roosevelt's appointment of the Charter Revision Commission, chaired by George Rieves, in 1900. Tammany's control of Manhattan politics meant that corruption had once again become rampant. Its excesses had been publicly played out before the state-appointed Mazet committee, which had questioned Mayor Robert Van Wyck about the operations of the Police Department. The major result of the revolt against Manhattan was the restructuring of the Board of Estimate. However, a subtheme in the proceedings of the charter commission report reads: "In considering the question of legislative powers to be conferred upon the city of New York, we have been met in the first instance by the question whether any city legislative should exist at all. It has been contended that the affairs of the city are entirely, or almost entirely, of a business nature, and that no city legislature is really necessary except for the adoption of what is commonly called administrative rules and regulations. In this view the Commission is unable to concur."[6]

Several arguments were advanced in favor of rehabilitating the local council. One suggested that the decline of the local legislature constituted a subordination of the principle of separation of powers, concentrating too much authority in the executive. It was thought that a council is more representative than a single individual.[7] Another argument suggested that the rehabilitation of the local council was necessary in order to avoid further intrusion by the state legislature. Some scholars at the time even argued that it was more feasible to elect a nonpartisan council than to have an independent chief executive, contrary to the reformist arguments of that period.[8]

The most significant outcome of the charter written by the Rieves commission in 1901 was the reduction of the mayor's power. Most important, the mayor no longer controlled the Board of Estimate and Apportionment, because the corporation counsel and the president of the Department of Taxes and Assessments (both mayoral appointees) were removed from it and the borough presidents were added. Under a new system of weighted voting, the mayor held only three of the sixteen votes. His power was further reduced by the abolition of the Board of Public Improvements, which had assigned the mayor considerable discretion over land use. Under the 1901 charter provisions, a newly composed one-house Board of Aldermen needed only a three-fourths majority to override the mayor's veto, instead of the previous five-sixths vote required of the Municipal Assembly. The mayor, in accordance with his executive power, was still allowed absolute veto power over franchises. Finally, the mayor's term was reduced from four years to two years in order to make him more accountable to the public. The terms of the comptroller and the president of the Board of Aldermen were also reduced to two years.

After 1901 the Board of Estimate and Apportionment was composed of three citywide elected officials and the five elected borough presidents. The citywide officials, which included the mayor, the president of the Board of Aldermen, and the comptroller, each had three votes on the board. The borough presidents of Manhattan and Brooklyn had two votes each, and the borough presidents of Queens, Richmond, and the Bronx were given one vote each. The newly structured board was an attempt to provide borough representation in the municipality, and it is important to note that the original representation was also weighted according to population. In 1905 the board received power over city franchises. In 1916 it was granted authority to regulate zoning, thereby creating an important role in city planning for itself as an institution and for its individual members.

It was assumed that the unicameral Board of Aldermen would work more efficiently than the previous bicameral Municipal Assembly. However, the size of this body, with sixty-five members, made doing business cumbersome and tended to mitigate its efficiency. The new legislature was empowered to pass local ordinances and to borrow money through the issuance of bonds. However, most of its powers were shared with the Board of Estimate and Apportionment. While this new body could overrule a mayoral veto with a three-fourths vote rather than a five-sixths majority, the mayor's veto power was still substantial. Thus, although the mayor's power was curbed, the hopes of some reformers to rehabilitate the local legislature were not realized.

By far the chief beneficiaries of the reallocation of authority by the Rieves commission were the borough presidents. As a group, they now controlled seven of the sixteen votes on the Board of Estimate and Apportionment, where they had previously had no voice. The new arrangement created opportunities for logrolling. Under the Rieves charter, borough presidents were also given substantial administrative authority over the construction and maintenance of public works in their respective boroughs and the power to enforce building-code violations. The range of duties granted to the borough presidents under the 1901 charter was a substantial rejection of the principle of separation of powers. Like the mayor, they were executive officials with administrative responsibilities who sat on the Board of Estimate and Apportionment, which performed legislature functions. They were also made members of the Board of Aldermen. The borough presidents continued to preside over their local boards, whose role in the initiation of public improvements was magnified with the demise of the citywide Board of Public Improvements. Local projects supported by the city's general funds still required the approval of the aldermen and the Board of Estimate and Apportionment, but they were now implemented by the borough presidents. And eventually, when the Board of Estimate and Apportionment was given discretion over zoning in 1916, the borough presidents became major participants in city planning.

Home Rule

Official charter commissions were established in 1907 and 1908 under the chairmanship of William Ivens, in 1909 under Fred Hammond, and again in 1921 under Henry de Forest Baldwin, but were of little consequence. While the struggle for institutional power continued between the mayor, the borough presidents, and the Board of Aldermen, the greatest check on any institution at the local level was found in the state government, particularly in the legislature. From the first days of statehood, the state government tended to pass special legislation, thus intervening in the affairs of local governments. One of the first concessions to local protests against intrusion came in 1894. The state constitution adopted in that year divided cities by population into three classes and stipulated that future state laws should apply to classes of cities rather than to specific ones. However, the state legislature continued to pass certain restrictions on the type of government that localities could employ. For example, the state prohibited the city-manager form of government and the commission plan.

And the constitution allowed the legislature to pass a special law affecting a particular city only with the approval of the local government, unless the legislature passed the law over a local veto a second time. The creation of the consolidated city of New York was, in fact, accomplished over the vetoes of the mayors of both New York City and Brooklyn. Between 1900 and 1921, more than 1,600 such special laws were passed regarding New York City. Of these, thirty-six were passed over the mayor's veto.[9]

In 1914 the state passed an "optional charter law," which allowed any city in the second or third class to select from a choice of six model charters designated by the state. The law only motivated these cities to demand the right to establish their own governments without unnecessary intrusion from the state. In 1923, a municipal home rule amendment was finally passed by the legislature for a second time and, upon receiving popular approval, was added to the state constitution in 1924. As a result of the Home Rule Law, a new Municipal Assembly was formed in New York City. The Board of Estimate and Apportionment was designated the upper house, and the Board of Aldermen functioned as the lower house. Any bill considered by the Board of Aldermen that amended the charter, reduced revenue, or concerned terms of employment had to be passed by the Board of Estimate and Apportionment before it could be submitted to the mayor. Many reformers hoped that the passage of the Home Rule Law in 1924 would finally allow the city to establish an assertive and competent legislative body, but the outcome proved to be disappointing. As Russell Forbes wrote in 1929: "In the five years of its existence, the Municipal Assembly has enacted seventy-four laws. The vast majority of these laws have been of trifling consequence and closely resemble the typical special law formerly passed by the state legislature at Albany. A great deal of the work of the municipal assembly has been concerned with such subjects as the creation of additional offices, increases in salaries, and changes in the pension allowance of civil servants."[10]

The Modern Municipality

Despite the efforts of reformers and the radical restructuring of the local legislature that they achieved, grave public concern arose again in the early 1930s about the quality, functioning, and integrity of the Board of Aldermen. Governor Franklin D. Roosevelt initiated an investigation of Mayor Jimmy Walker, who subsequently fled to Europe. Later, the Seabury committee, appointed by the state legislature, recommended another overhaul of the Board of Aldermen. Governor Alfred E. Smith actually chaired two consecutive charter commissions in 1933 and 1934. Then, in 1935, Mayor Fiorello LaGuardia appointed a charter commission, chaired by the Court of Appeals Judge Thomas Thacher, that produced the basic framework of the city government of New York as it is known today.

The overall effect of the Thacher charter was to increase the authority of the mayor. While the change was not dramatic, it began a trend that continued over the next three decades. The mayor's term had already been increased from two years to four years in 1905. He would now prepare the expense budget, a responsibility once held by the Board of Estimate and Apportionment. He also appointed six of the seven members of the newly created City Planning Commission. The commission was responsible for producing a master plan for the city and passed on all zoning changes subject to an override by a three-fourths vote of the Board of Estimate and Apportionment. The City Planning Commission was also responsible for preparing a capital budget for submission to the Board of Estimate and Apportionment. The board could delete from or modify the capital budget but needed a three-fourths majority vote to add items. The City Council also had the power to delete items, but it could not make any additions to the capital budget.

The renamed Board of Estimate ceased to be a legislative house and was treated instead as an executive board of directors. Despite its loss of legislative status and the transfer of some of its power to the mayor and planning commission, the board retained important powers over the budget and charter-related items. It set salaries, approved franchises, and authorized the sale or lease of property. While the Thacher commission removed the designation of the Board of Estimate as the upper chamber of the local legislature, any local law passed by the council that amended the charter, reduced revenue, or had anything to do with city employees still required approval by the board before submission to the mayor. The Thacher charter also gave the board the residual powers of the city, that is, those not specifically granted to any other institution of government or prohibited by state or federal law.

The bicameral Municipal Assembly was thus replaced by the one-chamber City Council. In another effort to improve the quality of its members and the efficiency of its operations, the size of the legislature was substantially reduced by linking it to voter turnout for councilmanic elections. One of the most controversial of the Thacher commission's charter changes created a system of proportional representation for the council that gave each borough one seat for every 75,000 votes cast. The terms of office for council members remained two years, until changed to four years in 1945, the last election for which proportional representation was used.

Redefining the Borough

The post–World War II era had brought significant changes in the distribution of the city population. With Veterans Administration mortgages available for buying homes, many inner-city residents from Manhattan and Brooklyn relocated to single-family suburban dwellings that were being built in Queens and, with the opening of the Verrazano Bridge, in Staten Island. The relocation of many middle-class and blue-collar voters to these outer boroughs was soon followed by demands for better representation. In 1958, the weighted voting scheme on the Board of Estimate was changed. All the borough presidents were given equal voting power — two votes each. The citywide officials (mayor, comptroller, and council president) were allowed to maintain a dominant position on the board, with four votes each. In the same year, Mayor Robert F. Wagner, concerned with the growing power of political bosses in the boroughs, asked the state legislature to allow him to appoint a new charter commission. Because the state had already initiated its own inquiries into the structure and operations of the city (the Moore commission), and the local Democratic party with which he was at odds obstructed action at the local level, Mayor Wagner did not succeed in setting up a charter commission until 1961. He appointed Judge John Cahill as chairman. Among the most notable changes brought about by the Cahill commission was a reduction in the role of the borough presidents. There was also a commensurate shift of power to the mayor and the City Council. The Cahill commission's work also resulted in the early definition of the structure of community government as it is known today.

Under the Cahill charter, the remaining administrative responsibilities held by the borough presidents, mostly concentrated in the area of public works, were transferred to the mayor. The mayor was authorized to appoint the chairman of the City Planning Commission, who would serve at his pleasure and oversee the Department of City Planning. Through the appointment of a personnel director, the mayor was given control over personnel matters once held by the Board of Estimate. As the city's chief executive, the mayor was granted power to reorganize the administrative structure of the municipality and to transfer funds between agencies. City Council approval was required for the former; Board of Estimate and City Council approval was required for the latter. The mayor, however, could make intra-agency transfers on his own. He retained responsibility for preparing the expense budget, and a two-thirds vote of both bodies was required to override his veto on a budget item. Finally, the residual powers of the city that were once held by the Board of Estimate were shifted to the mayor.

The Board of Estimate retained certain administrative functions, such as the supervision of franchises, leases, and concessions. Real-estate management, however, was moved to a mayoral agency. The board continued to approve both the overall expense budget and the capital budget. It retained final power over zoning regulations, but it lost most of its power to make laws.

The net effect of the Cahill commission charter was a reduction in the role of the borough presidents. The borough presidents did, however, assume new responsibilities in the area of community governance under the Cahill charter. They now appointed members of the community planning boards and chaired newly created borough-improvement boards. This community-based role in planning and land use complemented the citywide powers the borough presidents had as members of the Board of Estimate in these areas.

In order to provide opportunities for minority parties in city government, the Cahill charter alloted two at-large council seats per borough, and prohibited each party from nominating more than one at-large candidate in any borough. However, as with the allocation of equal votes to all borough presidents on the Board of Estimate, the allotment of two at-large council seats to each borough failed to recognize their differences in population. Finally, it was also declared in 1961 that all legislative powers were concentrated in the City Council. The council could override a mayoral veto with a two-thirds majority, but it still shared its authority to approve the budget with the Board of Estimate.

Community Government

Governor Nelson A. Rockefeller's appointment of the State Charter Commission in 1972 marked the culmination of years of planning, debate, and experimentation designed to effect a structure for neighborhood government in New York City.

One of the stated goals of the legislation creating the commission (chaired by New York State Senator Roy Goodman) was "to encourage genuine citizen participation in local city government." The plan produced by this commission in 1975 not only sought to create a government that was more responsive to New York City's diverse population but also sought to establish another check on the power of elected officials through the involvement of an informed citizenry at the neighborhood levels. Accountability was a prominent goal toward the end of the commission's work, as the city entered its most severe fiscal crisis in recent history. A central target of the new accountability measures was the mayor. The system of community government that emerged in 1975 and continues today is a two-level structure involving community boards and borough boards.

Under the Goodman commission charter, the mayor was given more latitude in reorganizing executive departments, but changes that altered the city charter required council approval. Although there were no structural changes made in the City Council and Board of Estimate, a number of measures were taken to increase the checks these bodies could exercise over the mayor. The mayor was required to submit a preliminary executive budget to both bodies for more extensive review. In response to the fiscal crisis of 1975, the charter itself required that this budget be balanced. As a member of the Board of Estimate, the mayor was no longer permitted to vote on the budget. Nor could he veto reductions made in the expense budget by either the Board of Estimate or the City Council. The mayor could veto any increase by either of these bodies, but the veto could be overridden by a two-thirds majority of either body with a simple majority of the other. The two bodies were also required to approve transfers of funds from one program to another.

As another means to increase the accountability of the city's chief executive, the mayor was required to submit a management report to the Board of Estimate and the City Council describing the operational goals and performance of mayoral agencies. The board and the council were expected to hold public hearings on this document. In order to provide the board and the council with an analytic capability to review financial and management reports, the Legislative Office of Budget Review was created. This office, headed by a professional director chosen by both bodies, was eliminated after considerable political infighting in 1981. Under the 1975 charter, the council was given the power of advice and consent on mayoral appointments to some boards and commisssions but not to major single-headed executive departments. The standing committees of the council were given the authority to conduct investigations and were given subpoena power, but they have not used these powers. The Board of Estimate retained final discretion with regard to planning, land use, and zoning.

Under the Goodman charter, the comptroller was required to establish a uniform system of accounts based on the system designed by the state comptroller. There was a substantial increase in the comptroller's audit role, although preaudits were relinquished to the departments, subject to oversight and review by the comptroller. The City Council president was given new responsibilities as a citywide ombudsman.

One Person, One Vote

In 1981, a federal district court in Manhattan ruled in *Andrews* v. *Koch* that the practice of electing two at-large council members per borough irrespective of the population of the boroughs violated the one-person, one-vote principle established by the Fourteenth Amendment of the Constitution. This decision was subsequently affirmed by the Second Circuit Court of Appeals and the United States Supreme Court. At about the same time, the U.S. Department of Justice rejected a plan proposed by a districting commission appointed by the City Council, resulting in a postponement of the council elections in 1981. In the meantime, the 1980 United States census revealed that many community districts in the city had fallen below the minimum 100,000 population required by the city charter.

In 1982 Mayor Edward I. Koch appointed a charter commission chaired by Michael Sovern, the president of Columbia University. Unlike previous charter commissions, which had conducted a full review of the structure and operations of the municipal government, the Sovern commission focused on the single issue of equal representation. In 1983, in accord with the recommendations of the commission, the city charter was amended to eliminate the two at-large council seats that had been allotted to each borough and to establish a new districting commission composed of nine members appointed by the mayor. Additionally, each community district was prohibited from having a population of more than 250,000.

In 1986 a federal district court ruled in *Morris* v. *Board of Estimate* that the practice of giving the representatives of all boroughs equal voting strength on the Board of Estimate despite differences in population violated the Fourteenth Amendment of the Constitution. In December 1986 Mayor Koch appointed a fifteen-person Charter Revision Commission, chaired by Richard Ravitch. The commission was charged to undertake a complete review of the structure and operation of city government. In October 1987, the district-court decision was affirmed by a three-panel Circuit Court of Appeals. The decision was subsequently appealed to the United States Supreme Court, which on 23 March 1989 found the Board of Estimate unconstitutional.

When its term of office expired at the end of 1988, the Ravitch commission was succeeded by a second charter commission, with eleven of the same members appointed by Mayor Koch for a two-year term. Chaired by former Corporation Counsel Frederick A. O. Schwarz, Jr., the new commission began its work in January 1989, in anticipation of the Supreme Court's action. Soon after the Court announced its decision, the commission proceeded to develop a new set of proposals for restructuring the city government that would be reviewed by the voters on election day in November 1989.

NOTES

1. On the early history of the city as a relatively autonomous corporation, see Gerald Benjamin, "The Political Relationship," in *The Two New Yorks*, ed. Gerald Benjamin and Charles Brecher (New York: Russell Sage Foundation, 1988), 115–17; Hendrik Hartog, *Public Property and Private Power* (Chapel Hill: University of North Carolina Press, 1983).

2. Frederick Shaw, *History of the New York City Legislature* (New York: Columbia University Press, 1954), 4.

3. Cited in Harold C. Syrett, *The City of Brooklyn, 1865–1898: A Political History* (New York: Columbia University Press, 1944), 109.

4. Shaw, 4.

5. Alfred R. Conkling, *City Government in the United States* (New York: Appleton, 1897), 224–96.

6. Cited in Frank J. Goodnow, *City Government in the United States* (New York: The Century Company, 1910), 147–48.

7. Edward Dana Durand, "Council Government versus Mayor Government," *Political Science Quarterly* 15 (December 1900): 675–709.

8. Dorman Eaton, *The Government of Municipalities* (New York: Columbia University Press, 1899), 252.

9. William B. Munro, *The Government of American Cities* (New York: The Macmillan Company, 1926), 77.

10. Russel Forbes, "The Municipal Assembly: New York's Home Rule Legislature," *National Municipal Review* 18 (October 1929): 633.

The Practical Lessons of Charter Reform

ERIC LANE

In November 1986, a federal district court judge declared the scheme of voting on New York City's Board of Estimate to be in violation of the constitutional doctrine of one person, one vote.[1] Mayor Edward I. Koch immediately appointed a charter revision commission, which defined its task broadly. It decided not only to examine alternative voting plans for the Board of Estimate but also to study whether other institutions could better perform the board's myriad powers, which include all final land-use and franchising decisions, the approval of certain types of contracts, and joint responsibility with the City Council for passing the budget. Richard Ravitch, then chairman of the Bowery Savings Bank and formerly head of the Metropolitan Transportation Authority and earlier the New York State Urban Development Corporation, was named chair of the commission by the mayor, who then added fourteen members, representing much of the city's geographic, demographic, and political diversity.

I was named the commission's executive director and counsel after several meetings with its chair, during which we discussed the extensive powers granted the commission by state law and the special opportunity it was being given to rewrite the city's governing document, or what was regularly referred to by some as the city's "constitution." Indeed, during the early proceedings, many members of the commission and its staff were infected by what one commissioner characterized as the "constitutional spirit" of our undertaking.

Now, however, more than two years have passed since the commission postponed its major reform efforts to await a decision of the United States Supreme Court, which took jurisdiction in the initiating case. Time has not dampened my enthusiasm for the task or diminished my sense of its importance (in fact, this sense has been enhanced by what I have learned), and it has forced me to refocus my attention from the hoped-for clean path of constitutional reform to a much

This essay, first published in 1988, does not reflect events since it was written. Reprinted, with minor stylistic changes, from *Urban, State and Local Law Newsletter* 11 (Summer 1988): 1, 17–18. Used with permission.

more thorny route of legal brambles and political prickles. From this focus I draw a series of lessons.

First, before you begin, know your limitations. Municipalities, for better or worse, continue to be legal dependencies, subject to numerous and frequently illogical state constitutional and statutory restraints. New York State's constitution, for example, contains home-rule provisions that are mandated to be read liberally but are interpreted narrowly. Furthermore, the state has adopted a local government bill of rights that promises much but delivers little. Thus, while the written law provides for municipalities "to have powers to adopt local laws" at least "relating to its property, affairs or government," and the state is constrained from regulating in these areas, except through general law, the power granted the state under this exception is, with judicial approval, frequently and liberally exercised. This leaves the municipality far less discretion in its affairs than may at first glance be imagined. This is particularly true for New York City, which everyone in state government wants to govern from afar. Examples abound, but a few will demonstrate the point.

The commission intends to reform New York City's arcane and inefficient procurement practices. Under the charter, all contracts over $15,000 have to be let under a system of competitive sealed bids (unless a different method is approved under special circumstances by the Board of Estimate). This is of particular significance in New York City, where $5 billion — one-quarter of the city's annual expenditures — is made through contracts. Three billion dollars is bid competitively. Many members of the commission consider this reliance on competitive sealed bids to be far too restrictive and wish to modernize the process through the introduction of other forms of competitive procurement and a reduction in the powers of the Board of Estimate. However, despite these exigencies and a consensus for reform, the commission must still contend with a state law that (except where a grandfather clause applies, as it does now for New York City) requires competitive sealed bidding for amounts substantially lower than currently in the charter.

A second example of our limitations is the state-imposed restriction on municipalities that seems to prevent them from restructuring their legislative bodies more than once a decade. This restriction potentially placed some limitation on the commission's goal of increasing the size of the council by reducing the size of each district. In New York City each council district has a population of 212,000, the largest in the United States, and the commission generally thinks that smaller districts will create more responsive representation and afford more election opportunity to the city's racial and political minorities. The pitfalls of this statute may be avoided by having the effective date of any such change fall in the next decade. Other examples were found in almost every substantive area of commission attention and even permeated the procedures for the commission's operations.

Second, while you are concerned about state law, do not forget to consider federal law. Early in the life of the commission, we became aware that any proposal the commission might adopt to change the structure of the Board of Estimate, its voting scheme, or its powers would have to be subject to U.S. Justice Department preclearance under section 5 of the Voting Rights Act of 1965. Moreover, we were concerned that many of the proposals before the commission might not receive such preclearance, nor be sustained in an action under section 2 of that act. Additionally, questions were raised under section 2 about the present board. A particular concern was whether weighted voting plans for the Board of Estimate submerged minority voting power in New York City, thus frustrating minorities' ability to participate in the political process and to elect representatives of their choice. Members of the commission were initially skeptical that the prohibitions of the act could apply to our work. After the presentation of opinions of five different legal experts, countless discussions on the matter, and a rending public debate with affected political figures, the members finally accepted the view that the adoption of any such plan would create an unacceptable risk. Nevertheless, at the time the commission postponed its consideration of alternatives to the Board of Estimate, it was still examining the impact of the Voting Rights Act on a series of alternatives that transferred the powers of the board to various other governmental institutions and officers.

Third, while you are considering state and federal law, do not forget to take into account politics. Changing the structure of a municipal government means affecting the power of its elected and appointed officers. Whether such change enhances or diminishes the power of such officials, it will generally disturb them, requiring enormous time, effort, and finesse to secure support or neutrality — if you want either. At the time the commission postponed its deliberation on structural reforms, all the proposals of its chairman were under assault by at least some elected officials, and his proposals were often found troublesome by many officeholders. This is particularly unpleasant because in New York City, at least, such matters quickly get personalized and also because charter proposals must be approved at a referendum.

Additionally, charter issues are frequently part of the agendas of those vying for political power (a perfectly legitimate and appropriate effort) and always part of the agendas of civic groups advocating their views of good government. Thus, many resources must be directed to considering all their interests and demands, the moderation of which is an exact art, recognized only in hindsight.

Fourth, while you are concerned about state law, federal law, and politics, do not forget to take into account the need for good government. The term *good government* reminds me of Oliver Wendell Holmes's apt phrase "delusive exactness." All the many groups and individuals who appear before, talk with, or lobby the commission, its members, and staff are for good government. Most of them are persuasive, and most of them disagree. While some of their positions, as well as the commissioners', cannot withstand research or logical reasoning, others — often competing ones — frequently make good sense. This leaves the question of how a commission's judgments are to be formed. Exhaustive research and analysis, experience, instinct, intuition, faith in the deliberative process, and the ability to tolerate a residuum of self-doubt seems a good place to start. There is, of course, also the assurance that the electorate will make the final decision.

Note

1. *Morris* v. *Board of Estimate*, 647 F. Supp. 1463 (1986). This case was subsequently affirmed by the United States Court of Appeals for the Second Circuit, 831 F.2d 384 (1987) and by the United States Supreme Court, 489 U.S. 103 (1989).

Taking Home Rule Seriously: The Case of Campaign Finance Reform

RICHARD BRIFFAULT

It is often contended that home rule has failed to fulfill its essential purpose of empowering local governments to act, on their own initiative, with respect to local matters. Many commentators have argued that the "narrow and restrictive judicial interpretation" given to local autonomy has stunted local initiative and discouraged local governments from utilizing the powers home rule may give them.[1] New York State, in particular, is said to have a constricted home rule tradition that provides local governments little real autonomy. Yet New York has just witnessed a striking example of municipal innovation: New York City's adoption of a program of optional partial public funding of campaigns for municipal offices.

Adopted in 1988 pursuant to a charter amendment and local laws, the New York City Campaign Finance Act provides public matching funds to candidates for mayor, other citywide offices, borough president, and city council in primary, runoff primary, and general elections. To qualify, candidates must limit campaign contributions and expenditures and abide by reporting and disclosure requirements. In terms of the number of offices and elections covered, the New York City law creates one of the most extensive public campaign finance programs at any level of government—federal, state, or local—in the country.

New York City's campaign finance program was adopted as a matter of local home rule, without any express state constitutional or statutory authorization. This essay examines the legal underpinnings of the city's power to enact such a significant local measure in the absence of express state authorization and in the face of considerable state legislation in the area of elections. It determines that, although existing judicial doctrines are too vague to be dispositive, a normative theory of home rule and preemption can be constructed that is both consistent with the case law and attentive to the competing concerns of empowering local governments while precluding local measures that interfere with state policies or impose extra-local costs. Such an approach would result in the validation of New

York City's campaign finance law. Indeed, treating the city campaign finanace law as a case study of the application of home rule and preemption theory to a major municipal innovation provides a welcome opportunity to demonstrate how the often-deprecated constitutional and statutory home rule grants and state preemption decisions can be used to vindicate municipal authority to engage in reforms in the structure and operations of local government.

State Constitutional and Statutory Framework

The fundamental source of local legislative power in New York is article IX of the state constitution. Article IX makes two general grants to local governments: first, "every local government shall have power to adopt and amend local laws not inconsistent with the provisions of this constitution or any general law relating to its property, affairs or government"; second, localities may adopt and amend laws in ten specified fields, whether or not these matters relate to local "property, affairs or government," but these local laws must not be "inconsistent" with the constitution or general laws, and local legislation not related to local "property, affairs or government" may be limited "to the extent that the legislature shall restrict the adoption of such a local law."

Among the fields in which a locality is specifically authorized to legislate are: "the . . . mode of selection . . . of its officers and employees"; and "the government, protection, order, conduct, safety, health and well-being of persons or property therein"— what is generally known as "the police power." In addition, article IX provides that "rights, powers, privileges and immunities granted to local governments by this article shall be liberally construed."

When article IX was revised in 1963, the legislature adopted the Municipal Home Rule Law to implement the constitution's grant of home rule powers. That law grants lawmaking authority with respect to local "property, affairs or government," the "mode of selection" of local officers, and the police power, and it also provides that such local powers "shall be liberally construed."

Courts have treated the "property, affairs or government" and "mode of selection" grants to authorize municipal regulation of local elections. Local control over the processes by which local officials are selected and local public policies are formulated is the core of municipal home rule. As the Court of Appeals, New York's highest court, observed in *Resnick* v. *County of Ulster*, "the idea that local officials should be chosen by local constituencies is one with deep roots in our democratic polity." Although New York has generally been seen as a weak home rule state, "there has been little dispute about the liberality with which municipalities have been given the power to devise their governmental structure and to provide for the allocation of responsibility for the discharge of government functions."[2]

Thus, in *Bareham* v. *City of Rochester*, decided under a much weaker home rule provision a half century ago, the Court of Appeals held that Rochester could depart from the state-prescribed municipal structure of a strong mayor and partisan elections and adopt a council-manager government with nonpartisan elections. According to the *Bareham* court, "the term 'mode of selection' expresses an intent to allow a city to determine not only that it shall cause its officers either to be elected or appointed but connotes also that a municipality may define the precise method by which either an election or appointment shall be effected."[3]

Other court decisions have looked to the "property, affairs or government" authority as the source of power to regulate local elections. In *Baldwin* v. *City of Buffalo*, for example, the Court of Appeals held that Buffalo could by local law change the boundaries of the wards in the city from which the Buffalo members of the Erie County Board of Supervisors were elected. Even though the city wards were used to elect county supervisors, "the alteration of ward boundaries is properly an affair of the municipality." In *Resnick* v. *County of Ulster* the Court of Appeals relied on both the "mode of selection" and "property, affairs or government" provisions to uphold a county law for filling vacancies in the county legislature that conflicted with the procedure provided in state law. Such a local law, the court said, was "well within both the philosophy and the explicit formulations" of home rule.

The General Municipal Law's grant of power to local governments to enact codes of ethics also supports local campaign finance legislation. Campaign finance laws are inspired as much by concerns about the postelection behavior of public officials as about the conduct of the electoral process. As distinct from earlier laws barring vote-buying and bribery of election officials, contemporary laws limiting contributions or providing public funds address the integrity of government between elections and the preservation of public trust in government operations. Campaign finance laws are comparable to restrictions on conflicts of interest and requirements of public disclosure. The State-City Commission on Integrity in Government took exactly this approach in including campaign finance reform in its package of ethics proposals.[4]

Section 806 of the General Municipal Law directs local governments to adopt codes of ethics "setting forth for the guidance of its officers and employees the standards of conduct reasonably expected of them." In *Belle* v. *Town of Onondaga*, the court relied on section 806, along with home rule, to uphold a town law banning officers and employees from holding political party positions, finding the town enactment "represents the kind of local initiative that section 806 of the General Municipal Law was designed to encourage."

Finally, cities possess the police power. The grant of the police power — the right to adopt and amend local laws concerning "the government, protection, order, conduct, safety, health and well-being of persons and property"— was a signal contribution of the 1963 constitutional amendment. Subject to whatever constitutional and statutory constraints may be applicable, a city may enact any measure that it deems will promote the local general welfare. By granting the police power, the constitution allows a city to legislate within its limits just as far as the state may legislate within its boundaries. As the state's own campaign finance laws indicate, campaign finance regulation clearly falls within the police power.

In sum, New York City has four grants of constitutional and statutory authority that support local regulation of the financing of campaigns in local elections: (1) "property, affairs or government"; (2) the "mode of selection" of local public officials; (3) the power to set ethical standards for local officials; and (4) the police power. Taken together, and supplemented by the constitutional and statutory injunctions that home rule powers be liberally construed, they provide broad support for local campaign finance measures.

Local Campaign Finance Regulation in Other States

In the federal system, the powers of a municipality turn entirely upon the laws of the state in which that municipality is incorporated. The laws of other states concerning the powers of local governments have no binding effect. Nevertheless, examples of other states permitting localities to regulate campaign finance support the idea that campaign finance is a proper matter of local concern.

In California, forty-four cities and counties have adopted charter provisions or ordinances relating to local campaign finance, including limits on cash or anonymous contributions, disclosure of contributors' names, and bans on contributions by city contractors, city licensees, or corporations.[5] Thirty-four jurisdictions, including the cities of Los Angeles, San Diego, and San Francisco and Orange County, have enacted limitations on the amount of contributions.

Prior to the adoption of New York's new law, the most ambitious local campaign finance regulation may have been that of Seattle, Washington. In 1976, the voters amended the Seattle city charter to require public disclosure of campaign contributions to and expenditures by or on behalf of candidates and ballot issues. In 1978, the city passed an ordinance setting limitations on campaign contributions, providing matching funds to candidates for local offices, and requiring candidates seeking matching funds to sign a "campaign contract" in which the candidate-recipient pledged to limit total spending and the size of the candidate's personal contribution to his or her own campaign.[6] In 1985, Seattle enacted a new program of partial public funding that followed the basic format of the 1978 ordinance.

The Supreme Court of Washington, in *City of Seattle* v. *State*, upheld the partial campaign funding program. The court found the program presented no danger of the improper diversion of public funds for private purposes—the principal issue in the case—and that the charter provision and ordinance, by curtailing the influence of special interest groups on local government, served a public purpose. The city had "the power to enact rules and spend funds with the purpose of protecting the authority and integrity of the ballot box." The court did not even consider the question of local power to act without express state authorization, apparently treating the scope of local autonomy over campaign finance not to be an issue at all.

The strongest explicit judicial affirmation of local home rule authority to regulate local campaign finance may be that of the Supreme Court of Utah in *State* v. *Hutchinson*, which found that a county could, as a matter of local police power and without further express state authorization, adopt an ordinance requiring candidates for county commissioner to file statements and disclose the size and source of contributions. As a matter of home rule, the "county has the power to preserve the purity of its electoral process," including the authority to require the disclosure of contributions.

Finally, Arizona voters passed an initiative measure in 1986 that set contribution restrictions on elections for state and local office and expressly authorized counties, cities, and towns to adopt contribution limits "that are stricter than those provided for" in the state law.

Home Rule and Preemption

In New York, each of the sources of home rule authority is subject to the restriction that any local enactment be "not inconsistent" with the state constitution or the state's general laws. The only provision of the constitution dealing with local elections is the requirement that such elections be held in odd-numbered years; the constitution does not address local authority to regulate campaign finances at all. The only provision of the Municipal Home Rule Law restricting local autonomy over elections relates solely to the dates and hours of voting.

The state has, however, legislated extensively in the area of elections — in particular, with respect to state and local election campaign finance. Local action in this area could, therefore, be arguably "inconsistent" with the state Election Law and, hence, preempted.

There are two strands to comtemporary preemption doctrine. The first focuses on whether the state and local governments have issued conflicting commands. A clear case of conflict would be a statute requiring motorists to drive on the right side of the road and a local ordinance requiring that they drive on the left. A motorist cannot comply with both laws at the same time. Most state-local conflicts, however, are more subtle than this example suggests. The most difficult issue is whether a limited state prohibition conflicts with a local measure extending that prohibition to conduct the state left alone.

The second strand of preemption analysis focuses not on conflict per se but on whether, given the fact of state regulation, any local enactment on the same subject — even one substantively consistent with the terms of the state law — would be inconsistent with the fact of state lawmaking in the area. This theory, known as "occupation of the field," recognizes that state and local laws may be formally consistent but that the local rule may still interfere with state policy. A court faced with a claim of occupation of the field must decide whether a field is to be regulated by the state *exclusively* or whether state law may coexist with local rules that reflect particular local concerns.

Outright Conflict

State courts have taken two different approaches to determining whether state and local laws are in conflict. The older approach, best exemplified in the 1962 decision in *Wholesale Laundry Board of Trade, Inc.* v. *City of New York*, would find a conflict and preempt local law whenever a local government seeks to extend the reach of a state prohibition. *Wholesale Laundry* concerned a New York City local law setting a minimum wage in the city of $1.25 an hour, while the minimum wage required by the state was only $1.00. The Appellate Division, in an opinion subsequently adopted by the Court of Appeals, found that the city minimum wage law conflicted with the state statute: "Generally speaking, local laws which do not prohibit what the State law permits nor allow what the State law forbids are not inconsistent . . . .However, where the extension of the principle of the State law by means of the local law results in a situation where what would be permissible under the State law becomes a violation of the local law, the latter law is unauthorized." Consequently, since the state law would permit employers to pay $1.00 an hour, a local law requiring a higher wage was preempted.

The *Wholesale Laundry* approach is a bad one because it ultimately subverts home rule. If any limited state prohibition is held to constitute an affirmative authorization of all conduct not prohibited, then, once the state has passed a law all local action that goes beyond mere duplication of the state's law is preempted. The dissenters to the Court of Appeals' affirmance in *Wholesale Laundry* recognized this. Judge Dye would have found a conflict only if the local law had sought to permit what the state law prohibited (e.g., to lower the minimum wage below $1.00) not the other way round. Judge Fuld would have found a conflict only if the city had permitted what the state had barred or if the "state statute *affirmatively* permits" what the city would prohibit.

In subsequent decisions, the *Wholesale Laundry* dissenters appear to have carried the day. The state's judges have increasingly held that localities may supplement state laws with additional restrictions or requirements unless the state has "affirmatively" or "specifically" sought to protect conduct from local regulation. In *People* v. *Cook*, for example, the Court of Appeals considered a New York City tax regulation requiring cigarette retailers to maintain a difference in price between high tar and nicotine cigarettes and those with a lower tar and nicotine content, with the price differential based on the differences in tax attributable to the difference in tar and nicotine. The defendant retailer contended that although the state taxed cigarettes according to their tar and nicotine content the state did not require the tax difference to be passed along in the price; and, therefore, the city requirement ran afoul of the rule that "a locality may not 'enact a local law which prohibits conduct which is permitted by State law.'"

A unanimous Court of Appeals strongly disagreed. Linking preemption to home rule, the court found that if the defendant's argument "were the rule, the power of local governments to regulate would be illusory. Any time that the State law is silent on a subject, the likelihood is that a local law regulating that subject will prohibit something permitted elsewhere in the State. That is the essence of home rule."

The Appellate Division for the Third Department, in *Town of Clifton Park* v. *C.P. Enterprises*, worked *Cook*'s insight concerning the connection between preemption and home rule into the language of the Home Rule Article and the Municipal Home Rule Law. *Clifton Park* involved a town procedure for the publication of new laws that differed from that required by the state in the Town Law. The defendant contended the town's procedure was, thus, "inconsistent" with state law, and therefore invalid. The court disagreed: "We do not perceive the use of the word 'inconsistent' to be the equivalent of 'different'. . . . To define the word 'inconsistent' narrowly as meaning merely 'different' would vitiate the flexibility of home rule. . . . Rather, it is a check against local laws which would contradict or would be incompatible or inharmonious with the general laws of the State."

Most New York courts have followed *Cook* and *Clifton Park* and have declined to find "inconsistency" in cases where a local government would prohibit what the state has permitted unless the state statute could be characterized as "specifically" allowing the conduct in question. Thus, in *Council for Owner Occupied Housing, Inc.* v. *Koch*, New York City's requirements that the sponsor of a cooperative conversion establish a reserve fund for capital repairs and post notice of the building's housing code violations were sustained. The sponsor argued that since the state law governing cooperative conversions had not included these rules the city law would prohibit a conversion that the state would allow, and, thus, the city's law was "inconsistent" with the state's. Relying on *Cook* and *Clifton Park*, the court found that "silence on this issue should not be interpreted as an expression of intent by the legislature. To interpret a statute in that manner would vitiate the concept of home rule." Similarly, in *People* v. *Ortiz*, the court rejected the argument that the city's "knife law," which proscribes the possession in public places of knives with blades four-inches or longer, is "inconsistent" with a section of the state Penal Law that bans the possession of certain weapons, including knives, but only if possession is accompanied by criminal intent. The court treated the "knife law" as a permissible extension of state law and not a conflict: "the 'knife law' does not prohibit what is specifically allowed under State law, nor does it allow what the State law specifically forbids. It merely supplements the Penal Law with additional reasonable requirements."

Which standard New York courts will apply to determine the existence of a conflict is not certain. *Wholesale Laundry* continues to be cited, and courts quote its phrase that a locality may not prohibit what the state permits, without adding the qualifier that the state's permission be "specific" or "affirmative."[7] These citations, however, are usually cursory or dicta,[8] and the rule in *Cook* and *Clifton Park* is applied more often.[9] The rule is also more in keeping with the spirit of home rule.

Occupation of the Field

Although the courts have generally rejected the notion that a state law constitutes affirmative permission of all conduct not proscribed, they have also refused to endorse the logical converse — that local legislation will be held "inconsistent" with state law only when the state has explicitly banned local lawmaking. Preemption, the Court of Appeals said in *Consolidated Edison* v. *Town of Red Hook*, "need not be express. It is enough that the Legislature has impliedly evinced its desire to do so." It is through the tension between these two principles — that state law is not automatically preemptive of local initiative, but that state law may be preemptive even when preemption is not expressly declared in the statute — that the doctrine of preemption by implication, or occupation of the field, has developed.

The courts have formally considered the question of occupation of the field to be a matter of legislative interpretation. Local action will be deemed preempted if the legislature so intended. The courts have relied on two indicators to divine the legislature's intent: statements of legislative policy and the scope of the state's regulatory scheme. These criteria, however, have often proved to be uncertain guides.

Sometimes the legislature gives a relatively clear indication of whether it intends to permit or preclude local lawmaking. In *Monroe-Livingston Sanitary Landfill, Inc.* v. *Town of Caledonia*, for example, the Court of Appeals found that the state law regulating solid waste disposal disclaimed any preemptive purpose and "speaks specifically, not of the preclusion, but rather the inclusion of local government in the planning and control of problems endemic to waste management." In *Consolidated Edison* v. *Town of Red Hook*, the Court of Appeals read the statement of purpose accompanying the state law dealing with the siting of major power plants, which stressed the goal of providing for the "expeditious resolution of all matters" related to the siting issues "in a single proceeding," to preclude local regulation.

More commonly, the legislature's declarations are difficult to fathom. The statement of legislative purpose accompanying the state law regulating the possession and sale of drug paraphernalia referred to the existence of local ordinances on the subject and declared it "the policy of the state to prohibit the sale of drug paraphernalia." Judges have divided over whether the state occupied the field. One court read that declaration, and a statement in the legislative history that the state law would be "one more weapon" in the attack on drugs, as indicating an intent to supplement and support local action.[10] Another court held that the state declaration "evinced an intent to make that article the sole remedy" and thus preempted local laws.[11]

Often, the state law says nothing at all about preemption. In these situations, courts focus on the scope of the state's regulatory scheme. If the state legislation is "comprehensive and detailed," setting forth numerous or interrelated standards, requirements or prohibitions or an administrative enforcement mechanism, it is likely to be preemptive. If the state has legislated "piecemeal" or in a "fragmented" fashion, then there has been no occupation of the field. As with the statements of legislative policy, this determination is sometimes straightforward. In *Red Hook*, the state provided substantive standards, extensive procedural detail, and an administrative mechanism that sought to have all the affected interests balanced by a single decision maker. The state was deemed to have occupied the field of major power plant siting. Conversely, the state laws in *Council for Owner Occupied Housing, Inc.* v. *Koch* mandated disclosure of only the facts considered necessary for investors considering the purchase of real estate securities and did not address the interests of tenants. The state was found to have not occupied "the entire multifaceted field of conversions"; thus, the city could regulate additional aspects of the field.

But the "scope of regulation" test usually yields less determinate results. It is rarely certain whether the several state laws on a subject add up to a "comprehensive regulatory scheme," and there is no obvious definition of what constitutes a "field."

Thus, the state's Penal Law regulates extensively and in detail the possession of dangerous weapons, yet numerous local laws criminalizing additional aspects of weapons possession have been upheld. In *People* v. *Judiz*, for example, the Court of Appeals upheld a New York City ordinance making it unlawful to possess a toy pistol that resembles a real gun. The state Penal Law criminalizes the possession of toy guns, and many other weapons, but only if possession is accompanied by an intent to use for an unlawful purpose. Even though the provisions of the Penal Law "evince[d] an intent to cover, quite broadly, most of the possible categories of weapons for which [the State] deems some sanction is necessary" the state had not occupied the field of weapons possession because the Penal Law is limited to possession with illegal intent—a narrower, and apparently different, field.

The question of the scope of the field occupied by the state badly split the Appelate Division in *Matter of Ames* v. *Smoot*, which considered whether the state law regulating pesticides preempted a local law prohibiting the aerial spraying of pesticides. The state law governs the uses of pesticides, provides for the testing and certification of pesticide applicators, and vests "jurisdiction in all matters pertaining to the distribution, sale, use and transportation" of pesticides in a state agency, but is silent on the subject of aerial spraying. Three justices concluded that the "complete and detailed nature of the State's scheme . . . clearly evince[d] the State's intention to preempt local regulation of pesticide use." Two other justices read the state law as focused only on permissible uses and the regulation of commercial applicators. That field had been occupied but not the broader field of all aspects of pesticides, such as aerial spraying.

As these examples indicate, neither legislative declarations nor the scope of state legislation constitutes a ready or determinate test for the resolution of the preemption question. A more normative framework is needed to reconcile the underlying policy goals of promoting local autonomy while controlling the costs of local variation from a statewide standard. Such an analysis, which is consistent with the decisions in many cases, would look to the nature of the matter regulated and consider whether it is a subject for which statewide uniformity is necessary or, rather, whether the variety of local conditions in the state make diversity in local lawmaking appropriate.

A proper commitment to home rule would require that there be at least a modest bias in the system in favor of local diversity so that the burden is on the party asserting preemption to demonstrate that the legislature has "evinced an unmistakable desire" to occupy the field.[12] The spirit of home rule requires that the balance be so struck since the essence of home rule is the authorization of nonuniformity for those matters about which localities may make law.

But nonuniformity has its costs, and in certain contexts those costs may be so much greater than the benefits of local diversity as to give rise to a presumption that state regulation occupies the field to the exclusion of local action. The costs of nonuniformity are greatest when local action has extra-local consequences or when it impairs free movement within the state.[13]

The problem of external effects is well illustrated in *Red Hook*: the town would have reaped all the benefits of the restriction, but the costs would have been borne throughout the area to be served by the projected power plant. Extra-local effects also figured in the invalidation of a Suffolk County law authorizing the formation of a local development corporation to acquire the Long Island Lighting Company. The state had just created a Long Island Power Authority with the authority to take over Lilco. Both measures were motivated by concerns over the Shoreham plant. The state and local laws were not in direct conflict, since the state did not mandate that its new state agency acquire Lilco. Nevertheless, in *Long Island Lighting Co.* v. *County of Suffolk*, the court held the Suffolk law preempted. Under the Suffolk plan the utility would be tax-exempt, while the state law required payments in lieu of taxes. Any savings under the Suffolk law "would only be to [Suffolk] ratepayers, and the resulting loss of tax revenues to the State would have to be shouldered by all its taxpayers." In addition, the state law prevented the Long Island Power Authority from acquiring preference hydrolectric power, whereas the local measure had no such restriction — another effort on the part of the county to prefer its residents at the expense of nonresidents.

Extra-local costs may also be imposed and free movement within the state impaired when many localities have different rules on the same matter. A business subject to varying local product safety requirements, for example, would have to either make products according to different specifications for different localities, which could be very inefficient, or run its entire operations statewide according to the rule of the most stringent locality, which would impose costs on all other localities in the state. Concern about the costs of multiple local lawmaking may be seen in the *Wholesale Laundry* and *Ames* decisions. In each case, the local rule would have affected companies operating in many localities, and complying with varying local laws could have been costly.

A good instance of judicial balancing of concerns for extra-local consequences and special local needs may be seen in the recent Fourth Department decision in *Morrell* v. *C.I.D. Landfill, Inc.*, which considered whether a state measure regulating the extractive mining industry preempted a local ordinance concerning the regrading of the land around a mining site. While local regulation would inevitably have some extra-local consequences, since mine products are consumed outside the locality, there was an appropriate local concern with the condition of the site after the mining had ended.The court found the state had occupied the field "relating to the extractive mining industry" but had not preempted local regulations designed to prevent nuisances.

Finally, occupation of the field because of a lack of statewide uniformity may occur when local laws threaten to impinge on the free movement of people across local boundaries. New York is a highly mobile society. New Yorkers, particularly those living in metropolitan areas, may live in one locality, work in another, shop in a third, seek recreation in a fourth, and travel through many others in the course of a day. People frequently change their residences or places of work within the state. Mapping variant local laws across a mobile population makes it difficult for people to know what laws they are subject to or to determine whether their conduct violates a local rule. The lack of proper notice, and the resulting unfairness, may be greatest when the ordinances impose criminal penalties for behavior not obviously wrongful.

Thus, state occupation of the field has been found, and local laws preempted, most commonly when localities have sought to criminalize behavior that might be characterized as only borderline criminal or antisocial but not obviously dangerous or unlawful, such as gambling at home, patronizing after hours clubs, certain aspects of disorderly conduct, and possessing drug paraphernalia.[14] In each case the local ordinance could have been characterized as merely supplementing provisions of the Penal Law in a manner consistent with the opinions in *Cook* and *Clifton Park*. But, in this context, the danger that "different standards, definitions, and penalties would lead to confused and inconsistent enforcement"[15] rendered local regulation inconsistent with fundamental fairness.[16]

The law of preemption should be viewed as an attempt to reconcile the deep-seated tension between the local diversity that home rule creates and the need, in certain areas, for statewide uniformity. The argument for uniformity and for presuming, without an express declaration, that the state has occupied the field is strongest when a local law will have considerable effects outside the local boundaries, when multiple local laws could drive up the costs of doing business or traveling in the state, or when local criminal ordinances could have an unfair impact on unsuspecting citizens who have no reason to know that their behavior is subject to an unusual local law. The argument against presuming uniformity is strongest when the local law reflects unusual local conditions or special local needs, when the effect of the local rule is borne almost entirely within the locality, when multiple local rules would not disrupt commerce, and when the subjects of the local law have reason to know of the laws and to modify their behavior accordingly. These concerns — special local needs, local impact, nondisruption of statewide activity, and fairness to persons regulated — are, of course, also the core concerns of home rule.

Preemption and the New York City Campaign Finance Law

State law extensively regulates various aspects of elections for public and party office in New York State. The seventeen articles of the Election Law address: party organization; election officials; proceedings preliminary to registration, enroll-

ment, and elections; registration and enrollment of voters; designation and nomination of candidates; the ballot, the conduct of the election, and the count of the
results; and judicial proceedings and violations of the elective franchise. But the
Election Law does not preempt all aspects of the regulation of local elections. By
its terms, the state law permits "any other law which is inconsistent with the provisions of this chapter" to govern unless specifically precluded. In addition, as previously indicated, there is considerable case law upholding local election laws despite the existence of extensive state elections legislation.

Moreover, although the Election Law generally speaks in broad terms applicable
to all jurisdictions in the state, on occasion it authorizes local deviations from
the statewide standard. While some matters — the date and hours of polling, which
local governments are specially precluded from regulating by the Municipal Home
Rule Law — require uniformity, there are other aspects of elections that have no
external effects or where a variety of local rules will not be disruptive of statewide
concerns, so there is no need for statewide uniformity.

Although the Election Law is not completely preemptive of all local initiatives,
it could be argued that article 14, which regulates campaign finance, preempts
local campaign finance measures. Article 14 requires political committees and candidates to keep and file records concerning campaign receipts, contributions,
transfers, and expenditures; to file copies of political advertisements and literature; and to maintain treasurers, depositories, and certain accounting procedures.
Most important, it bans corporate political contributions and sets limits on the
dollar value of contributions that may be made to candidates or political
committees — although it still permits fairly large contributions within those limits.
Moreover, a provision added in 1986 explicitly sets lower limits on contributions
to candidates for positions on the Board of Estimate by applicants or bidders in
matters before the board. The central issue, then, for New York City's campaign
finance law is whether it is preempted by article 14 of the State Election Law.

The Case Against Preemption

The New York City law has three basic elements: public money, candidate expenditure limitations, and contribution limitations. The Election Law is silent on the
first component, neither providing for nor prohibiting the public funding of campaigns. Nor does the Election Law preclude expenditure restrictions. It addresses
campaign expenditures, but only by requiring records, accounting procedures,
and disclosure. The only limit on expenditures is that imposed on "constituted
committees," e.g., the standing state and county party committees, which are subject to a limit of one cent per voter. Do these provisions render the local public
funding expenditure restrictions "inconsistent" with the Election Law? Do they reflect the legislature's affirmative intent to protect unlimited candidate spending?
That seems unlikely. The Election Law's silence on expenditure limits no doubt
reflects the effect of the First Amendment, as construed by the Supreme Court
in *Buckley* v. *Valeo* and later cases, to forbid quantitative limits on candidate

spending except in the context of public funding. As the state has not provided public funding, it cannot impose expenditure limits. The state's silence on expenditure limits follows from its silence on public funding and should not be interpreted as a commitment to unrestricted campaign spending.

The contribution limits in the city's public funding law, which are lower than those set by the state, create a closer question. But the argument against a conflict ought to prevail. Under *Cook* and *Clifton Park* the state contribution limits should not preclude lower local limits. Contribution restrictions are intended to reduce the influence of large contributors on elections and on the postelection behavior of government—what the Supreme Court refers to as the dangers of corruption and the appearance of corruption. Lower limits on contributions are, in the words of *Clifton Park*, "compatible" or "harmonious" with the state's goal, supplementing the state's anticorruption purpose. Nothing in article 14 suggests that the state sought to immunize large contributors from further restrictions or that the state was, in effect, licensing large contributors to spend up to the state's ceilings.

Moreover, the state's restrictions on individual contributions are set according to a formula based on the number of registered voters in the relevant electorate, with donors in local elections permitted to give up to five cents per voter. This guarantees different dollar ceilings in every locality. Donors in citywide elections in New York City may contribute fifteen times as much as contributors in citywide elections in Buffalo and far more than that when compared with donors in elections in smaller cities. To treat this law as a "contributors' rights" statute, rather than as a measure setting baseline limits, would entail a conception of contributors' rights that turns entirely on the jurisdiction in which the contributions are made. Such a conception of "contributors' rights" is highly implausible. The lack of statewide uniformity certainly distinguishes the state contribution restriction from the state minimum wage law in *Wholesale Laundry*, which set the same minimum wage throughout the state.

For a different reason, lower contribution limits, when part of public funding, probably raise no issue of conflict at all. Governments generally have the power to impose reasonable requirements as a precondition for the receipt of public money. So long as the recipient is truly free to decline the public grant, those requirements will be treated as consensually assumed, in the nature of a contract. The contract analogy explains the Supreme Court's determination that, the First Amendment notwithstanding, expenditure limitations may be required as a condition for granting public funds, since a candidate accepting public money "voluntarily" accepts the expenditure limits. Requiring candidates who accept public money also to decline contributions above a certain amount may be characterized not as a general regulation of public behavior, arguably inconsistent with the state's much higher contribution restriction, but merely as one of the permissible restrictions that the city may impose on parties voluntarily agreeing to a city contract.

The public funding law is, thus, not in direct conflict with any provisions of state law. Nevertheless, it may be contended that article 14 has occupied the field of local campaign finance regulation to the exclusion of all municipal initiatives.

Despite the lack of an outright conflict with state law, is the New York City measure preempted?

The formal judicial criteria for resolving preemption questions are not of much help here. The legislature has not made any declaration of intent as to the preemptive effect of article 14. The state has written a "detailed" law, but whether it is "comprehensive" to the exclusion of a public funding plan is unanswerable. Article 14 addresses record keeping, accounting, and reporting, and it regulates several aspects of contributions but says little about expenditures and nothing about public funding. Certainly, some campaign finance specialists would say that any code that omits public funding is not comprehensive.[17]

The normative framework for the resolution of preemption claims, however, cuts strongly in favor of a finding of no preemption.

First, there is no extra-local impact. The effects of a campaign finance plan for elections for local offices would be borne entirely by New York City voters, taxpayers, and candidates; there would be no costs outside the city's borders. It is this very "localness" of local election rules that places local elections at the core of home rule.

Second, no costs are imposed on the election process statewide. Even if several localities were to adopt different campaign finance plans, no candidate runs for local office in more than one place at a time, so no candidate would have to sustain the costs of having to comply with different local campaign finance rules simultaneously. There would be no effect on statewide elections, on elections in districts that are partly within and partly outside the city, or on elections in other localities. There would be no effect on combined state-local slates, since the state constitution, which requires that elections for city offices be held in odd-numbered years while elections for state offices are held in even-numbered years, precludes the formation of such slates.

Third, a public finance plan carries with it little danger of unfair surprise to the persons regulated. Public funding primarily regulates candidates; it operates by providing candidates with campaign money in exchange for their voluntary agreement to accept certain restrictions. Participation in public funding is consensual. Candidates and other campaign participants affected by it are politically sophisticated people, likely to be aware of the law and capable of taking the steps necessary to ensure compliance. Indeed, since contributions are already subject to record keeping, reporting, and disclosure requirements, as well as some dollar limits, candidates and large donors are already on notice that their activities are subject to regulation.

These three arguments, with their emphasis on the "localness" of campaign finance regulation, would all be applicable to any local campaign finance measure. A very different argument would emphasize just how distinct public funding is from the campaign finance system codified in article 14. Even if article 14 occupied the field of the regulation of privately funded campaigns, public funding creates a wholly new field about which the state has been silent.

Article 14 is built entirely around private contributions and unlimited spending. The state law assumes that campaigns will be privately financed, with the dangers of corruption warded off by record keeping, disclosure, and relatively high contribution limits. The reporting and disclosure requirements give the public an opportunity to learn the identity of a candidate's backers and the intensity of their support. The contribution limits provide some upper bound on the ability of the wealthy to support candidates.

But the system is an entirely private one. A candidate's financial success will turn entirely on his or her ability to raise private contributions, with large donations the most prized. Candidates are able to spend the contributions received under the state's high limits without restriction. Moreover, state law permits particularly large contributions in New York City. In several opinions, the state courts have indicated in dicta that even where state law has occupied the field local laws may be sustained "if there exists 'a real distinction between the city and other parts of the State,'" or if "special conditions exist in the city."[18] The "special conditions" in New York City may be said to arise out of the unusually weak effect the state's limits have in the city, the large number of people in the city with the wealth to make large donations; and the demoralizing effect on confidence in city government stemming from the recent municipal scandals.

Individual contributions in statewide elections are subject to a half-cent per registered voter limit. There are about 9 million registered voters in the state, so in statewide elections the contribution limit is approximately $45,000. In nonstatewide elections, however, the contribution limit is set at five cents per voter. New York City's large population — about 3 million registered voters — yields an unusually high individual contribution limit for citywide elections of $150,000. This is triple the limit for statewide elections and dramatically higher than the limit on contributions in any locality in the state. Indeed, the state limits have less restrictive effect on citywide elections in New York City than the limits anywhere else in the United States where there are limits.[19] Thus, a "real distinction" exists between New York City and the rest of the state with respect to contribution limits.

If the relatively large number of people in New York City with the wealth and incentive to make large contributions is also taken into account, it can be seen that state law allows a far greater potential in New York City than in other localities for corruption and the appearance of corruption during the course of financing campaigns. The recent municipal scandals and the report of the State-City Commission on Integrity in Government suggest that the matter may have gone beyond being merely potential and that public confidence in the integrity of government has been impaired. These special local needs justify public funding and lower contribution limits in New York City.

New York City's public funding law addresses these problems by creating a very different system. Underlying a public funding system is the goal of reducing the role of private wealth in the election process. To that end, public funding provides that a substantial portion of candidates' funds will come from the public fisc. Dependence on private donors is mitigated. By matching private grants only up to a certain amount, public funding particularly reduces the importance of large contributions while comparably increasing the role of small donations. By including expenditure limits, public funding lessens the ability of candidates who participate in the program to translate financial resources into campaign spending. With candidates of unequal financial resources, public funding may lessen the gap in their relative strengths.

Public funding tends to promote equity and public concerns and to move away from private wealth. A public funding system is quite different from the one regulated in article 14. Thus, even if the state has occupied the field of privately funded campaigns, public funding constitutes a different "field" not regulated by the state. As a matter of home rule the city has the autonomy to move into this new "field."

The issue of occupation of the field is not completely clear. A proponent of preemption would note that article 14 addresses all municipal elections, as well as state elections, regulates campaign finance in some detail, provides its own enforcement mechanism, and, since the enactment in 1986 of special restrictions on candidates for the Board of Estimate, contains a provision specifically geared to campaign funds and the danger of corruption in New York City. The 1986 amendment, it may be said, indicates the state's awareness of the problems posed by large contributions in New York City. The state has arguably taken all the action it deems necessary to deal with it.

But the argument against preemption is compelling. The state law's silence concerning public funding and spending restrictions, and the fundamentally different approach to campaign finance that public funding constitutes, provide a substantial legal basis for a determination that the city's measure is not preempted. Moreover, few matters come as close to the heart of local autonomy or have as few external effects as the process by which candidates for local offices are selected. A commitment to home rule principles, including a willingness to accept local diversity where the effects of local measures are felt entirely within the locality, should lead to a finding that the state's constitution and statutes have left the city with authority to act in this area.

Conclusion

As this essay indicates, existing home rule grants and state case law, when properly considered, may provide much more extensive authority for municipal innovation than is usually believed. The contours of most home rule grants, as in New York, are quite broad; the real concern about the scope of local initiative has been state preemption. Most preemption questions arise in settings where the state has not expressly barred local laws but has instead passed laws that address some aspects of a problem, thus raising the issue of occupation of the field. By adopting a home-rule-centered approach to preemption that emphasizes the need to accept local variations from state law where the local interest is strong and the impact on statewide or extra-local interests is slight, the fields occupied by state laws can be cabined. This can encourage localities to experiment with municipal reforms, exercise their home rule authority, and expand their capacity for local self-determination.

NOTES

1. K. Vanlandingham, "Constitutional Home Rule Since the AMA (NLC) Model," *William and Mary Law Review* 17 (1975): 1, 33. See also G. Frug, "The City as a Legal Concept," *Harvard Law Review* 93 (1980): 1057; and Stephen L. Elkin, *City and Regime in the American Republic* (Chicago: University of Chicago Press, 1987), 176.

2. J. D. Hyman, "Home Rule in New York 1941–1965: Retrospect and Prospect," *Buffalo Law Review* 15 (1965): 335, 338.

3. In 1983, the attorney general interpreted *Bareham* as providing authority for local regulation of campaign contributions in local elections. *Opinions of the Attorney General*, I 83–57 (28 Sept. 1983).

4. "The Quest for an Ethical Environment," Final Report of the State-City Commission on Integrity in Government (1986), 10–11.

5. "Summary of Local Campaign Disclosure and Contribution Limitation Ordinances," California Fair Political Practices Commission (March 1985).

6. See *City of Seattle* v. *State*, 668 P.2d 1266, 1267–68 (S. Ct. Wash. 1983); see also "An Analysis of Campaign Contributions in Closely Contested Seattle City Campaigns, 1975–1983," City of Seattle, Office of Elec. Admin. (5 June 1984).

7. See *Consolidated Edison* v. *Town of Red Hook*, 60 N.Y.2d 99, 108 (1983); *Jancyn Mfg Co.* v. *County of Suffolk*, 125 A.D.2d 641, 644 (2d Dept. 1986) (3 to 1 vote); *Matter of Ames v. Smoot*, 98 A.D.2d 216, 219 (2d Dept. 1983) (3 to 2 vote); *Davis Constr. Corp.* v. *County of Suffolk*, 95 A.D.2d 819 (2d Dept. 1983); *Seacoast Products, Inc.* v. *City of Glen Cove*, 50 A.D.2d 579 (2d Dept. 1975); *Kindermann Fireproof Storage Warehouses, Inc.* v. *City of New York*, 39 A.D.2d 266 (1st Dept. 1972).

8. Of the cases in note 7 in which *Wholesale Laundry* was cited, three — *Seacoast, Davis,* and *Jancyn* — were memorandum opinions. *Consolidated Edison* found preemption based on both occupation of the field and outright conflict, but the local law in that case clearly interfered with the operation of state law. *Jancyn* found preemption based on occupation of the field; the citation of *Wholesale Laundry* was dicta. *Ames* was also based on a finding of occupation of the field, not outright conflict. *Kindermann* was decided before *Cook* and *Clifton Park*.

9. In addition to the cases discussed in the text, see *New York State Club Association* v. *City of New York*, 69 N.Y.2d 211 (1987); *People* v. *New York Trap Rock Corp.*, 57 N.Y.2d 371 (1982); *People* v. *Judiz*, 38 N.Y.2d 529 (1976); *Matter of Albert Simon, Inc.* v. *Myerson*, 36 N.Y.2d 300 (1975).

10. *Gless* v. *City of New York*, 121 Misc.2d 1030, 1035–36 (Sup. Ct. N.Y. Co. 1983), *rev'd* 107 A.D.2d 607 (1st Dept. 1985).

11. *Dougal* v. *County of Suffolk*, 102 A.D.2d 531, 533–34 (2d Dept. 1984).

12. *People* v. *New York Trap Rock Corp.*, 57 N.Y.2d, 371, 378 (1982).

13. See, e.g., Report of the California Commission on the Law of Preemption, 1970 Urb. L. Ann. 130.

14. *People* v. *DeJesus*, 54 N.Y.2d 465 (1981) (after hours club); *Dougal* v. *County of Suffolk*, 102 A.D. 2d 531 (2d Dept. 1984) (drug paraphernalia law); *People* v. *Autieri*, 120 Misc.2d 725 (City Ct. Mt. Vernon 1982) (harassment of a police officer); *People* v. *Wilkerson*, 73 Misc.2d 895 (Co. Ct. Monroe Co. 1973) (gambling at home).

15. *Dougal* v. *County of Suffolk*, 102 A.D.2d at 534.

16. A concern that varying local standards could impinge on an unknowing population in a manner unjustified by any particular local concern may also be seen in *Robin* v. *Village of Hempstead*, 30 N.Y.2d 347 (1972), which held preempted a local ordinance requiring that abortions be performed only in hospitals. The Court of Appeals found there was nothing in the nature of a nonhospital abortion or in local conditions in Hempstead to alert women seeking abortions about Hempstead's unique rule. *Robin* was decided before *Roe* v. *Wade* created a constitutional basis for challenges to abortion restrictions.

17. Larry Berg et al., *Corruption in the American Political System* (Morristown, N.J.: General Learning Press, 1976); David W. Adamany and George E. Agree, *Political Money: A Strategy for Campaign Financing in America* (Baltimore: Johns Hopkins University Press, 1975). In addition to the public financing of the presidential primary and general elections provided by the Federal Election Campaign

Act, sixteen states have adopted some type of public funding mechanism. See Herbert Alexander, *Financing Politics: Money, Elections & Political Reform* (Washington: Congressional Quarterly, 1984).

18. *Robin* v. *Village of Hempstead*, 30 N.Y.2d 347, 351 (1972).

19. Twenty-five states impose some limits on the size of campaign contributions. Most statewide individual contribution limits range from $1,000 to $3,000 per election or per calendar year. Where separate limits are set for nonstatewide elections, those limits are usually lower. The limits on individual contributions in federal elections under the Federal Election Campaign Act is $1,000.

SUPREME COURT OF THE UNITED STATES

Nos. 87–1022 AND 87–1112

BOARD OF ESTIMATE OF CITY OF NEW YORK,
ET AL., APPELLANTS
87–1022
v.
BEVERLY MORRIS ET AL.

FRANK V. PONTERIO, APPELLANT
87–1112
v.
BEVERLY MORRIS, JOY CLARKE HOLMES
AND JOANNE OPLUSTIL

ON APPEALS FROM THE UNITED STATES COURT OF APPEALS
FOR THE SECOND CIRCUIT

[March 22, 1989]

JUSTICE WHITE delivered the opinion of the Court.

The Board of Estimate of the City of New York consists of three members elected citywide, plus the elected presidents of each of the city's five boroughs. Because the boroughs have widely disparate populations — yet each has equal representation on the board — the Court of Appeals for the Second Circuit held that this structure is inconsistent with the Equal Protection Clause of the Fourteenth Amendment. We affirm.

Appellees, residents and voters of Brooklyn, New York City's most populous borough, commenced this action against the city in December 1981. They charged that the city's Charter sections that govern the composition of the Board of Estimate[1] are inconsistent with the Equal Protection Clause of the Fourteenth Amendment as construed and applied in various decisions of this Court dealing with districting and apportionment for the purpose of electing legislative bodies. The District Court dismissed the complaint, 551 F. Supp. 652 (EDNY 1982), on the ground that the board was not subject to the rule established by *Reynolds* v. *Sims*, 377 U. S. 533 (1964), its companion cases, and its progeny, such as *Abate* v. *Mundt*, 403 U. S. 182 (1971), because in its view the board is a nonelective, nonlegislative body. The Court of Appeals reversed. 707 F. 2d 686 (CA2 1983). Because all eight officials on the board ultimately are selected by popular vote, the court concluded that the board's selection process must comply with the so-called "one person, one vote" requirement of the reapportionment cases. The court remanded to the

---

Notes 1 and 3 in the original were deleted and the remainder renumbered.

District Court to ascertain whether this compliance exists. Bifurcating the proceedings, the District Court determined first, that applying this Court's methodology in *Abate* v. *Mundt, supra,* to the disparate borough populations produced a total deviation of 132.9% from voter equality among these electorates, 592 F. Supp. 1462(EDNY 1984); and second, that the city's several explanations for this range neither require nor justify the electoral scheme's gross deviation from equal representation. 647 F. Supp. 1463 (EDNY 1986). The court thus found it unnecessary to hold that the deviation it identified was *per se* unconstitutional.

The Court of Appeals affirmed. 831 F. 2d 384 (CA2 1987). Tracing the imperative of each citizen's equal power to elect representatives from *Reynolds* v. *Sims* to *Abate* v. *Mundt* and beyond, the court endorsed the District Court's focus on population per representative. The court held that the presence of the citywide representatives did not warrant departure from the *Abate* approach and that the District Court's finding of a 132% deviation was correct. Without deciding whether this gross deviation could ever be justified in light of the flexibility accorded to local governments in ordering their affairs, the court of appeals, agreeing with the District Court, held inadequate the city's justifications for its departure from the Equal Protection requirement that elective legislative bodies be chosen from districts substantially equal in population, especially since alternative measures could address the city's valid policy concerns and at the same time lessen the discrimination against voters in the more populous districts. We noted probable jurisdiction in both Nos. 87–1022 and 87–1112, 485 U. S.– (1988).

As an initial matter, we reject the city's suggestion that because the Board of Estimate is a unique body wielding nonlegislative powers, board membership elections are not subject to review under the prevailing reapportionment doctrine. The Equal Protection guarantee of "one person, one vote" extends not only to congressional districting plans, see *Wesberry* v. *Sanders*, 376 U. S. 1 (1964), not only to state legislative districting, see *Reynolds* v. *Sims, supra,* but also to local government apportionment. *Avery* v. *Midland County,* 390 U. S. 474, 479–481 (1968); *Abate* v. *Mundt, supra,* at 185. Both state and local elections are subject to the general rule of population equality between electoral districts. No distinction between authority exercised by state assemblies, and the general governmental powers delegated by these assemblies to local, elected officials, suffices to insulate the latter from the standard of substantial voter equality. See *Avery* v. *Midland County, supra,* at 481. This was confirmed in *Hadley* v. *Junior College Dist. of Metropolitan Kansas City,* 397 U. S. 50 (1970):

> "[W]henever a state or local government decides to select persons by popular election to perform governmental functions, the Equal Protection Clause of the Fourteenth Amendment requires that each qualified voter must be given an equal opportunity to participate in that election, and when members of an elected body are chosen from separate districts, each district must be established on a basis that will insure, as far as is practicable, that equal numbers of voters can vote for proportionally equal numbers of officials." *Id.,* at 56.

These cases are based on the propositions that in this country the people govern themselves through their elected representatives and that "each and every citizen has an inalienable right to full and effective participation in the political processes" of the legislative bodies of the Nation, state, or locality as the case may be. *Reynolds* v. *Sims*, 377 U. S., at 565. Since "[m]ost citizens can achieve this participation only as qualified voters through the election of legislators to represent them," full and effective participation requires "that each citizen have an equally effective voice in the election of members of his . . . legislature." *Ibid.* As Daniel Webster once said, "the right to choose a representative is every man's portion of sovereign power." *Luther* v. *Borden*, 7 How. 1, 30 (1849) (statement of counsel). Electoral systems should strive to make each citizen's portion equal. If districts of widely unequal population elect an equal number of representatives, the voting power of each citizen in the larger constituencies is debased and the citizens in those districts have a smaller share of representation than do those in the smaller districts. Hence the Court has insisted that seats in legislative bodies be apportioned to districts of substantially equal populations. Achieving " 'fair and effective representation of all citizens is . . . the basic aim of legislative apportionment, '[*Reynolds, supra*], at 565–566; and [it is] for that reason that [*Reynolds*] insisted on substantial equality of populations among districts." *Gaffney* v. *Cummings*, 412 U. S. 735, 748 (1973).

That the members of New York City's Board of Estimate trigger this constitutional safeguard is certain. All eight officials become members as a matter of law upon their various elections. New York City Charter § 61 (1986). The Mayor, the comptroller, and the president of the City Council, who comprise the board's citywide number, are elected by votes of the entire city electorate. Each of these three cast two votes, except that the Mayor has no vote on the acceptance or modification of his budget proposal. Similarly, when residents of the city's five boroughs — the Bronx, Brooklyn, Manhattan, Queens, and Richmond (Staten Island) — elect their respective borough presidents, the elections decide each borough's representative on the board. These five members each have single votes on all board matters.

New York law assigns to the board a significant range of functions common to municipal governments.[2] Fiscal responsibilities include calculating sewer and water rates, tax abatements, and property taxes on urban development projects. The Board manages all city property; exercises plenary zoning authority; dispenses all franchises and leases on city property; fixes generally the salaries of all officers and persons compensated through city monies; and grants all city contracts. This array of powers, which the board shares with no other part of the New York City government, are exercised through the aforementioned voting scheme: three citywide officials cast a total of six votes; their five borough counterparts, one vote each.

In addition, and of major significance, the board shares legislative functions with the City Council with respect to modifying and approving the city's capital and expense budgets. The Mayor submits a proposed city budget to the board and City Council, but does not participate in board decisions to adopt or alter the proposal. Approval or modification of the proposed budget requires agreement between the board and the City Council. Board votes on budget matters, therefore, consist of four votes cast by two at-large members; and five, by the borough presidents.

This considerable authority to formulate the city's budget, which last fiscal year surpassed twenty-five billion dollars, as well as the board's land use, franchise, and contracting powers over the city's seven million inhabitants, situate the Board comfortably within the category of governmental bodies whose "powers are general enough and have sufficient impact throughout the district" to require that elections to the body comply with Equal Protection strictures. See *Hadley* v. *Junior College Dist.*, 397 U. S. at 54.

The city also erroneously implies that the the Board's composition survives constitutional challenge because the citywide members cast a 6–5 majority of board votes and hence are in position to control the outcome of board actions. The at-large members, however, as the courts below observed, often do not vote together; and when they do not, the outcome is determined by the votes of the borough presidents, each having one vote. Two citywide members, with the help of the presidents of the two least populous boroughs, the Bronx and Staten Island, will prevail over a disagreeing coalition of the third citywide member and the presidents of the three boroughs that contain a large majority of the city's population. Furthermore, because the Mayor has no vote on budget issues, the citywide members alone cannot control board budgetary decisions.

The city's primary argument is that the courts below erred in the methodology by which they determined whether, and to what extent, the method of electing the board members gives the voters in some boroughs more power than the voters in other boroughs. Specifically, the city focuses on the relative power of the voters in the various boroughs to affect board decisions, an approach which involves recognizing the weighted voting of the three citywide members.

As described by the Court of Appeals, 831 F. 2d, at 386 n. 2 (the city's description is essentially the same, Brief for Municipal Appellants 35–36), the method urged by the city to determine an individual voter's power to affect the outcome of a board vote first calculates the power of each member of the board to affect a board vote, and then calculates voters' power to cast the determining vote in the election of that member. This method, termed the Banzhaf Index, applies as follows: 552 possible voting combinations exist in which any one member can affect the outcome of a board vote. Each borough president can cast the determining vote in 48 of these combinations (giving him a "voting power" of 8.7%) while each citywide member can determine the outcome in 104 of 552 combinations (18.8%). A citizen's voting power through each representative is calculated by dividing the representative's voting power by the square root of the population represented; a citizen's total voting power thus aggregates his power through each of his four representatives—borough president, Mayor, comptroller, and council president. Deviation from ideal voting power is then calculated by comparing this figure with the figure arrived at when one considers an electoral district of ideal population. Calculated in this manner, the maximum deviation in the voting power to control Board outcomes is 30.8% on non-budget matters, and, because of the Mayor's absence, a higher deviation on budget issues.

The Court of Appeals gave careful attention to and rejected this submission. We agree with the reasons given by the Court of Appeals that the population-based approach of our cases from *Reynolds* through *Abate* should not be put aside in this case. We note also that we have once before, although in a different context, declined to accept the approach now urged by the city. *Whitcomb* v. *Chavis*, 403 U. S. 124 (1971). In that case we observed that the Banzhaf methodology "remains a theoretical one" and is unrealistic in not taking into account "any political or other factors which might affect the actual voting power of the residents, which might include party affiliation, race, previous voting characteristics or any other factors which go into the entire political voting situation." *Id.*, at 145–146.

The personal right to vote is a value in itself, and a citizen is, without more and without mathematically calculating his power to determine the outcome of an election, shortchanged if he may vote for only one representative when citizens in a neighboring district, of equal population, vote for two; or to put it another way, if he may vote for one representative and the voters in another district half the size also elect one representative. Even if a desired outcome is the motivating factor bringing voters to the polls, the Court of Appeals in this case considered the Banzhaf Index an unrealistic approach to determining whether citizens have an equal voice in electing their representatives because the approach tends to ignore partisanship, race, and voting habits or other characteristics having an impact on election outcomes.

The Court of Appeals also thought that the city's approach was "seriously defective in the way it measures Board members' power to determine the outcome of a Board vote." 831 F. 2d, at 390. The difficulty was that this method did not reflect the way the board actually works in practice; rather, the method is a theoretical explanation of each board member's power to affect the outcome of board actions. It may be that in terms of assuring fair and effective representation, the equal protection approach reflected in the *Reynolds* v. *Sims* line of cases is itself imperfect, but it does assure that legislators will be elected by and represent citizens in districts of substantially equal size. It does not attempt to inquire whether, in terms of how the legislature actually works in practice, the districts have equal power to affect a legislative outcome. This would be a difficult and ever-changing task, and its challenge is hardly met by a mathematical calculation that itself stops short of examining the actual day-to-day operations of the legislative body. The Court of Appeals in any event thought there was insufficient reason to depart from our prior cases, and we agree.[3]

Having decided to follow the established method of resolving equal protection issues in districting and apportionment cases, the Court of Appeals then inquired whether the presence of at-large members on the board should be factored into the process of determining the deviation between the more and less populous boroughs. The court decided that they need not be taken into account because the at-large members and the borough presidents respond to different constituencies. The three at-large members obviously represent citywide interests; but, in the Court of Appeals' judgment, the borough presidents represent and are responsive to their boroughs, yet each has one vote despite the dramatic inequalities in the boroughs' populations. Consideration of the citywide members might be different, the court explained, "If the at-large bloc was not simply a majority, but a majority such that it would always and necessarily control the governing body, and the district representatives play a decidedly subsidiary role. . . ." *Id.*, at 389, n. 5. Like Judge Newman in concurrence, however, the court noted that this was decidedly not true of the board.[4]

The Court of Appeals then focused on the five boroughs as single-member districts, electing five representatives to the board, each with a single vote. Applying the formula that we have utilized without exception since 1971, see *Abate* v. *Mundt*, 403 U. S., at 184 and n. 1; *Gaffney* v. *Cummings*, 412 U. S., at 737; *Brown* v. *Thompson*, 462 U. S. 835 (1983), the Court of Appeals agreed with the District Court that the maximum percentage deviation from the ideal population is 132.9%.[5]

We do not agree with the Court of Appeals' approach. In calculating the deviation among districts, the relevant inquiry is whether "the vote of any citizen is approximately equal in weight to that of any other citizen," *Reynolds* v. *Sims*, 377 U. S., at 579, the aim being to provide "fair and effective representation for all citizens," *id.*, at 565–566. Here the voters in each borough vote for the at-large members as well as their borough president, and they are also represented by those members. Hence in determining whether there is substantially equal voting power and representation, the citywide members are a major component in the calculation and should not be ignored.[6]

Because of the approach followed by the District Court and the Court of Appeals, there was no judicial finding concerning the total deviation from the ideal that would be if the at-large members of the board are taken into account. In pleadings filed with the District Court, however, appellees indicated, and the city agreed, that the deviation would then be 78%. See App. 47, 206, 375–376. This deviation was confirmed at oral argument.[7] Tr. of Oral Arg. 14–15, 39–40. And as to budget matters, when only two citywide members participate, the deviation would be somewhat larger. We accept for purposes of this case the figure agreed upon by the parties.

We note that no case of ours has indicated that a deviation of some 78% could ever be justified. See *Brown* v. *Thompson*, *supra*, at 846–847; *Conner* v. *Finch*, 431 U. S. 407, 410–420 (1977); *Chapman* v. *Meier*, 420 U. S. 1, 21–26 (1975); *Mahan* v. *Howell*, 410 U. S. 315, 329 (1973). At the very least, the local government seeking to support such a difference between electoral districts would bear a very difficult burden, and we are not prepared to differ with the holding of the courts below that this burden has not been carried. The city presents in this court nothing that was not considered below, arguing chiefly that the board, as presently structured, is essential to the successful government of a regional entity, the City of New York. The board, it is said, accommodates natural and political boundaries as well as local interests. Furthermore, because the board has been effective it should not be disturbed. All of this, the city urges, is supported by the city's history. The courts below, of course, are in a much better position than we to assess the weight of these arguments, and they concluded that the proffered governmental interests were either invalid or were not sufficient to justify a deviation of 132%,[8] in part because the valid interests of the city could be served by alternative ways of constituting the board that would minimize the discrimination in voting power among the five boroughs.[9] Their analysis is equally applicable to a 78% deviation, and we conclude that the city's proffered governmental interests do not suffice to justify such a substantial departure from the one-person, one-vote ideal.

Accordingly the judgment of the Court of Appeals is *Affirmed.*

JUSTICE BRENNAN, concurring in part and concurring in the judgment.

I agree with the opinion of the Court except insofar as it holds that the Court of Appeals should have taken the at-large members of the Board into account in calculating the deviation from voter equality. For the reasons given by the Court of Appeals, I would exclude those members from this calculation.

JUSTICE BLACKMUN, concurring in part and concurring in the judgment.

I, too, would affirm the judgment below and share many of the Court's reasons for doing so.

I agree with the majority that measuring the degree of voter inequality in this case requires inclusion of the at-large members of the Board of Estimate. I also suspect the Court is correct in rejecting the Banzhaf Index here. But, as the Court itself notes, *ante,* at 8, under the Index the deviation from voter equality measures 30.8% for nonbudget matters, and a still larger figure for budget issues. Even this measure of voter inequality is too large to be constitutional and, for the reasons given by the District Court, 647 F. Supp. 1463 (EDNY 1986), cannot be justified by the interests asserted by the city.

NOTES

1. Section 61 of the New York City Charter (1986) reads: "Membership. The mayor, the comptroller, the president of the council, and the presidents of the boroughs shall constitute the board of estimate." Section 62 reads: "Voting in the Board. a. As members of the board of estimate, the mayor, the comptroller and the president of the council shall each be entitled to cast two votes, and the president of each borough shall be entitled to cast one vote. b. Except as otherwise provided in this charter or by law, the board shall act by resolution adopted by a majority of the whole number of votes authorized to be cast by all the members of the board. . . . d. A quorum of the board shall consist of a sufficient number of members thereof to cast six votes, including at least two of the members authorized to cast two votes each." Section 120(d) provides that the Mayor may not vote as a board member when the adoption or modification of his proposed budget is at issue.

2. The District Court correctly observes that the board's powers are set forth in the City Charter, state legislation, and the New York City Administrative Code. Plaintiffs-appellees submitted to the District Court the following list of board powers:

"A. The Board of Estimate exclusively

"i. determines the use, development and improvement of property owned by the City;

"ii. approves standards, scopes and final designs of capitol [sic] projects for the City;

"iii. negotiates and enters into all contracts on behalf of the City;

"iv. negotiates and approves all franchises that are granted by the City;

"v. grants leases of City property and enters into leases of property for City use;

"vi. sets the rates for purchases of water from the City;

"vii. sets the charges for sewer services provided by the City;

"'viii. approves or modifies all zoning decisions for the City; and

"ix. sets tax abatements.

"B. The Board of Estimate acting in conjunction with the New York City Council

"i. recommends and approves the expense budget of the City without the participation of the Mayor;

"ii. recommends and approves the capital budget of the City without the participation of the Mayor;

"iii. periodically modifies the budgets of the City;

"iv. confers with the City Council when agreement on the budget between the two bodies is not reached;

"v. overrides mayoral vetoes of budget items without the participation of the Mayor; and

"vi. holds hearings on budgetary matters.

"C. The Board of Estimate also

"i. administers the Bureau of Franchises;

"ii. administers the Bureau of the Secretary;

"iii. holds public hearings on any matter of City policy within its responsibilities whenever called upon to do so by the Mayor or in its discretion for the public interest;

"iv. holds hearings on tax abatements that are within the discretion of City administrative agencies; and

"v. makes recommendations to the Mayor or City Council in regard to any matter of City policy."

Statement of Facts Pursuant to Local Rule 9(g) in No. 8–CV–3920 (EDNY), App. 44–46; See also W. H. K. Communications Associations, Inc., The Structure, Powers, and Functions of New York City's Board of Estimate (1973), App. 54 (Kramarsky Report).

3. Similarly, we reject Appellant Ponterio's submission, which disagrees with both the Court of Appeals and the city. Ponterio puts aside a citizen's theoretical ability to cast a tie-breaking vote for their representative and focuses only on each borough representative's tie-breaking power on the board. The formula suffers from the criticisms applicable to the Banzhaf Index generally. Ponterio's argument in some ways is also inconsistent with our insistence that the equal protection analysis in this context focuses on representation of people, not political or economic interests. See, e.g., Reynolds v. Sims, 377 U. S. 533, 561, 562 (1964); Dunn v. Blumstein, 405 U. S. 330, 336 (1972).

4. The Court of Appeals writes: "Through [sic] the appellant Board insists on referring to 'an at-large majority voting bloc,' in fact there is no such 'bloc.' Rather, this supposed 'bloc' consists of three persons having two votes each who are free to, and do, vote on different sides of various issues. Only if all three vote together are they bound to carry the day. Furthermore, on certain budget issues, on which the mayor does not vote, the at-large members cannot win a vote without the support of a borough president. It follows that there is no majority-at-large voting bloc bound to control the Board and that this case is far removed from the hypotheticals offered by the Board and Amicus Banzhaf." 831 F. 2d, at 389, n. 5 (citation omitted).

5. That percentage is the sum of the percentage by which Brooklyn, the city's most populous district (population 2,230,936), exceeds the ideal district population (1,414,206), and the percentage by which Staten Island, the least populous (352,151), falls below this ideal. Queens' population was stipulated to be 1,891,325; Manhattan's, 1,427,533; and Bronx's, 1,169,115. The parties stipulated, therefore, that the city's total population is 7,071,030. See App. to Juris. Statement in No. 87–1112, pp. 9–10, 11.

6. Appellees point out that in Avery v. Midland County, 390 U. S. 474 (1968), we struck down a county apportionment scheme consisting of four district representatives and one at-large member without considering the effect of the at-large representative. In that case, however, we were not faced with the task of determining the disparity in voting power among districts of different population; the issue before the Court was whether our decision in Reynolds v. Sims, requiring that state legislatures be apportioned on the basis of population, applied as well to local government legislative bodies. 390 U. S., at 478–479. Nothing in Avery even remotely suggests that the impact of at-large representa-

tives is to be ignored in determining whether an apportionment scheme violates the Equal Protection Clause.

7. At oral argument in this Court, the city conceded this point: "QUESTION: . . . If we use the Abate method and took the three at-large officers and factored them into the analysis, what would the population deviation be? Or can we not determine that based on this record? Mr. ZIMROTH [counsel for the City]: It depends on how you factor them in. There's one way of factoring them in which would divide the number of city-wide votes proportionately among all of the counties [sic].
. . . If you use that method, you come up with a number of 76 [sic] percent. . . . [T]hat's the answer to your question. That's the result you get if you use that methodology." Tr. of Oral Arg. 14–15. Appellees' counsel also stated that the deviation "came to 78 percent when you allocated that way." Id., at 39–40. Although Ponterio rejected the 78% figure in the District Court, he did so only in reliance on his modified Banzhaf test. For reasons already stated, that reliance was misplaced.

8. We note also that we are not persuaded by arguments that explain the debasement of citizens' constitutional right to equal franchise based on exigencies of history or convenience. See *Reynolds*, 377 U. S., at 579–580 ("Citizens, not history or economic interests, cast votes"); see also *Maryland Committee for Fair Representation* v. *Tawes*, 377 U. S. 656, 675 (1964); *Lucas* v. *Forty-Fourth Colorado General Assembly*, 377 U. S. 713, 738 (1964).

9. We are not presented with the question of the constitutionality of the alternative board structures suggested by the District Court and the Court of Appeals.

Voting Rights and the Board of Estimate: The Emergence of an Issue

FRANK J. MAURO

Early in its deliberations, the New York City Charter Revision Commission decided to respond to the *Morris* v. *Board of Estimate* decision by placing its primary focus on the major functions of the Board of Estimate — budgeting, contracting, land use, and franchising. Its goal was to determine how each of these critical processes should best be organized and conducted. While emphasizing this functional approach, the commission also voted to include the more general topic of the structure and election of the Board of Estimate on its research agenda.

During the summer of 1987, concomitantly with the commencement of its studies of the board's major functions, the commission staff began analyzing the various proposals that had been advanced for complying with the one-person, one-vote principle by changing the board's voting structure, its composition, or both. As part of this analysis, the staff attempted to identify the various legal requirements that a new system would have to satisfy. Because the Voting Rights Act of 1965 requires some jurisdictions, including New York City, to obtain advance federal approval (known as "preclearance") of proposed changes in the stucture or powers of elected offices, it was clear that particular attention needed to be given to the act's provisions and to the manner in which they had been applied in the past.[1]

The central question under the Voting Rights Act is whether a governmental system abridges the right of racial and language minorities to fair and effective political representation. Put another way, the act seeks to ensure that minorities have an equal opportunity to participate in electoral politics and to elect representatives of their choice. The courts, in determining whether particular governmental stuctures violate the Voting Rights Act, have scrutinized systems involving at-large (jurisdictionwide) elections and unusually large electoral districts. Such systems are viewed with concern because substantial minority populations may be "submerged" within a citywide or other large district and thereby be effectively precluded from electing representatives of their choice. This "submergence" of minority voting power was also a major focus of the 1982 amendments of the act, Congress's most recent changes to it.

Because the current structure of the Board of Estimate, and most of the proposed options for restructuring it, involve citywide elections and elections from unusually large districts — four of the five boroughs have populations of over one million and the fifth is larger than any other city in New York State — the commission staff, in early September 1987, asked one of its principal legal advisers, Richard Briffault of the Columbia University School of Law, for a preliminary review of the problems posed by such options under the act. Additionally, in mid-September, the staff, as a result of its initial discussions with Professor Briffault, also recommended that a detailed analysis be solicited from an expert in this field. M. David Gelfand of Tulane Law School was selected for this assignment because of his scholarly writings on voting rights and his experience as a special master in voting-rights cases.[2]

On 12 October 1987, Professor Gelfand met with commission staff members and Professor Briffault for a preliminary discussion of the issues involved. Public discussion of these issues began that same day at a panel sponsored by the commission as part of the annual Northeast Regional Conference of the American Society for Public Administration. In addition to Professor Gelfand, other participants in this panel on "The Federal Constitution and Local Government Structure" included commission member Frank J. Macchiarola, commission research director Frank J. Mauro, commission advisers Joseph P. Viteritti of New York University and Gerald Benjamin of the State University of New York at New Paltz, and James Jacobs of New York University School of Law.

At an initial briefing for Chairman Richard Ravitch early in 1988, Professors Briffault and Gelfand indicated that a credible case could be made that both the existing stucture of the Board of Estimate or a similarly structured board with the members casting weighted votes violated the Voting Rights Act because of the use of citywide elections and districts as large as the current boroughs. They thought that an electoral structure with such large districts faced severe legal obstacles under both the act's preclearance process and under the provisions that provide affected parties with the standing to challenge state and local governmental structures in federal court.

After Professors Briffault and Gelfand made this preliminary presentation to the commission chairman, Professor Gelfand was asked to prepare a formal memorandum for the commission covering several specific proposals for structural changes in the board. Additionally, Chairman Ravitch decided that it would be worth soliciting the opinion of a voting-rights expert with experience in defending municipalities against Voting Rights Act challenges. On the basis of her background, including scholarly writings on voting rights and experience as an attorney on the staff of the Justice Department's voting rights section, Katharine I. Butler of the University of South Carolina Law School was retained to prepare an additional analysis of the matter. Professor Butler was asked to focus particularly on the difficulties that New York City might face during the preclearance process.

When Professor Butler reported concerns similar to those expressed by Professors Briffault and Gelfand, and also identified additional potential problems based on the mechanics of the preclearance process, Chairman Ravitch concluded that a serious problem existed and arranged for the entire commission to be briefed on the details of the issue. Because of the controversial nature of this matter, a private hearing of the commission, allowable under a special provision of state law, was scheduled for 28 January 1988. At that hearing, Professor Gelfand reviewed the issue for the entire commission and presented copies of a memorandum that he had prepared for the commission with his colleague, Terry E. Allbritton. A condensed version of that analysis appears in this volume.

Because of the gravity of the findings presented by Professors Gelfand and Butler regarding the legality of the Board of Estimate's structural arrangements, the commission decided to solicit the opinions of additional experts before ruling out, on the basis of voting-rights concerns, the weighted-voting option for complying with the one-person, one-vote requirement. Commissioner Fred W. Friendly thought that it would be useful for the members of the commission to have the advice of Judge Arlin M. Adams, a widely respected federal jurist, who had recently retired from the United States Court of Appeals for the Third Circuit. Other members thought that the commission should also solicit opinions from a dean of a major law school and from a lawyer experienced in representing plaintiffs in Voting Rights Act litigation. To that end, the commission retained Norman Redlich, dean of New York University Law School, and Frank R. Parker, director of the Voting Rights Project of the Lawyers' Committee for Civil Rights Under Law and one of the most experienced lawyers in this field.

Immediately after Professor Gelfand's presentation at the commission's private hearing and well before receipt of the additional opinions from Adams, Redlich, and Parker, members of the Board of Estimate and commission member W. Bernard Richland began to respond to the problems identified by Gelfand and Butler. In addition, reacting to the newspaper publicity given to the fact that the commission was being advised that the structure of the board raised significant Voting Rights Act questions, the members of the board asked for an immediate meeting with the chairman of the commission. On 3 February 1988, Chairman Ravitch, accompanied by Professors Gelfand and Butler and commission staff, met with members of the Board of Estimate and their representatives. Edward N. Costikyan, who had previously served, at the board's request, as a specially designated assistant corporation counsel in the *Morris* litigation, and who had experience in voting-rights matters as a representative of the City Council in its efforts to obtain U.S. Justice Department preclearance of its 1981 and 1982 redistricting plans, accompanied the members of the board to this meeting and served as their primary spokesperson. Shortly thereafter, the board retained Costikyan's law firm (Paul, Weiss, Rifkind, Wharton & Garrison) as its consultant "in connection with any and all proposals to alter the structure or power of the Board of Estimate."

On 29 February 1988, Manhattan Borough President David N. Dinkins, accompanied by a number of other past and present elected officials, held a press conference at which he argued that the Board of Estimate provided the best vehicle for effective minority representation in the New York City government. In addition to his own press release, Dinkins released both a statement, in which he was joined by Congressman Charles B. Rangel and former Congressman Herman

Badillo, and a letter to Messrs. Rangel and Badillo from Julius L. Chambers, director and general counsel of the NAACP Legal Defense and Education Fund, Inc. Chambers expressed the belief that Gelfand and Butler had identified the relevant legal principles and had, for the most part, correctly applied them to the hypothetical situations specified, but he criticized the commission for not asking its consultants to consider a broader range of alternatives. Specifically, Chambers raised questions about the plan to transfer power from a multimember Board of Estimate, though flawed, to a single citywide elected mayor.

In early March, the commission received the opinions of its additional advisers (Adams, Redlich, and Parker). They all arrived at the same conclusion as Gelfand. In summarizing these opinions for the members of the Charter Revision Commission on 10 March, Eric Lane, the commission's executive director and counsel, wrote: "All of the consultants raised the fundamental objection that [weighted] voting plans submerge minority voting power in New York City. In specific terms, weighted voting continues a system in which a white plurality in at least Brooklyn, Queens, and citywide elections, voting as a bloc, is able to frustrate minorities' ability to participate in the political process and to elect representatives of their choice." Lane concluded that submergence of minority voting power could jeopardize preclearance and create the risk of subsequent private litigation under the act, and that such litigation would have a reasonable likelihood of success.

In March, Costikyan's law firm, as consultants to the Board of Estimate, submitted an extensive memorandum to the commission on this subject. Later in the year, Costikyan submitted for the commission's consideration a decision by a federal district court judge in a Voting Rights Act case involving the city of Norfolk, Virginia, and copies of opinion letters from three subconsultants: Henry P. Monaghan of the Columbia University School of Law, Gary J. Simson of Cornell Law School, and Michel Rosenfeld of New York Law School. The Monaghan and Simson opinions were cautious in their critique, concluding only that the commission should not yet discard as unlawful a proposed weighted-voting structure for the Board of Estimate. Only the Rosenfeld opinion affirmatively concluded that a weighted-voting system would, in fact, be lawful under the Voting Rights Act.

On 17 March 1988, the commission found that the Voting Rights Act questions raised by weighted-voting plans were indeed significant and decided to proceed with its deliberations by considering the advantages and disadvantages of alternative means of handling the board's major functions. At the commission's request, at its next meeting on 28 March 1988, Chairman Ravitch presented his recommendations on how those functions should be organized and conducted.

A week later, however, the United States Supreme Court announced its decision to entertain full briefing and argument in the *Morris* case and, on 14 April 1988, the commission decided to defer any further consideration of proposals to restructure the Board of Estimate until it had the benefit of the Supreme Court's final decision in that case. The commission then turned its attention to several other matters. These were presented to, and overwhelmingly approved by, the voters in the 8 November 1988 general election.

When the commission reorganized in 1989 under its new chairman, Frederick

A. O. Schwarz, Jr., it stepped up its analysis of the Board of Estimate's major functions, holding full-day, fact-finding hearings on contracting, land use, franchising, and budgeting. Following the Supreme Court's 22 March 1989 unanimous affirmation of the Second Circuit Court's decision in the *Morris* case, the commission was asked once again to consider the alternative of weighted voting before proceeding with a discussion of other options. By that time the risks of weighted voting under the Voting Rights Act were almost universally accepted by the members of the commission. While some saw these risks as fatal and therefore dispositive of the issue, others viewed them as only one of many factors to be considered in reaching a conclusion on this approach. Consequently, the commission's 1989 discussion of the weighted-voting alternative focused primarily on other legal and policy questions. During the previous year when only one issue, though an important one — the fair and effective representation of groups protected by the Voting Rights Act — was the focus of the commission's discussions of weighted voting, these other questions had received virtually no attention.

The voting-rights problems with weighted voting were underscored in 1989 by virtue of public and commission discussion of another option for responding to the *Morris* decision. On 24 April 1989, Chairman Schwarz invited comments on the idea of a bicameral legislature, consisting of an expanded City Council of about fifty members and a new nineteen-member body. This latter body would have consisted of the borough presidents and fourteen other members selected from the boroughs in a manner that would ensure population equality. So, for example, Staten Island would have had one representative on this body, its borough president; and Brooklyn six, its borough president and five others.

In presenting this idea for comment, Schwarz said that in his judgment, there was a lot to be said for it but that before he would feel comfortable recommending it one "threshold question" would have to be answered affirmatively: "Can such a second house be structured in a way that will in fact result in, and that will be seen as likely to result in, fair and effective representation of the people of the city, including the members of racial and language minority groups?" Schwarz argued that if, and only if, this threshold question were answered "yes," should the commission debate the governmental pros and cons of having such a second body.

The commission examined two approaches to meeting this threshold test. The first was to elect the additional members (two from the Bronx, three from Manhattan, four from Queens, and five from Brooklyn) by a system of boroughwide elections using cumulative or limited voting. The second was to divide those boroughs into the specified number of single-member districts of equal size and to elect a representative from each such district with traditional winner-take-all primary and general elections.

While cumulative and limited voting have recently been adopted in a number of southern and western jurisdictions to settle voting-rights suits,[3] individuals with practical experience in New York City electoral politics were skeptical that such an approach would provide fair and effective representation in this context. The major impediments were seen as the overwhelming size of the electoral districts involved, ranging from 1.2 to 2.2 million people, the cost of running for office in such large districts, the different nature of political communication and voter coordination in such large, impersonal districts, and the complexity of New York State's election laws and practices.

The commission's attention therefore turned to the second alternative as the more viable option for a relatively small governing body. Even here, however, there was significant skepticism regarding the feasibility of creating a nineteen-member body that would be as representative as a fairly and effectively districted thirty five-member council, let alone a fifty-member body that would undoubtedly be more reflective of the city's diversity. Consequently, at its 2 May 1989 meeting, the commission decided to drop the idea of bicameralism from active consideration.

While explicit comparisons were never made between these nineteen-member body alternatives and the Board of Estimate (with or without weighted voting), the fact that, with relative dispatch, the former were found wanting in their ability to provide fair and effective representation for racial and language minorities served to emphasize the shortcomings of the Board of Estimate on these grounds. Both the nineteen-member body alternatives and the Board of Estimate options included the borough presidents, although their share of total voting power was greater on the board than on the nineteen-member body alternatives. The remainder of the voting power on the Board of Estimate was vested in members elected from citywide electoral districts that substantially submerged minority voting strength, but in the proposals for a nineteen-member body the remainder of the members would be elected in ways that would be superior in terms of fair and effective representation.

Despite the absence of direct, explicit comparisons, the voting-rights concepts with which the commission became familiar during its extensive 1988 discussions of weighted voting certainly affected its 1989 consideration of bicameralism. In addition, these concepts played an important part in the discussions leading up to the commission's decisions to propose an increase in the size of the council from thirty-five to fifty-one and a change in procedures for council redistricting after each decennial census. It was clear that the commission had come to view fair and effective minority representation as an important policy objective as much as a legal requirement.[4] The concepts that form the intellectual foundation of the Voting Rights Act had, in effect, been accepted by and become a part of the commission's thinking.[5]

NOTES

1. Based on criteria set forth in the act, three counties in New York State — Bronx, New York (Manhattan), and Kings (Brooklyn) — are "covered jurisdictions." As a result, New York State and New York City are required to obtain preclearance for any changes in electoral arrangements that affect these three counties. While the preclearance requirement applies only to covered jurisdictions under

a separate section of the act, all state and local governments are subject to legal challenge, by the U.S. Justice Department or affected parties, for alleged violations of the act.

2. See, e.g., his *Federal Constitutional Law and American Local Government: A Treatise for City Attorneys, Public Interest Litigators and Students* (Charlottesville, Va.: Michie, 1984).

3. For a review of such recent actions, see Pamela S. Karlan, "Maps and Misreading: The Role of Geographic Compactness in Racial Vote Dilution Litigation," Harvard Civil Rights–Civil Liberties Law Review 24 (1989): 174–248; and Richard L. Engstrom, Delbert A. Taebel, and Richard L. Cole, "Cumulative Voting as a Remedy to Minority Vote Dilution: The Case of Alamogordo, New Mexico," *Journal of Law & Politics* 5, no. 3 (Spring 1989): 469–97.

4. The commission's redistricting proposals included several relevant provisions, including, for example, the establishment of "the fair and effective representation of the racial and language minorities protected by the United States Voting Rights Act of 1965, as amended" as the highest priority criterion, after compliance with the one-person, one-vote requirement that districting commissions must utilize in dividing the city into council districts.

5. While this undoubtedly resulted, at least in part, from the exposure to the intellectually compelling concepts that underlie the Voting Rights Act and its judicial interpretations, it is probably also the result of a change in the commission's composition. Following the 1988 election, when Mayor Edward I. Koch reappointed eleven of the commission's fifteen members and appointed four new members, he increased the number of African-American and Latino members of the commission from four to six. In addition, the new chairman of the commission, Frederick A. O. Schwarz, Jr., was familiar with the implications of the Voting Rights Act from his work as corporation counsel and was personally supportive of the underlying concepts.

Voting Rights and the Board of Estimate: Prospects and Pitfalls

M. DAVID GELFAND
TERRY E. ALLBRITTON

In March 1989, the New York City Board of Estimate sustained a mortal injury at the hands of the United States Supreme Court, which, in *Morris* v. *Board of Estimate*, found the current structure to violate the constitutional requirement of "one person, one vote." Any restructuring of the Board to eliminate this deficiency must also take into account other voting-rights requirements that have been imposed by Congress and the Constitution. This essay describes and explains the constitutional and statutory framework for the protection of the voting rights of racial and language minorities, and it analyzes how specific proposals for restructuring the Board of Estimate are likely to fare in the courts, given this legal framework.[1]

The Supreme Court has interpreted the Equal Protection Clause of the Fourteenth Amendment of the Constitution to require a one-person, one-vote standard for election districts for state and general-purpose local governments, as well as in school districts. It was on this basis that the constitutionality of the structure of the New York City Board of Estimate was successfully challenged in the *Morris* case. In addition to that requirement, state and local electoral arrangements must provide for the "fair and effective representation" of members of racial and language minorities. This requirement derives from the Equal Protection Clause of the Fourteenth Amendment, the Fifteenth Amendment, and the Voting Rights Act of 1965. Consequently, any new structure for the Board of Estimate, or any body (or office) assuming its functions, must not only meet the one-person, one-vote standard but must also provide for fair and effective representation.

The Constitutional and Statutory Framework

The Thirteenth, Fourteenth, and Fifteenth Amendments, along with a number of

---

civil-rights statutes, were adopted shortly after the Civil War to outlaw slavery, remove its vestiges, and grant to newly freed blacks the basic political and civil rights possessed by white male citizens. Subsequently, the Fifteenth Amendment, which is specifically addressed to equal voting rights, became a vehicle for suits challenging certain direct and obvious barriers to registration and voting by members of minority groups. For example, the Supreme Court in a line of "White Primary Cases," culminating in 1953 in *Terry* v. *Adams*, held that various attempts to exclude blacks from official and unofficial political party primaries violated the Fifteenth Amendment. In 1960, in *Gomillion* v. *Lightfoot*, the Court invalidated, under the Fifteenth Amendment, an alteration of a city's boundaries (from a square to a twenty-eight-sided figure) that excluded almost 400 black voters but no white voters from the city. In 1980, in *City of Mobile* v. *Bolden*, 446 U.S. 55, 65 (1980), however, the Supreme Court ruled that plaintiffs suing under the Fifteenth Amendment must prove a "purposefully discriminatory denial or abridgment by government of the freedom to vote," thereby greatly reducing the utility of the Fifteenth Amendment in many voting-rights situations. In addition, the plurality opinion in *Mobile* required that plaintiffs challenging an electoral structure under the Equal Protection Clause of the Fourteenth Amendment (or under section 2 of the Voting Rights Act) must prove discriminatory intent on the part of the state or local government employing the challenged structure. (Justice Stewart's opinion was joined by Chief Justice Burger and Justices Powell and Rehnquist. Justice Stevens filed a separate opinion concurring in the judgment.)

In *Rogers* v. *Lodge*, 458 U.S. 613, 618 (1982), however, a clear majority of the Court ruled that "discriminatory intent need not be proved by direct evidence" in Equal Protection cases. Discriminatory intent can be inferred from circumstantial factors, including electoral patterns, historical discrimination of various forms, unresponsiveness of elected officials, and the existence of certain structural factors, such as large electoral districts, majority-vote requirements, and "anti-single-shot" provisions. (Justice White's opinion for the Court was joined by Chief Justice Burger and Justices Brennan, Marshall, Blackmun, and O'Connor.)

Examples of anti-single-shot provisions include rules requiring electors to vote for each available position (e.g., vote for five separate candidates in a five-member district) or have their ballots invalidated. Such provisions, according to the Senate Report on the 1982 Amendments of the Voting Rights Act, "may enhance the opportunity for discrimination against the minority group" by, in effect, requiring minorities to "waste" votes for candidates who may not be perceived as representatives of their interests. Single-shot voting can also be thwarted by requirements that each candidate run for a specific seat.

Though *Rogers* greatly reduced the burden for plaintiffs suing under the Equal Protection Clause, most racial voting-rights cases today are brought under the Voting Rights Act of 1965. That Act arose out of many years of struggle in the streets, in Congress, and in the courts to protect and expand the rights of members of racial and language minority groups. Litigation under prior legislation had encountered fundamental constraints. The Civil Rights Act of 1957, for example, empowered the United States attorney general to bring suits challenging discrimination in voting, but the Justice Department was hampered by inaccessibility of local registration records and the limited remedies available under the Act. A 1960 Act provided assistance with both problems for cases challenging a clear pattern or practice of discrimination, and the number of suits brought by the Justice Department increased. Soon afterward, the voting-rights provisions of the 1964 Act established expedited procedures in federal voting-rights cases and outlawed certain types of literacy tests in federal elections. However, it remained difficult to challenge minority vote dilution caused by more subtle practices or electoral arrangements.

As late as the 1960s, large numbers of blacks remained disenfranchised, especially in the South, and many Hispanics were excluded from voting in various cities and towns around the country. Recognizing the ineffectiveness of the existing statutory and case law, blacks mobilized to register large numbers of new voters in southern communities. For example, a massive voter registration campaign culminated in the celebrated march from Selma to Montgomery in early 1965. The purposes of this march were to dramatize black disenfranchisement and to petition Governor George Wallace to discontinue obstructionist tactics.

These attempts were frequently met with violence. Bloody confrontations during the Selma to Montgomery march had a tremendous impact on much of the American public and many national political leaders. On 25 March 1965, the marchers reached Montgomery. Less than five months later, President Lyndon B. Johnson signed the Voting Rights Act into law.

The Voting Rights Act of 1965, as amended over the years, provides a nearly comprehensive structure for preserving and protecting the voting rights of racial and language minorities. Not only does the Act ban overt barriers to registration, such as literacy and language tests, but it also forbids the use of electoral arrangements that "dilute" the votes of members of protected minority groups. The provisions most relevant to reform of New York City's Board of Estimate are sections 2 and 5 of the Act. Section 2 currently outlaws the use of standards, practices, or procedures that result in denial or abridgement of the right to vote on account of race or membership in a language minority. Section 2 suits can be initiated either by private plaintiffs or by the United States attorney general.

Section 5 requires state and local governments "covered" by formulas specified in the Act to obtain approval before implementing any change in a "standard, practice, or procedure with respect to voting." This mandatory prior approval is generally referred to as "preclearance" and must be obtained from the United States attorney general or from the United States District Court for the District of Columbia. If a covered jurisdiction proceeds with a change in electoral arrangements without seeking preclearance, a private party can sue under section 5 to require that preclearance be obtained. The "preclearance" system was established in recognition of the inherent inability of the Justice Department to conduct ongoing investigations of all electoral changes proposed by each covered jurisdiction.

The formulas for determining whether a jurisdiction is "covered" for purposes of preclearance are contained in section 4 of the Act. They focus on the jurisdictions' historical use of a voting "test" or language requirement, voter registration levels, and voter turnout. Although most covered jurisdictions are in the South, some states and counties in other parts of the nation also are subject to the preclearance requirement. In New York City, three boroughs are covered jurisdictions — Manhattan, Brooklyn, and the Bronx.

Preclearance can be denied for any electoral change that has a discriminatory "purpose" or "effect." In particular, a proposed electoral change will be denied preclearance under section 5 of the Act if the attorney general determines that it would have "retrogressive effect." This test involves a determination whether the proposed change, when compared with the existing electoral arrangement, would make members of minority groups protected by the Act "worse off" with respect "to their opportunity to exercise the electoral franchise effectively."[2] In practice, the Justice Department exercises broad discretion in the preclearance process.[3]

Among the several significant changes wrought by the 1982 amendments to the Voting Rights Act was the amendment of section 2 to allow a "results" test, rather than the more onerous "intent" test that the Supreme Court had required in *Mobile* v. *Bolden*. According to the Senate report on the 1982 amendments, the intent test was rejected because it was "unnecessarily divisive [because it involved] charges of racism on the part of individual officials or entire communities," it imposed an "inordinately difficult" burden of proof on plaintiffs, and it "asked the wrong question." Instead, the report insisted, the question should be whether "as a result of the challenged practice or structure plaintiffs do not have an equal opportunity to participate in the political processes and to elect candidates of their choice." The report also noted that "voting practices and procedures that have discriminatory results perpetuate the effects of past purposeful discrimination."[4] The Supreme Court has treated the Senate report as an "authoritative source for legislative intent." (*Thornburg* v. *Gingles*, 478 U.S. 30, 43 n.7 (1986).)

Hence, it is now quite clear that section 2 does much more than simply outlaw purposeful exclusion from voting. As James Blacksher, attorney for the plaintiffs in *City of Mobile* and in numerous other voting rights cases, has observed:

> The results test of amended section 2 of the Act extends the need for consideration of race beyond mere avoidance of retrogression to full consideration of a plan's racial fairness. The importance of a clear mandate for planmakers to be aware of racial results ought not to be underestimated. There has always been a facile attractiveness to claims that redistricting was accomplished by the use of "neutral lines." . . . But the idea is wrong, as a matter of fact. . . .[A] so-called "neutral" or "racially blindfolded" districting plan most likely will result in racial unfairness and thus will be unlawful under amended section 2 of the Voting Rights Act.[5]

The Supreme Court, in *Thornburg* v. *Gingles*, 478 U.S. at 47, announced that the "essence of a section 2 claim is that a certain electoral law, practice or structure interacts with social and historical conditions to cause an inequality in the opportunities enjoyed by black and white voters to elect their preferred representatives." The *Gingles* Court established an elaborate, multipart test for plaintiffs in section

2 suits. In briefest terms, plaintiffs challenging multimember districts and similar electoral structures are required to prove that "a bloc voting majority must *usually* be able to defeat candidates supported by a politically cohesive, geographically insular minority group." (478 U.S. at 49.) The *Gingles* Court also considered other factors, drawn from the Senate report and prior cases, important in determining whether the challenged electoral arrangements, under the "totality of the circumstances," violate the Act.

In sum, challenges to state and local electoral arrangements can be based on the Fifteenth Amendment (with direct proof of intentional discriminatory exclusion from voting), the Fourteenth Amendment (with direct or circumstantial proof of purposeful discriminatory practices), or the Voting Rights Act (with proof of discriminatory effects or results). Given the lower burden of proof, plaintiffs generally prefer to base such suits on the Voting Rights Act.

The Voting Rights Act and the Current Structure of the Board of Estimate

Although it is difficult to predict the outcome of any lawsuit, it seems that the structure of the New York City Board of Estimate, which was successfully attacked under the Equal Protection Clause in *Morris*, would also have been vulnerable to a successful challenge under section 2 of the Voting Rights Act. The Board of Estimate was an elected body with substantial powers. As of 1988, it consisted of three members who were elected citywide — the mayor, president of the City Council, and comptroller — and the five borough presidents. In most matters, the citywide officials, when voting together, commanded a majority on the Board.

This arrangement presents problems under the Voting Rights Act because of the substantial influence on the Board of members who are chosen primarily by white voters. The citywide officials, who have a majority on the Board, have always been white; more important, the demographic and bloc-voting patterns in New York City suggest that these at-large members are likely to continue to represent white voters. Much the same can be said of the presidents of the larger boroughs. Although members of minority groups have occasionally served as borough presidents of Manhattan and the Bronx, that has not been the general pattern. (Indeed, in most cases, these minority borough presidents were initially appointed to fill vacancies in the office.) It must also be remembered that the Act provides that the "extent to which members of a protected class have been elected to office in the State or political subdivision is [only] one circumstance which may be considered" in evaluating a section 2 claim. The focus of the Voting Rights Act is on the "opportunity" of members of protected minority groups, under the "totality of the circumstances," to "participate in the political process and to elect representatives of their choice."

Moreover, most of the boroughs are extremely large, and concentrations of minority groups within them are often relatively small. For example, assuming racial bloc voting, only the Bronx, which in 1980 had a 34 percent white population and a voting-age citizen population that was 42 percent white, would appear to offer the structural likelihood of the election of a representative preferred by the black and Hispanic communities, and then only if members of these minority groups vote together. The borough representatives of Queens and Staten Island would almost certainly represent white majority populations. Much the same would be true (from a structural and demographic perspective) of the borough representative from Brooklyn, which has a 49 percent white population. Moreover, 59 percent of its voting-age citizens were white. In short, the Board's structure, as of 1988, presented many of the difficulties that have led courts to invalidate at-large and large multimember district systems.

Proposals for a Restructured Board of Estimate

This section evaluates six possible changes in the structure of the Board of Estimate, designed to satisfy the *Morris* one-person, one-vote requirement, in terms of whether they comply with the requirements of the Voting Rights Act.[6] Initially, it should be noted that prior to implementation any of the six proposed changes in the structure of the Board of Estimate discussed below would have to be submitted for preclearance by the U.S. Department of Justice, under section 5 of the Act. This would require proof, at least, that the proposed change would not result in retrogression; as noted above, other factors may also be considered by the Justice Department. Preclearance for some of the proposed changes might be possible if the submission were made in proper form. A shift from the current system to one involving representatives from single-member districts or multimember districts and retaining or reducing the proportion of the votes held by the citywide officials would probably not constitute retrogression. Shifting to the use of "weighted voting" for borough representatives (either with or without citywide representatives), however, would likely be viewed as retrogression by the Justice Department. Retrogression would occur because such a system (in order to meet the one-person, one-vote requirement) would need to grant relatively *more* votes than the present system to representatives from Queens and Brooklyn, elected primarily by white voters. Furthermore, even preclearance of a proposed plan would not insulate it from subsequent suits under section 2.

Nearly all the proposed structural changes would be vulnerable to a suit under section 2 of the Act. (The only exception is a system composed solely of properly drawn and moderately sized single-member districts, with few or no votes on the new board given to the citywide officials). Many of these suits would have a likelihood of success for appropriate plaintiffs. It must be remembered that, under section 2, a legal challenge to a restructured board would be based on the results of its electoral arrangements on racial or language minority groups. Plaintiffs would not need to prove that the challenged arrangements were designed or operated for a discriminatory purpose.

1. Single-member districts. A system of single-member districts is the electoral arrangement most favored by the courts. A single-member district system involves the election of one representative from each of several equally populated districts. Each representative, in turn, has one vote on the governing body. A restructured board of estimate composed solely of representatives from single-member districts will be used here as the "standard" model against which other proposals will be evaluated.

To provide for adequate representation of minority interests under sections 2 and 5 of the Voting Rights Act, the population of the individual districts cannot be set too high. For example, one approach to *Morris* might be to divide the city into only five equal districts, which would have to cross borough boundaries in order to meet the one-person, one-vote requirement. Each district would contain approximately 1.5 million persons. Such districts, while meeting the one-person, one-vote requirement, would not provide any effective voice to the less numerous minorities, such as Asians, and would also pose serious barriers to the election of representatives of the black and Hispanic communities. To put these 1.5 million person districts in perspective, the at-large systems invalidated in *City of Rome* v. *United States* and *Rogers* v. *Lodge* had only 30,759 persons and 19,349 persons, respectively.

It may well be possible to establish less populous districts that both respect borough boundaries and provide for adequate representation for members of minority groups. Various districting plans, with smaller districts, could be drawn so as to give members of the city's principal minority groups a fair opportunity to elect representatives of their choice. An example of such a set of districts would involve sixty single-member districts of approximately 117,000 persons each. These districts could probably meet the one-person, one-vote requirement of the Constitution (with a maximum population deviation of about 1.81 percent—well within the variation permitted by the courts) with no districts crossing borough lines. Under this plan, seats would be allocated as follows: the Bronx, 10; Brooklyn, 19; Manhattan, 12; Queens, 16; and Staten Island, 3. In practice, however, the actual drawing of district boundaries may not work out neatly and simply. For example, the establishment of districts that give various minorities the fairest opportunity to elect representatives might require crossing borough boundaries. Also, various changes will be necessary once the 1990 census figures are available.

Guaranteed proportional representation of particular minority groups on a governing body is specifically disavowed in the 1982 amendments to section 2 of the Voting Rights Act. Rather, the districts in such a plan could (and under the Voting Rights Act should) be drawn so that members of protected minority groups will have a fair opportunity to elect persons to represent their interests.

The drawing of single-member districts has, on occasion, generated litigation regarding the "packing" or "fracturing" of minority population concentrations. "Packing" occurs when members of a minority group are concentrated into very few districts, thereby reducing their electoral strength in other districts. On the other hand, "fracturing" occurs when geographically concentrated minority-group members are split among many districts, thereby reducing their voting effectiveness in any particular district. For example, in *Ketchum* v. *Byrne*, the federal Court

of Appeals for the Seventh Circuit found that Chicago's redistricting plan for al-
dermanic seats violated section 2 by "fracturing" black and Hispanic concentrations among several districts and, in certain other districts, "packing" more black
voters than needed to obtain a substantial majority. Both packing and fracturing
"waste" the votes of impacted minorities.

  2. *Single-member districts plus citywide officials.* The addition of the citywide
officials to such a system of moderately sized, fairly drawn single-member districts would create a "mixed" electoral system. A restructured board of estimate
composed of representatives elected from single-member districts and officials
elected from the entire city would be similar to a number of city councils around
the country.

  Citywide officials, by their very nature, are not intended to serve the interests
of any particular racial, ethnic, or geographic group. Indeed, citywide positions,
for the most part, were established by "reform" movements that sought to avoid
the parochialism they believed arose from ward-based electoral systems. Some
political scientists and historians, however, have concluded that these "structural
reformers" were motivated primarily by their dissatisfaction with the enfranchise-
ment of growing immigrant populations. Including citywide representatives in
a mixed system governing board today could raise concerns regarding the dilution
of minority voting strength. If the citywide officials are allocated a sizable proportion (or an absolute majority) of the total votes on that mixed system governing
board, there could be claims that the careful drawing of single-member districts
to allow minority representation has been negated by the power of the representatives of the majority group — usually whites.

  The courts have tolerated some mixed systems but have invalidated others. Since
these cases have been decided on their particular facts, under the "totality of the
circumstances" approach,[7] it is difficult to articulate any absolute standard to measure particular proposals. Generally, however, the less power wielded by the
citywide officials, the greater the likelihood that a court would uphold the proposed plan. On the other hand, plans in which citywide officials have a clear
majority would probably be viewed with extreme disfavor by the courts and would
be more likely to invite legal attacks.

  The Board of Estimate could be restructured so as to contain representatives
of a number of single-member districts, with the citywide officials being allocated
the same proportion of the total votes on that larger board as they had on the
Board in 1988. Thus, if there were sixty single-member districts, the citywide officials would be given twenty-four votes each. These three citywide officials could
still command a majority. In reality, such a system would be little different from
the current Board, except that the board members (and votes) on the new board
would be more numerous, with sixty-three board members casting 132 votes, rather
than the eleven votes currently cast by the eight Board members. Even if this proposal were precleared by the Justice Department, the larger board would be nearly
as vulnerable as the current structure to attack by a private plaintiff under section
2 of the amended Voting Rights Act, for the reasons explained above. Reducing

the proportion of votes given to the citywide officials and drawing districts so as to maximize minority representation, however, would clearly improve such a mixed system's chances of surviving a section 2 challenge.

3. *Multimember districts.* If each borough were treated as a "multimember district," the number of representatives from each borough could equal the number of districts used in the first model. Thus, Staten Island would elect three representatives, Manhattan twelve, and so forth. Again, this system (by choosing a varying number of representatives from each borough) could be designed to meet the one-person, one-vote requirement. But it would be quite difficult, if not impossible, to address fully the issue of fair and effective representation.

When multimember districts are used, two or more representatives are elected from one relatively large district rather than from separate, smaller districts of equal size. Like at-large elections, multimember district elections "tend to minimize the voting strength of minority groups by permitting the political majority to elect *all* representatives of the district."[8] This dilution of the voting strength of racial minorities may be especially severe when racial bloc voting is combined with a majority vote requirement. Unless specialized electoral arrangements — single-shot voting, cumulative voting, or single transferable voting — are employed to ameliorate majority domination of a multimember system, members of minority groups probably could not elect representatives in numbers reflecting their true population strengths in the city.

For example, a multimember system would allot sixteen members to the Queens "district." On a strictly proportional basis, whites would have ten representatives, blacks three, Hispanics two, and Asians one. If racial bloc voting occurs in the elections for each of the sixteen positions, however, the white population — 62 percent of the total borough population according to the 1980 census — would have a clear majority and could possibly elect all sixteen representatives in the Queens multimember district. Indeed, representatives of minority interests could be elected only if a substantial portion of white voters cast "crossover" votes for candidates representing minority-group interests. Thus, multimember elections often produce virtually the same practical effect as several simultaneous at-large elections.

Multimember systems also present other, more subtle, barriers to full electoral participation by minority groups. As in at-large systems, candidates for multimember seats must campaign in larger geographic areas, especially when their specialized electoral base is widely dispersed throughout the district. Larger areas require higher campaign costs, which can deter the entry of candidates whose supporters and contributors are poorer. These candidates are precisely the ones who should be encouraged to participate in the electoral process, if the fair and effective representation requirement is to be fully satisfied.

4. *Multimember districts with citywide officials.* Adding citywide members to such a multimember district system would give rise to defects similar to the single-member/at-large mixed system. The unacceptable dilution of minority group representation, generally operating in multimember systems, can be exacerbated if the citywide officials are given too large a share of the board's total votes. The

larger the share of votes those officials are given, the greater the likelihood that the plan would be invalidated by the courts in any section 2 litigation.

5. *Weighted voting.* An alternative approach would restructure the Board of Estimate based on "weighted voting." Under such an approach, the representative elected from each borough would be given multiple votes, based on the population of his or her borough. A number of counties in New York State have employed weighted voting as a mechanism for satisfying the one-person, one-vote requirement while preserving electoral districts that vary widely in population. (None of the cases upholding these systems on one-person, one-vote grounds, however, analyzed Voting Rights Act challenges.)

Weighted-voting systems allow a representative body to be kept to a smaller size, while respecting existing political subdivisions. For example, if the least populous entity (e.g., city or town) in a county were allocated a single representative on the county governing body and the more populous entities were given proportionally more representatives, the size of the county governing body could become quite large. With "weighted voting," however, the representatives from the more populous subdivisions are given more votes to account for the greater populations they represent. (In effect, the votes of the representatives from a multimember district are aggregated and placed in the hands of a single representative). As a result, the representative body is smaller—which some policymakers prefer—than a body based on multimember (or numerous single-member) districts.

Even before analyzing the fair and effective representation aspects of weighted voting, the special one-person, one-vote aspects of such a system must be considered. In the past, New York courts have required that the counties employing weighted voting assign votes to representatives based on complex models of the representatives' "voting power." These models consider and measure "voting power" on the governing body, rather than weighting the representatives' votes on a simple arithmetic basis. In practice, high-speed computers generate and tabulate all possible voting combinations by the representatives. (A computer model is necessary because the voting combinations increase exponentially with the size of the body. For example, a thirty-member body would have over a billion possible voting combinations.) The combinations in which a particular representative can influence the outcome of the governing body's vote are totaled. The computer program then makes incremental changes in the numbers of votes assigned until each representative is able to influence the outcome of the governing body's decisions in the same proportion as the total population he or she represents. This influence is known as "voting power."

The principal reason for focusing on voting power has been to counteract the tendency of simple population weighted voting to exaggerate the influence of populous districts. In Nassau County, for example, simple weighted voting would have given 56 percent of the county board's weighted votes to a single representative from the town of Hempstead. This person could never have been outvoted and would, therefore, actually have held 100 percent of the voting power. By contrast, weighting votes on the basis of voting power means that the representative from

Hempstead should be able to cast the crucial vote 56 percent of the time. Some recent judicial decisions have treated weighted voting only as an interim or last-choice approach. Furthermore, the Supreme Court's decision in *Morris* rejected the use of voting-power analysis as a means of measuring the extent of deviation from population equality on the current Board of Estimate. Hence, the appropriate method for measuring the one-person, one-vote aspect of weighed voting systems now appears to be in some doubt.

The fair and effective representation litigation to date has not directly examined the racial and language minority representation aspects of weighted-voting systems. It appears, however, that weighted-voting systems can run afoul of the fair and effective representation requirement in three ways: the difficulty in electing minority representatives to the governing body; the submersion of minority interests by the practical necessity of a representative casting all of his or her weighted vote as a unit; and the severe inhibition of informal alliances on the governing body.

First, election of a single representative from a large "district," like one of New York City's boroughs, suffers from many of the defects of at-large elections. In one sense, such borough representatives serve subcity "districts," but these districts are extremely large and minority group populations are usually too small within any particular borough to have a significant impact on the election.

The second fair and effective representation problem with weighted-voting systems is that the aggregation of votes in the hands of a single individual tends to submerge minority group interests. Weighted-voting systems, which entail casting all of a representative's weighted votes as a unit, resemble multimember systems but without one of the potential advantages of a multimember system. When multiple representatives are elected from a single (usually large) district, racial and ethnic minorities have at least a chance of electing one or more representatives, especially if specialized electoral arrangements (e.g., single-shot or cumulative voting) are employed. But when weighted votes are consolidated into the hands of a single representative who must cast them as a unit, it becomes extremely difficult, if not impossible, to address adequately the concerns of racial and language minorities.

The third fair and effective representation problem arises directly from one of the principal perceived attractions of weighted-voting — the small size of the resulting governing body. With fewer representatives on that body, there are fewer opportunities for coalitions to form. In larger bodies, certain voting blocs coalesce around issues, into racial and ethnic coalitions or into smaller political party caucuses. Such issue-oriented groups and coalitions cross district lines; indeed, they can transcend all geographic demarcations, including New York City borough boundaries.

These more or less informal alliances provide additional, diverse input into the governing process that cannot occur when the number of participants is too small. A small body with weighted voting can greatly deter, if not completely eliminate, the formation of such single- or multiple-issue coalitions on the governing body.

Because a weighted-voting system suffers from the same, or worse, defects that the courts have found in at-large election schemes, such a system could confront serious barriers in the Justice Department's preclearance process. Even if a weighted-voting plan were precleared, it might be subject to a serious challenge under the Equal Protection Clause and under section 2 of the Voting Rights Act.

6. *Weighted voting plus citywide officials.* This approach can be evaluated by considering four possibilities, which differ in the power wielded by citywide officials. All four involve weighted voting by the borough presidents but differ in terms of whether the citywide officials would be allocated the same share of the board's votes as they now have, a greater share, or a smaller share.

The proposal closest to the current structure of the Board of Estimate would retain the same ratio of power between the citywide and the borough officials. To meet the one-person, one-vote requirement, the board's members could be assigned approximately the following set of votes: mayor, 2.0; comptroller, 2.0; City Council president, 2.0; Bronx borough president, 0.8; Brooklyn borough president, 1.6; Manhattan borough president, 1.0; Queens borough president, 1.3; and Staten Island borough president, 0.3. A majority would be 5.6 votes. A major voting-rights problem with this plan, as with the current system, is that the three citywide officials, when voting together, can always garner a majority. This absolute majority possessed by the citywide officials, who in all likelihood will not be representatives of minority group interests, would further restrict the possibilities for minority groups to gain an effective voice on the board.

Another variation, originally proposed by David Dinkins, the Manhattan borough president, would assign votes in a manner similar to the first proposal but would eliminate fractional votes by multiplying all votes by ten. In addition, this plan would require a supermajority of fifty-eight votes, rather than a simple majority of fifty-six votes. The votes would be distributed as follows: mayor, 20; comptroller, 20; City Council president, 20; Bronx borough president, 8; Brooklyn borough president, 16; Manhattan borough president, 10; Queens borough president, 13; and Staten Island borough president, 3. This plan would also assign more than the required fifty-eight vote supermajority to citywide officials. But if only two of the citywide officials voted together, even the addition of the votes of the Brooklyn representative would be insufficient to pass a measure; this bloc would have only fifty-six votes, rather than the required fifty-eight votes. Under these circumstances, the voting influences of the four remaining boroughs become equal, as *any* borough representative could provide the necessary supermajority. Therefore, this proposal would face some, but not all, of the difficulties presented by the first plan.

A plan, originally proposed by Andrew Stein, the president of the City Council, and Ralph Lamberti, the Staten Island borough president, would provide the citywide officials with a greater share of votes on the Board than they now possess. This plan would assign 141 votes as follows: mayor, 35.0; comptroller, 35.0; City Council president, 35.0; Bronx borough president, 5.9; Brooklyn borough president, 11.4; Manhattan borough president, 7.3; Queens borough president, 9.6; and Staten Island borough president, 1.8. The required majority would be 71.6 votes. This plan provides the citywide officials with 105 votes out of a total of

141 votes, or nearly 75 percent of the total. Even if all the boroughs were to vote together, the vote of at least one citywide official would be needed for a majority.

The great weight that would be given to the citywide officials by this plan also, paradoxically, overvalues Staten Island's voting influence, thereby creating a one-person, one-vote problem. If two citywide officials vote together — a total of seventy votes — only one additional vote would be needed to garner a majority. Staten Island's 1.8 votes would be just as valuable in that situation as Brooklyn's 11.4 votes; either borough could supply the necessary "swing vote." Since the representative from Staten Island would almost certainly not represent racial or language minorities, this plan would appear extremely vulnerable to a successful challenge under the Voting Rights Act.

Another variation presented to the commission would have given the citywide officials a smaller share of the restructured board's total votes than they now have: mayor, 7.0; comptroller, 7.0; City Council president, 7.0; Bronx borough president, 3.3; Brooklyn borough president, 6.3; Manhattan borough president, 4.0; Queens borough president, 5.4; and Staten Island borough president, 1.0. A majority would be 20.6. This plan provides a marginally smaller share of the vote to the citywide officials (21 of 41, or 51 percent) than does the current Board (6 of 11, or 55 percent). These officials, though still commanding an absolute majority, would have a smaller majority than that provided by the Stein-Lamberti plan. The dilution of the votes of minority groups, however, would differ only in degree and not in kind.

Other plans could be devised to give the citywide officials an even smaller share of the vote than does this fourth plan. However, as demonstrated above, weighted-voting systems using boroughs (or the city as a whole) as the representational units appear to have innate deficiencies in terms of fair and effective representation for minority groups. It is not at all clear that a court would overlook these deficiencies of weighted voting, even if the current influence of citywide officials were reduced. Thus the specter of a successful voting-rights challenge against any of these weighted-voting plans remains a very real possibility.

Conclusion

Most of the proposals for restructuring the Board of Estimate considered here, while possibly meeting the constitutional standard of one person, one vote, would not fully address the fair and effective representation requirement of the Voting Rights Act of 1965. Of the alternatives discussed, the most favorable, in terms of the twin mandates of the Constitution and the Voting Rights Act, involve a governing board with: (1) members elected from numerous, relatively small single-member districts and few, if any, members elected citywide; or (2) members elected from larger multimember districts, specialized voting arrangements to ensure the opportunity for minority representation, and few, if any, members elected citywide. Even these plans would have to be carefully crafted to avoid preclearance problems under section 5 or challenges under section 2 of the Act.

NOTES

1. This essay is a condensed version of the report that the authors submitted to the New York City Charter Revision Commission in 1988. For a detailed discussion of the charter-revision process that followed, see Frank J. Mauro, "Voting Rights and the Board of Estimate: The Emergence of an Issue," in this vol., pp. 62–68. The present authors' full report and others that followed are reprinted in Frank J. Mauro, ed. *Voting Rights and the Board of Estimate: A Compilation of Advisory Opinions, Memoranda, Correspondence, and Related Materials* (New York City Charter Revision Commission, 1988).

2. 28 C.F.R. Section 51.54(a) (1987); see also *City of Pleasant Grove v. United States*, 479 U.S. 462 (1987); *Beer v. United States*, 425 U.S. 130, 140–42 (1976).

3. See Katharine Butler, "An Evaluation of Whether a Weighted Voting System for the Board of Estimate Would Comply with Section 5 of the Voting Rights Act," in Frank J. Mauro, ed., *Voting Rights and the Board of Estimate*, 108, 112–16.

4. See Senate Rep. No. 417, 97th Cong., 2d sess., 1982, 28, 36, 40, reprinted in *1982 U.S. Code Congressional & Administrative News*, 61.

5. James Blacksher, "Drawing Single-Member Districts to Comply with the Voting Rights Amendments of 1982," 17 *Urban Lawyer* (1985): 347, 352.

6. These proposals were current in January 1988, when the present authors issued their report to the Charter Revision Commission, and several have been revived in the wake of the Supreme Court's *Morris* decision.

7. See generally *Thornburg v. Gingles*, 478 U.S. 30, 45–46 (1986); *Rogers v. Lodge*, 458 U.S. 613, 623–27 (1982).

8. *Rogers v. Lodge*, 458 U.S. 613, 616 (1982).

On the Size of the City Council: Finding the Mean

DOUGLAS MUZZIO
TIM TOMPKINS

"No political problem is less susceptible to a precise solution than that which relates to the number convenient for a representative legislature. . . ."

James Madison,
The Federalist, No. 54

For two centuries, the problem of the appropriate size of a legislative body has remained unsolved. The difficulty, as Madison described it in the celebrated *Federalist* No. 10, is to find "a mean, on both sides of which inconveniences will be found." The dilemma was well put by the State Commission on the Governmental Operations of the City of New York, which examined the conveniences and inconveniences of city councils of various sizes in 1961. The commission found that "few guidelines exist to help fix size." A council should be "large enough to be truly representative, to provide for a deliberation of public issues, to prevent control by corrupt influences, and to guard against too easy a combination for improper purposes." But at the same time it should be "small enough to get capable men and women, to avoid confusion and expedite action, to avert excessive involvement by its members in administrative details, and to center responsibility for its action or inaction."[1] In sum, there is neither an abstract optimal size for a national, state, or city legislature nor an accepted formula for establishing legislative size, because decisions on size involve fundamental matters of representation, governmental effectiveness, political accountability, and the competitiveness of the city's political system.

The purpose of this essay is to review what is known about the effects of the size of legislative bodies and to examine the implications of altering the size of the current New York City Council (which has thirty-five members elected from single-member districts). The essay addresses the central issue of representation, the problem of definition and comparison, the effect of changing size on core values, and, finally, the effect of changes in the electoral system on city politics.

Representation

The issue of representation is paramount. The question remains that Melancton Smith posed at the New York State constitutional ratifying convention in Poughkeepsie in June 1788: "How was the will of the community to be expressed?" To Smith and other opponents of the Constitution, the proposed national legislature was "too small to possess the sentiments, be influenced by the interests of the people." (The House was to have had sixty-five members, the Senate twenty-six.) A large body, with small electoral districts, would more likely produce representatives who "resemble those they represent." The legislature would be "a true picture of the people, possess a knowledge of their circumstances and their wants, sympathize in all their distresses, and be disposed to seek their true interests."

Alexander Hamilton, in reply to Smith, offered a different concept of representation and of the representative. Hamilton's representative, who was to be elected in a large electoral district, was supposed to "refine and enlarge public views, to act as a filter for impassioned and intemperate opinions and interests." This tempering function, Hamilton believed, would work best in the large district because men of factious tempers, of local prejudices, and of sinister designs would have less influence.

More than a century later, the conflict between the progressive municipal reformers and the supporters of the political machine in New York and elsewhere during the late-nineteenth and early-twentieth centuries was, at its root, a debate over both the method of representation and who should be represented. The reformers echoed Hamilton; the defenders of the machine, Smith.

Most American cities at the turn of the century had large councils drawn from numerous wards. Reformers, in their assault on the machines, advocated (and were often successful in effecting) smaller councils, often elected from at-large districts, to weaken the power of lower- and working-class neighborhood and other interests that formed the cornerstones of the machine. To the reformers, a smaller council would be more efficient and effective; small councils were also more likely to attract "better" candidates (that is, candidates more like the reformers themselves) and, hence, "better" public officials. These officials would be more powerful, independent, and effective. The small at-large city council would take a citywide perspective on issues and policy decisions; the municipal legislature would be free from the direct control of spatially ordered interests. Finally, small councils would be less expensive.

The reformers were opposed by locally based lower- and working-class groups (and, to an extent, middle-class groups) who held that geographic neighborhood and group interests ought not be sacrificed. Local ward leaders, overwhelmingly drawn from the same classes and communities as their constituents, spoke for their local areas, the economic interests of their inhabitants, their residential concerns, and their recreational and religious interests.

Recent reform, driven by the "one person, one vote" standard and the Voting Rights Act of 1965 as amended in 1982, favors district systems to enhance at least the possibility of minority-group representation from areas with concentrated minority populations. Historically, the general pattern in New York City has been to expand the council in order to accommodate newly emerging groups while protecting incumbents. If the size of the New York City Council were to be altered, it would doubtless be expanded in this classic pattern, and to avoid running afoul of proscriptions against the "dilution" of minority group representation.[2]

The Problems of Definition and Comparison

A central problem in "finding the mean" is the lack of consistent definitions of *large* and *small*. Today, for example, the "small" house at the national level, the Senate, is larger than the "large" house in more than a third of the states and has twice the membership of the largest city councils. Small state chambers are larger than or about the same size as large city councils. Yet, at each level the same arguments are made about the relative virtues of "small" or "large" bodies.

The notion of size itself is complicated because two distinct but related factors can make a council "large" and "small" simultaneously: (1) the number of members in the body, irrespective of the number of constituents served by each member; and (2) the number of constituents represented by each member, regardless of the number of members.

The sizes of American city councils vary widely, both in the number of council members and in the number of constituents per council member. In the mid-1980s, the councils of the twenty largest American cities ranged in absolute size from seven (Columbus) to fifty (Chicago). New York's thirty-five–member council ranked second to Chicago's, making it a "large" council. The number of constituents in these twenty councils ranged from 24,000 in Indianapolis to 202,000 in New York, making New York's council "small." In 1984, each New York City councilmanic district was approximately the size of Mobile, Alabama, the seventy-third largest United States city, which had a city council of seven members.

The unique size and scope of New York City government suggest that comparative analysis should be approached with caution, since the appropriate universe for comparison is unclear. Comparisons to other cities are natural. It also seems appropriate to examine the experiences of large counties. They are similar to cities in their geographic expanse, range of function, and relationships with smaller governmental units within their boundaries. Finally, New York City, given its size, composition, and level of governmental activity, may be appropriately compared to a state.

The average council in cities responding to a survey by the International City Management Association in the early 1980s had six or seven members. The average was depressed, however, by the large number of smaller cities in the sample. For larger cities, there was a direct relationship between city size and council size. Cities with a population of 1 million had an average council size of 22; those with 0.5 to 1 million, 13.25; and those with 0.25 to 0.5 million, 10.19.

The five largest American cities (excluding New York) now have an average council size of twenty-two members. The average number of constituents per council member in these five cities is 122,600. If the New York City Council were to have twenty-two members elected from single-member districts, each district would contain 341,190 people — or two-thirds more constituents than the current 202,000 people per district. To have the average number of constituents per representative (122,600), the council would need fifty-eight members.

Although the New York City Council is far smaller than either the New York State Senate or the State Assembly, it is now equal to or larger than the upper houses of twenty-two of the states. Before the abolition of its ten at-large seats in 1983, the council was larger than the upper houses of thirty-three states and both houses of three of these (Alaska, Delaware, and Nevada). Of the seventy-seven United States counties with populations greater than half a million, forty-one have boards with five or fewer members. The mean size of legislatures in New York State counties is 18.5 members, and the average number of constituents per legislator (excluding New York City) is 11,177. Five counties in New York State have legislatures larger than the New York City Council.

Much of the thinking about the effect of the size of legislative bodies on their functioning comes from a comparison of the United States Senate and the House of Representatives. Though recently challenged, the conventional view is that size differences largely account for the fact that the Senate has functioned as a "forum," whereas the House has been a "workshop." More informal, decentralized, and deliberative, the Senate — the "upper house"— is more prestigious and visible. In contrast, the House has been portrayed as a body where strong leadership and strict procedures hold sway, "more formal, more impersonal, more hierarchically organized."[3]

State legislatures have had similar experiences. The observations of Alan Rosenthal provide a useful summary: "The size of a legislative chamber has much to do with its norms and its behavior. A body of 80, 100, and 150 members, as in most houses, or of 400 as in New Hampshire, is likely to be institutionally dissimilar from one with 20, 30, or 40 members, as in most senates. Size has its effects on the following: the atmosphere, with more confusion and impersonality in larger bodies and friendlier relationships in smaller ones; hierarchy, with more elaborate and orderly rules and procedures and greater leadership authority in larger bodies and informality and collegial authority in smaller ones; the conduct of business, with a more efficient flow and less debate in larger bodies and more leisurely deliberation and greater fluidity in smaller ones; the internal distribution of power, with more concentrated pockets possible in larger bodies and greater dispersion of power in smaller ones."[4]

Why Council Sizes Change

Legislative size changes as a result of internal and external factors. Changes in district size of the New York City Council have reflected political, economic, and demographic developments in the city and state as well as attempts to achieve

TABLE 1

Councils of the Twenty Largest United States Cities
Ranked by Population per Representative
and Size of Single Member Districts

City	Population	Council Size			Persons per Representative	Rank	District Size	Rank
		Total	District	At-Large				
New York	7,071,639	35	35	—	202,046	1	202,046	1
Chicago	3,005,072	50	50	—	60,101	12	60,101	14
Los Angeles	2,966,850	15	15	—	199,790	2	199,790	2
Philadelphia	1,688,210	17	10	7	98,130	5	168,821	4
Houston	1,595,138	15	9	6	106,342	4	177,237	3
Detroit	1,203,339	9	—	9	133,704	3	—	—
Dallas	904,078	11	8	3	82,188	8	113,010	6
San Diego	875,538	9	8	1	97,282	6	109,442	7
Phoenix	789,704	9	8	1	87,745	7	98,712	8
Baltimore	786,775	19	18[a]	1	41,409	17	131,129[a]	5[a]
San Antonio	785,880	11	10	1	71,443	10	78,587	11
Indianapolis	700,807	29	25	4	24,165	20	28,032	16
San Francisco	678,974	11	—	11	61,725	11	—	—
Memphis	646,356	13	6	7	49,720	14	92,337	9
Washington	638,333	13	8	5	49,102	15	79,792	10
Milwaukee	636,212	16	16	—	39,763	18	39,763	15
San Jose	629,442	11	10	1	57,222	13	62,944	12
Cleveland	573,822	21	21	—	27,328	19	27,328	17
Columbus	564,871	7	—	7	80,696	9	—	—
Boston	562,994	13	9	4	43,307	16	62,555	13

Note: Population data are 1984 Census Bureau estimates from the Statistical Abstract of the United States, 1987, table K. Council size and composition data drawn from The Municipal Year Book 1987, city charters, and personal communication with city council staffs.

[a] Baltimore has multimember districts; that is, three representatives are elected from each of six districts, for a total of eighteen district representatives. The nineteenth member is the city council president, elected citywide.

a number of (sometimes conflicting) objectives. These have included enhancing competitiveness, attracting quality candidates for office, meeting the one-person, one-vote standard, recognizing the integrity of traditional geographic boundaries, and ensuring equitable representation of minority groups, among others. Of course, changes in council size also reflect attempts by various parties, party factions, and other interests to gain the upper hand in city government.

A classic strategy for altering the power relationships in a legislative body is to alter its size. William Riker, in his influential *A Theory of Political Coalitions* (1962), noted that "expansion and contraction of membership [in legislatures] has been a persistent and standardized technique for changing the relative weights of members." Riker offered three examples: the expansion of the United States House of Representatives throughout the nineteenth century to minimize the loss of influence by older states; the controversies surrounding the admission of new states to the union, particularly the effect on the partisan and regional balance in the Senate; and American resistance to admitting China to the United Nations, not because of the possible effect in the larger General Assembly but in the smaller Security Council.[5]

Local examples of "legislative size" strategy abound. In the 1940s, for instance, fusion forces in New York City attempted to contract the City Council and thus reorder power relationships within it. More recently—in 1965 and 1973—reapportionments have expanded the council's size to protect incumbents while responding to pressures from minorities for increased representation. Finally, the increase in the size of the New York State Senate after recent reapportionments has helped ensure Republican dominance of that body.

Thus the conflict between reformers, who in general have advocated smaller legislatures, and incumbent politicians, who have defended larger ones, have at least as much to do with who has power in those bodies as with the trade-off between enhanced efficiency and greater representation. Those in control have sought to protect established power relationships and expand available political opportunities for themselves and their allies. Those critical of incumbents have sought to disrupt established relationships in a variety of ways, one being the contraction of the decision arena.

Legislatures, when left to their own devices, almost always expand rather than diminish in size. When reduction has occurred in recent years, such as in a number of state legislatures during the mid-1960s and in the New York City Council in 1983, it is often as a result of the intervention of an extrinsic actor—in these cases, the federal courts concerned about reapportionment or voting rights. In Illinois in 1980, the reduction in the size of the house, sought for many years, was finally triggered by a popular reaction to legislative pay raises.

The size of the New York City Council and its predecessor, the Board of Aldermen, has been changed twelve times since 1901 (see table 2). The number of members has varied from seventeen (between 1943 and 1945) to seventy-three (between 1901 and 1915). Under the system of proportional representation used from 1937 through 1949, the membership varied, depending on voter turnout. As a result, the size changed with every election, a total of five times in a twelve-year period. District size has varied widely as well. In 1901 there were 49,000 New Yorkers for each alderman; in 1943, each council member represented 439,000 people.

Most changes in City Council size have been incremental, with little discernible impact on the organization and composition of the body. An exception was the dramatic reduction in membership following the adoption of proportional representation. Some reformers regarded this reduction in the size of the body as an end in itself, for the seats eliminated were denied to the Democratic machine. In the hearings before the Thacher commission in 1936, Richard Childs, one of the leaders of the municipal reform movement, thanked the commission because it "cut out thirty-six useless jobs by reducing the Board of Aldermen."[6]

The variable-sized council that operated under proportional representation was considered a more effective, issue-oriented body that attracted "better quality" membership, but these characteristics are generally attributed only minimally to its

TABLE 2

Size of City Council and Predecessors since 1902

Dates	Number of Single Member District	Number of Borough At large	Period in Office	Population	Average Size of District
1902–3	73	5	2	3,437,152	47,084
1904–5	73	5	2		
1906–7	73	5	2	4,013,781	54,983
1908–9	73	5	2		
1910–11	73	5	2	4,766,883	65,299
1912–13	73	5	2		
1914–15	73	5	2		
1916–17	73	5	2	5,047,221	69,140
1918–19	67	5	2		75,331
1920–21	67	5	2	5,560,048	82,985
1922–23	65	5	2		85,539
1924–25	65	5	2		
1926–27	65	5	2	5,373,356	82,667
1928–29	65	5	2		
1930–31	65	5	2	6,954,491	106,622
1932–33	65	5	2		
1934–35	65	5	2		
1936–37	65	5	2	6,930,446	
1938–39	0	26	2		
1940–41	0	21	2	7,454,995	
1942–43	0	26	2		
1944–45	0	17	2		
1946–49	0	23	4		
1950–53	25	0	4	7,891,957	315,678
1954–57	25	0	4		
1958–61	25	0	4		
1962–63	25	0	2	7,781,984	311,279
1964–65	25	10	2		
1966–69	27	10	4		288,221
1970–73	27	10	4	7,895,563	292,428
1974–77	33	10	4		239,259
1978–82	33	10	5		
1983	35	10	0.5	7,071,639	202,046
1983–85	35	0	2.5		
1986–89	35	0	4	(7,262,700)	207,505

Note: The heading "Period in Office" is used because some terms were extended and others truncated because of unusual circumstances.

reduced size. The key factor seems to have been the enhanced competition that resulted from changes in the electoral system.

The reduction in the size of the City Council in 1983 (from forty-three to thirty-three, with the loss of the ten borough at-large seats), like the earlier incremental changes, seems to have had little effect on the organization or operation of the body. The proportion of minority and women members did increase as a result of this change, however, since no at-large members at the time of the change were drawn from these groups.

How Changing Size Affects Core Values

Ultimately, the size of the New York City Council depends on which and whose values are to be effected. The 1988 New York City Charter Revision Commission has posited eight "core values": representativeness; responsiveness; public participation and confidence in government; limiting the concentration of governmental power (that is, creating checks and balances and competition); attracting quality people to public service; accountability; increasing the ability of officials to make difficult and wise decisions for the public good; and enhanced effectiveness and efficiency.

Clearly, no set of institutional arrangements (including the size of the council) can serve all of these values. Goals conflict; trade-offs are often necessary. Most important, an effective democratic electoral system must strike a balance between two basic goals. On the one hand, an electoral system ought to give each voter an adequate range of choices to allow expression of his or her true preferences and then give representation to the preferences expressed roughly in proportion to their popular support. On the other hand, when the results are aggregated, a stable government must emerge that can be said to be the choice of the people.

Also, any changes in basic governmental structures in a complex sociopolitical system will likely produce effects that are unforeseen or unintended by policymakers. How changes in council size will ultimately affect both internal dynamics and constituent representation cannot be predicted with certainty. Alterations in the size of the body will have effects in combination with other changes. The core values will be influenced by myriad structural, political, economic, demographic, social, and other changes. Moreover, the consequences of changes in council size are unlikely to be immediately evident; for instance, incumbent leaders will probably continue to hold sway for a time, whatever the size of the body.

Representativeness. Logically, the larger the council, the smaller the councilmanic district, and the fairer the representation of ethnically, racially, or religiously defined neighborhoods. If representation means the election of a member of the group to the council ("descriptive representation") suggested by most Supreme Court decisions,[7] there is evidence that small city councils adversely, yet differentially, affect the equity of representation of blacks, Hispanics, and Asians. The greater the number of districts, the greater the equity of representation of these three groups. (A larger City Council might also lead to the election of more women, Republicans, and gays).

An enlarged council that increased the equity of representation of ethnic and racial minorities would probably by looked on with favor by federal courts and the U.S. Department of Justice. A council with fewer members might violate the Voting Rights Act of 1965 by diluting black and Hispanic membership on the council. One critic of traditional reformers has called the small council "'gerrymandering by numbers' rather than by geography" and sees it as the "Achilles' heel" of the municipal reform movement.[8]

Furthermore, a larger council will likely have both stronger leadership and more vigorous public dissent by individual members. The presence of more people with dissimilar backgrounds would produce a greater diversity of voices and interests in the council. While strong leadership (one possible consequence of increased size) might limit the effectiveness of those voices, the mere presence of a greater range of opinion might make the council a more vigorous forum. Clearly, however, if the talk is not connected to action, it may be ignored.

Moreover, substantially enlarging the council could improve the institution. Newly defined districts will enhance the prospects of competition, especially within primaries, for established members. Membership turnover is likely to increase, at least in the short run. New members may challenge the norms of the council, as was the case in the United States House of Representatives in 1975, making it more internally democratic in its procedures and distributing power more widely within the body.

A larger council with a higher proportion of minority-group members might lead to the formation of new alliances within the body. Judging from issues that have been given substantial publicity in the recent past — the selection of Peter Vallone to the majority leadership in 1986, for example — the dominant cleavages in the New York City Council have been along geographic and ideological lines.[9] Although the protection of borough interests and ideological differences among members will surely remain important, a larger body may reduce the salience and importance of the geographically defined divisions and — given the strong overlap of race and ideology — may produce cleavages more influenced by race or ethnicity.

Responsiveness. Smaller districts enhance the capacity of a council member to serve constituents and communities. Studies suggest that there is an increasing "case" orientation among American city council members, especially those based in districts or wards. In fact, the two-century-old conception of the representative as "trustee" or "delegate" has been expanded to include the "ombudsman."[10]

Increasing the size of the council is likely to affect the balance between the legislator's district-service function and his or her larger policy-making role. If smaller districts result in a greater focus on local and parochial matters and interests and if homogeneity in district opinion offers members less room to compromise on the legislative floor, the development of a broader policy perspective in the council may be retarded.

This change may be addressed in two ways. A well-staffed and structured legislative body with effective leadership could develop an institutional perspective that, in turn, could foster a citywide perspective, even in a larger body. Experience in the New York State Legislature, for example, indicates that members of an effective legislative body come, in part, to identify their personal interests and goals with the strength of the institutions in which they serve. This, in turn, inclines them to support positions that can be presented as broadly beneficial to the state as a whole. Other institutional changes can be made to promote a legislative body that has a greater policy focus. Community boards, for example, can be given ombudsman and "case" functions, freeing legislators, to a degree, from this role.

Public participation and confidence in government. Proponents of a larger council have argued that it would increase citizen participation in government, since people's feeling that their actions could influence government might increase. Increased voter participation would follow, it is said, because there would be fewer people per representative and a greater range of interests represented. There is no empirical evidence, however, that smaller district size increases participation. In fact, voter participation in the United States is lowest in low-visibility local elections.[11]

Limiting the concentration of governmental power. Following Madison (*The Federalist*, No. 58), some municipal reformers have suggested that "the greater the number composing [a body] may be, the fewer will be the men who will in fact direct their proceedings." Large bodies must delegate power, it is argued, and therefore become leadership-dominated. In contrast, each member of a smaller body (particularly, if it is significantly smaller) would be a more powerful, independent, and effective political figure. This is one of the reasons that the National Municipal League's Model City Charter ("the orthodox text of the municipal reform movement"[12]) recommended a small council—four to six members—in its first six editions and a five- to seven-member council in its seventh edition.

The argument in support of a larger body is that the internal power structure of the council depends significantly on its rules and its role in city government as a whole. Increasing the size of the body might lead to delegation of power to committee chairs, thus reducing the role of a single leader. Also, the combination of a strong leadership and powerful committee chairs could serve as an effective check on the executive branch. But, again, greater size could lead to increased factionalism and a reduced check on the executive.

Finally, for a larger body made up of smaller single-member districts, it is likely that election campaigns would be both less costly and less difficult to conduct than a broader campaign. Certainly, when boroughwide elections prevailed for the twelve-year period under proportional representation, campaigns were more costly and harder to mount. Moreover, incumbents may face more serious challenges in smaller districts.

Attracting quality people to public service. No structural change, such as enlarging or reducing the size of the council, can "guarantee the personal characteristics, quality, or performance of those who seek or are elected to the Council."[13] There is general agreement that the average ability of members elected to the smaller councils under proportional representation (1937–45) was higher than those who had been elected to the boards of aldermen.[14] It is not clear whether this was simply the result of a great reduction in council size (from sixty-five to twenty-six), the new voting system, happenstance, or some combination of these and other factors.

Accountability. Smaller districts conform to the American belief that the closer the government is to the citizenry, the more responsive it is to their demands. This view appears to have a basis in fact in many American cities.[15] For example, a larger council, as noted above, would appear to enhance member availability for constituent and community service. But smaller councilmanic districts in New York City (which in all likelihood would contain more than 100,000 constituents) would inhibit accountability if a citizen found it harder to keep informed, that is, if the change resulted in less media coverage.

Proponents of a large council argue that it would be subject to less control by corrupt influences. Their view is that a smaller body means fewer conspirators have to be recruited to make a cabal and perform corrupt acts. This argument runs counter to the views of late-nineteenth and early-twentieth century municipal reformers, who assaulted the "machine" control of large bodies. Reformers advocated at-large elections and reductions in the size of city councils to weaken the power of neighborhood and other parochial interests. Small districts were seen to be the building blocks from which machines were usually constituted. They argued that the electorate could better hold a fewer number of more visible legislators responsible and, therefore, a smaller council would be less corruptible. Opponents also suggest that a larger council, if elected exclusively from districts, could become less sensitive to citywide needs and interests.

There are also fears that with the abolition of the New York City Board of Estimate, with its citywide and boroughwide representation, a larger district-based City Council could further weaken the representation of such citywide or boroughwide interests that are not also neighborhood ones. But it is unclear that the Board of Estimate has been indeed less parochial than the current City Council. The board is a forum in which the interests of key city political leaders, each with his or her own agenda, are pursued. In contrast, the council has an institutional interest as the city's legislature, one that might be developed further if it is enlarged and may generate a more vital and effective committee structure. Moreover, in its internal structure, the council takes account of geographic interests.

Increasing the ability of officials to make difficult and wise decisions for the public good. Better decisions might be made in a larger body because of a greater development of expertise and the more likely availability of expert staff. More members might allow fewer committee assignments per member and consequently allow each to concentrate his or her energy in a few policy areas. A greater range of opinion and more genuine deliberation and exchange may produce a greater number of alternatives and more thoughtful consideration of them (see the discussion of effectiveness below). Also, members might be more willing to make difficult decisions because of a diffusion of responsibility. On the other hand, in accord with the traditional view, members may be more myopic and parochial because their districts are smaller.

Enhanced efficiency and effectiveness. The question of effectiveness is primarily an internal one: How does its size help or hinder the council in getting its work done? Traditionally, municipal reformers have argued that substantially smaller councils would be more efficient and effective, since they do not require the degree of consultation, debate, and discussion of large legislatures. A larger council could widen the dispersal of power and make it harder to get council members to act in unison.

However, more recent thinking suggests that larger bodies are more formalized in their structure, with concentrations of power centered on the leadership and more specialized committees. Because of their size, larger legislatures are more attentive to procedures that are likely to foster greater productivity. Despite strong leadership, there tend to be less groupthink among members, and a more vigorous public dissent in larger bodies, and a greater tendency to organize in coalitions.

Research in social psychology, done principally with groups smaller than the current New York City Council, indicates that size is a significant factor in influencing the "quality" of decision making. In general, there is a trade-off between efficiency (more likely in smaller bodies) and full availability of alternatives (more likely in larger ones). Optimal size appears to be linked to the nature of the task, an observation that is minimally helpful for the design of a body, such as a city council, which performs diverse functions (but the observation may be relevant to committees and subcommittees). One author has offered the following "tentative generalizations:" (1) larger groups tend to be more productive and develop higher quality products; (2) as size increases, members feel freer to express dissatisfaction; (3) smaller groups provide greater opportunities for leadership; (4) as group size grows, cohesiveness declines; and (5) member satisfaction declines with group size.[16]

The efficiency and effectiveness of a legislature depends, in part, on the size and number of committees and subcommittees as well as on the size of the entire body. Larger legislatures are likely to have more committees than smaller ones. A study of state legislatures identified the "optimum committee size"— that is, one that both minimized "decision costs" and "external costs" for legislators — for a small chamber to be about nine members and for a large body, thirteen.[17] Though this is hardly a well-established principle, the "optimal" size for committees of the current thirty-five member New York City Council, which is about the size of the average state upper house, would be around nine members. Thus, since the current average council committee has fewer than nine members, it could be argued that increasing the size of committees as a consequence of enlarging council size would not be damaging to the council or its operations.

Research also suggests that larger legislatures (which are likely to have more committees than smaller ones) afford their members more opportunity to develop substantive expertise. (But members' expertise and participation may be hampered if each has a considerable number of committee assignments.) Also, as the number of members in a chamber increases, there is a tendency toward longer sessions and more coalition formation (with its attendant logrolling). Debate is more constrained and decision on the floor less likely in a larger body. Throughout, the question of what is "large" and "small" remains.

Finally, greater size (and, perhaps, greater proportionality of representation) may lead to greater factionalism and conflict in the council, which might become a cause — as well as an effect of — ethnic, racial, or class conflict. The council could be even less a check on the mayor than it is now.

A larger city council will inevitably be more expensive than a smaller one, all other things being equal, but experience suggests that making bodies smaller does not reduce their cost. Once a critical mass of central staff is established, increases in cost are linked entirely to the level of support given individual members. The issue is whether incremental increases in cost are worth the gains that might accrue from a larger body.

Conclusion

There are few empirical analyses of the effects of city council size, either in the political science or legal literature, and the federal courts have largely ignored the number of seats in a legislature. Thus, much of the available information on the effects of legislative size is speculative and anecdotal. It is certain, however, that changes in a city council's "electoral system"— that is, the number, size, and type of election districts and the procedures for casting and counting votes — will affect, often profoundly, the character of city politics. Like all rules, electoral procedures are not neutral, for, as E.E. Schattschneider has said, "all organization is bias."[18] An electoral system influences the number and nature of political parties, the type of candidates for public office, and the appeals they make and the policies they pursue. Ultimately, an electoral system influences the political stability and legitimacy of the system itself.

However, the electoral system (and specifically here the number and size of New York City Council districts) is only one among many interacting factors that affect city politics. It is difficult if not impossible to isolate its effects and those of its constituent elements from the influence of other factors, such as social cleavage, party structure, organization of interest groups, political culture, and socio-economics.

But the city's electoral system is subject to direct manipulation through charter changes in ways that these other elements are not. Moreover, it provides the channels through which ethnic, racial, religious, geographic, economic, and ideological divisions are played out. Therefore, efforts to change fundamentally the distribution of power within the city (indeed, any political system) are often directed toward changing elements of the electoral system.

Despite the acknowledged importance of the electoral system, there is a large subjective or arbitrary element in finding the mean and determining the conveniences and inconveniences of legislatures of various sizes. At best, one size cannot be called better than others; rather, different sizes are conducive to different goals. And even then, the connection between the number of seats and the size of districts is not satisfactorily established, if not plainly ambivalent.

Notes

1. New York State Commission on Governmental Operations of the City of New York, *Background Research on the Top Structure of the Government of the City of New York*, vol. 3, Feb. 1961, 57.
2. For a discussion of the Voting Rights Act of 1965, see Alta Charo, "An Overview of the Voting Rights Act" (1987), prepared for the New York City Charter Revision Commission.
3. David Vogler, *The Politics of Congress* (Boston: Allyn and Bacon, 1974), 152.
4. Alan Rosenthal, *Legislative Life* (New York: Harper and Row, 1981), 133–34.
5. William Riker, *The Theory of Political Coalitions* (New Haven: Yale University Press, 1962), 201.
6. Frederick Shaw, *The History of the New York City Legislature* (New York: Columbia University Press, 1954), 73.

7. Hanna Pitkin, ed., *Representation* (New York: Atherton Press, 1969), 60–91.

8. Delbert Taebel, "Minority Representation on City Councils: The Impact of Structure on Blacks and Hispanics," *Social Science Quarterly* 59 (June 1978): 147–48, 151.

9. *New York Times*, 1 Jan. 1986, 8 Jan. 1986.

10. Peggy Heilig and Robert Mundt, *Your Voice at City Hall: The Politics, Procedures and Policies of District Representation* (Albany: State University of New York Press, 1984), 83–91. However, constituent service "may be more a function of staff and logistical support" than the size of a constituency. State Charter Revision Commission for New York City, *The City Council of New York and The President of the City Council* (December 1973), 57.

11. Nicholas Henry, *Governing at the Grassroots*, 3d ed. (Englewood Cliffs: Prentice Hall, 1987), 52.

12. Edward Banfield and James Q. Wilson, *City Politics* (New York: Random House, Vintage Books, 1963), 89.

13. State Charter Revision Commission on Governmental Operations of the City of New York, *The City Council of New York and The President of the City Council* (New York, December 1973), 48.

14. Belle Zeller and Hugh Bone, "The Repeal of P.R. in New York City: Ten Years in Retrospect," *American Political Science Review* 57 (December 1948), 1137; and Shaw, chap. 10.

15. Edward Banfield and James Q. Wilson, *City Politics* (New York: Random House, Vintage Books, 1963), 91.

16. Walter S. Swap and Associates, *Group Decision Making* (Beverly Hills: Sage, 1984), 54–55.

17. Wayne L. Francis, "Legislative Committees, Optimal Committee Size and the Costs of Decision Making," *Journal of Politics* 44 (1982), 831–32.

18. Elmer Eric Schattschneider, *The Semisovereign People: A Realist's View of Democracy in America* (New York: Holt, Rinehart and Winston, 1960), 87.

Community Governance: A Decade of Experience

ROBERT F. PECORELLA

The New York State Charter Revision Commission (SCRC) of 1975, created immediately after a massive effort focused on decentralization and community control of the New York City government, was charged with increasing citizen awareness of and influence over the operations of the city. In designing the community-board system, the SCRC produced a form of decentralization that went far beyond any other such experiment in the New York City experience. That system coupled the notion of political decentralization with administrative decentralization.

The 1975 charter revisions created fifty-nine community boards, each with a maximum of fifty members selected by borough presidents and local city councilors. The boards receive expense-budget funding for such operating purposes as rent, office supplies, clerical assistance, and the services of a full-time district manager who serves at the pleasure of the board. The revised charter allocated to the community boards advisory responsibility in three major areas: local budget priorities, land-use planning, and service monitoring. The charter revisions provided a process for the boards to present proposals for inclusion in the city's expense and capital budgets, each of which was to be broken down by community districts. Community-board influence over land-use planning was codified in the Uniform Land Use Review Procedure (ULURP), which increased the importance of and standardized the process for board input on land-use matters. And the new charter augmented and standardized the boards' service-monitoring role through the establishment of district service cabinets, which formalized agency relationships with community boards. Moreover, the charter mandated coterminality of community and service districts, a reform intended to organize interactions between city officials and community representatives.

In evaluating community-board effectiveness since the adoption of charter reform, it is useful to separate the analysis into two periods. The first, from January 1977 to early 1982, was one of adjustment both for the community boards and for the city agencies dealing with them. It was a time of severe fiscal stress in city government, with the consequent retrenchment and constraints on policy making such retrenchment implies. The second period, from 1982 to 1987, was character- ized by the community-board system already in place as well as an economic recovery that served to loosen some of the fiscal and legal constraints on city policymakers.

Evaluating Budget Reforms

Under New York City's system of geographically based budgeting, community- board and agency representatives at the district level meet every June to discuss districts' needs and their respective expense and capital-budget priorities. In early July, the boards submit District Needs Statements, which outline board analyses of community needs, to the Department of City Planning. For the remainder of the summer and into early fall, the boards hold public hearings on the budget requests and the District Needs Statements and prepare agendas for borough-level consultations. Starting in mid-September, board representatives meet with agency commissioners or deputy commissioners at the borough level.

Following public hearings and votes of the membership, each board may submit up to forty capital and fifteen expense budget proposals to the Office of Manage- ment and Budget (OMB) in November. The OMB staff gives special attention to the boards' top ten priority requests. OMB's input is reflected in the mayor's pre- liminary budget that is made public in mid-January, serves as the focus of com- munity and citywide public hearings during January and February, and evolves into the executive budget. By early June, the City Council and the Board of Esti- mate approve some version of the executive budget, which after adoption becomes operative for the fiscal year starting that July.

Early experiences with community-based budgeting were mixed. David Leben- stein, for example, found that "the overall quality of community board budget proposals vary greatly from excellent to very poor."[1] Several boards did not even submit board-initiated proposals to OMB, and those that did frequently made procedural mistakes hampering their efforts. Moreover, the boards that correctly submitted budget proposals tended to favor "hard" services — those that did little to assist people in need of expanded social services.[2]

This early confusion about community-based budgeting is not surprising. The municipal budget process is complex, and board involvement with the process was an innovation when these initial studies were done. Furthermore, a city in fiscal crisis without real home rule is hardly the optimal locale in which to imple- ment geographical decentralization. Nor is it particularly puzzling, with the de- terioration of the city's infrastructure obvious and a focus of concern, that suc- cessful board proposals tended to emphasize "hard" rather than "soft" services.

Several studies attempted to determine whether the boards influenced the budget process by calculating their success in having their proposals included in the city's expense, capital, and community-development budgets during this early period.

Summarizing the findings from studies of fiscal years 1979 through 1981, John Mudd reported: "With some minor variation, the funding approval rate has remained in the 40 to 50 percent range for capital items and the 30 to 40 percent range for expense budget priorities."[3]

Among the strongest predictors of success on budget matters was the number of years a proposal has been in process and whether it had an agency cosponsor. Moreover, for the expense budget, the socioeconomic status of the district represented by the board was related to board success — that is, the poorer the district, the less successful it was in obtaining its locally initiated proposals.

Since those early years, the city's fiscal situation and board budget capabilities have improved dramatically. Despite some questions concerning the breadth of the city's recovery, the aggregate data indicate clear signs of renewed economic health. New York's expense budget has produced surpluses for five consecutive years and the city's debt is once again marketable. In fact, because of the city's recent fiscal performance, provisions of state legislation that eased the most pervasive oversight functions brought on by the fiscal crisis went into effect in August 1986.

Paralleling the recovery, community-board budgetary success has increased over the years. Since fiscal year 1982, each of the city's fifty-nine boards has submitted proposals to OMB and most submitted their full complement of prioritized proposals. OMB can take four actions in response to board-initiated proposals to either the capital or expense budgets. First, these proposals can be included in the respective budget as either a line-item or a lump-sum appropriation; this action could be considered a first-time success for a board-initiated proposal. Second, OMB can approve a request for continued funding. Third, the proposal can be rejected for lack of information. And, fourth, the proposal can be rejected for cause.

Table 1 reveals that the percentage of board-initiated proposals included in the capital budget as line-item, lump-sum, or continued funding stayed at roughly 50 percent between 1982 and 1985. It is important to note, however, that between the fiscal years in question, the percentage of first-time board-initiated proposals (those not involving continued funding) included in the city's capital budget increased over 50 percent while the percentage of proposals rejected for cause decreased over 60 percent.

Overall increases in board budgetary success notwithstanding, the boards differed significantly in their capacity to secure local budgetary priorities. As table 2 indicates, there are two independent explanations for board budget success: the presence of agency cosponsorship and the income level of the community.

Overall, proposals cosponsored by city line agencies are nearly three times as likely to be included in the city's capital budget as those submitted alone and nearly five times as likely to be accepted as proposals cosponsored by community groups. The strong relationship between agency cosponsorship and eventual inclusion of the proposal in the city's capital budget held in each of the three fiscal years examined and across each of the three community demographic types involved.

TABLE 1

The Disposition by Percentage of 2,274 Board-Initiated Capital Budget Proposals Between Fiscal Years 1982 and 1985

Proposal Disposition	Total (1982–85)	FY 1985	FY 1984	FY 1983	FY 1982
Included: line item*	18%	11%	20%	20%	20%
Included: lump sum*	9	22	7	5	2
Included: continued‡	19	17	18	26	14
Rejected: lack of information**	17	28	25	12	5
Rejected: merits**	37	22	30	37	59
Total percentages	100	100	100	100	100
Average success rate	27	33	27	25	22
Number of proposals	2,274	589	562	555	568

Source: R.F. Pecorella, "Community Input and the City Budget: Geographically Based Budgeting in New York City," *Journal of Urban Affairs* 8 (Winter 1986): 62.
* Considered successful proposals.
** Considered unsuccessful proposals.
‡ Because not all the "continued proposals" originated with the boards, they were excluded from the analysis.

Table 3 presents specific data that both reconfirm and qualify these findings. Boards from low-income, minority districts submit a greater number of their proposals with community-group cosponsors and fewer with line agencies than do either middle-income or upper-middle-income areas. This parochial tendency among community boards from low-income districts explains in part their lower success rates. But their lower-income status independently causes these communities to be less successful than the other community types. Indeed, a linear relationship exists between community wealth and acceptance rates.

Four characteristics, then, summarize the evolution of board budget responsi-

TABLE 2

Method of Board-Initiated Proposal Submission and the Percentage of 1,358 Proposals Accepted for Inclusion in the Capital Budget Between Fiscal Years 1982 and 1984

Manner of Submission of Board-Initiated Proposal	Overall Average Success Rate	Average Success Rate By Year			Average Success Rate By Community		
		FY 1984	FY 1983	FY 1982	Low Income	Middle Income	Upper Income
Submitted alone	22%	26%	28%	11%	13%	21%	31%
With line-agency cosponsor	61	60	66	59	57	63	63
With community-group cosponsor	14	25	10	8	7	16	20

Source: R.F. Pecorella, "Community Input and the City Budget: Geographically Based Budgeting in New York City," *Journal of Urban Affairs* 8 (Winter 1986): 66.
Note: Number of proposals: 1,358.

TABLE 3

The Disposition of 1,358 Board-Initiated Proposals Between Fiscal Years 1982 and 1984 by Manner of Submission and Community District Socioeconomic Statuses

Disposition of Board-Initiated Proposals	Lower-Income Districts			Middle-Income Districts			Upper-Income Districts		
	Board Alone	With Agency	With Community	Board Alone	With Agency	With Community	Board Alone	With Agency	With Community
Accepted	7%	14%	2%	13%	16%	3%	17%	18%	3%
Rejected	47	10	20	46	9	13	38	10	13
Totals	54	24	22	59	25	16	55	28	16
Number of proposals by district income	366			731			261		

Source: Joseph P. Vitteritti and R.F. Pecorella, Community Governance and the Decentralization of Service Delivery (New York: Charter Revision Commission, 69).

bilities since 1977. First, overall board success rates have remained constant. The boards succeeded roughly one-half of the time in having their proposals included in the capital budget. Second, overall constancy notwithstanding, the boards have become more active in submitting and more successful in obtaining first-time budget priorities in the past five fiscal years. Third, city budget officials have apparently adopted decision rules that reward boards for vertical but not horizontal integration; board budgetary success is enhanced by cooperation with city agencies but not with community organizations. And, fourth, community-based budgeting favors the proposals of middle-class boards, which have a greater percentage of their proposals funded than lower-income boards.

Land-Use Reforms

The Uniform Land Use Review Procedure established by the 1975 charter revisions gave the boards a standardized role in land-use decisions. Although the boards were given only advisory power, once considered more a strategy for co-optation of community interests by citywide officials than a meaningful attempt at decentralization, such authority has taken on renewed import in recent years. The new land-use review procedures ensured that development decisions, previously a function of the economic marketplace and the central-city political arena, were now at least formally constrained by community input. One 1974 commission report suggested that "because local rulings would probably be upheld in the majority of cases, developers would be forced to negotiate with the board about their projects, thereby insuring increased responsiveness to community interests and needs."[4] Writing a decade later, Howard Hallman noted that indeed since the 1960s "many citizens have learned to use the advisory role as an entry point for bargaining and exerting influence, and there are public officials who genuinely seek participation and respond to what they hear."[5]

From the beginning, many observers saw ULURP as an important source of board power. In 1980, Glenn Fowler argued: "The most dramatic change experienced by the community boards occurred three years ago when . . . they assumed a formal place in the process for dealing with zoning changes, disposition of municipally owned property, and franchises granted by the city."[6] This view is supported by a Center for Responsive Government report suggesting that land-use review "may offer the boards their most direct opportunity to shape the futures of their districts because of the relatively immediate and highly visible economic and social consequences of land-use decisions."[7]

David Lebenstein has been more critical. He pointed out that many board members had extensive experience in land-use issues because of their prior involvement with community planning boards. Additionally, they were receiving technical assistance from the borough offices of the Department of City Planning. Nevertheless, Lebenstein argued that "the boards still function in a 'reactive' fashion" and should be encouraged "to take the initiative more often on planning and development issues."[8]

Conversely, some observers complained that the boards actually had too much influence over land-use issues and that their parochial input threatened the overall planning ability of the city. Arthur Zabarkes, for example, argued that "the absolute right of a community to veto a project (even if only through delay) is unconscionable."[9] And Mimi Ellis, reacting to a Queens board's ability to block an Urban Homesteading Program near John F. Kennedy International Airport, contended that "the growing influence of the boards has also, unfortunately, magnified their ability to impede needed projects by unreasoned obstructionism or by holding them ransom to parochial interests."[10]

In order to determine how successful or obstructionist—depending on one's point of view—the community boards have been under ULURP, one needs some idea of how often their recommendations on proposed projects are accepted by city officials. Although the data are sketchy, estimates for the early years are generally high. One study reported that the Department of City Planning "goes along with roughly 80 percent of board recommendations."[11] City Planning itself claimed that it approved more than 90 percent of community-board decisions, while the Board of Standards and Appeals claimed an 82 percent approval rating. And Robert Wagner, Jr., then chair of the City Planning Commission, contended that the commission went along with the boards "in 98 percent of the cases before us."[12]

During the early years, several boards used land-use powers to influence their districts' overall development. In 1979, Community Board 17 in Brooklyn successfully challenged a Community Development Agency report recommending that the board's Carnarsie-East Flatbush district be classified as a "neighborhood development area." Community Board 7 in Queens helped establish a community-development corporation and a community-stabilization organization in Flushing to guide that community's future growth. Community Board 7 in Booklyn assisted in bringing about a comprehensive development strategy for Sunset Park. And Community Board 7 in Manhattan was able to leverage a large urban renewal grant for its West Side district.

Generally, however, early experiences of the boards with ULURP were mixed. One report notes that "some community boards function better than others with about two-thirds being adequate or exceptional and a bottom third being weak and ineffectual."[13] Generally, the better-functioning boards represented middle-class community districts, while the weaker boards were in the poorer communities. A study commissioned by the Community Services Society reports:

Our findings indicate that many community boards in the city have serious problems. This is particularly true in poverty neighborhoods, where conditions for community boards are often decidedly different from those in middle-class communities. Factors which enable some boards to work effectively—well established community organizations, continuity of leadership, professionals who make their skills and expertise available to the board, attentive elected officials, easy access to high-level policymakers—are not available to many boards. The 20–30 boards in poverty and lower-middle-class areas lack most or all these ingredients.[14]

In recent years, land-use issues in New York City have centered on tensions brought on by the city's real-estate boom. As development in Manhattan proceeds, the saturation of that borough's markets has produced spillover pressures in the outer boroughs. Such spatial pressures are particularly intense because of dislocation threats. Peter Marcuse contended that in such a gentrifying climate, even boards representing poor areas "have major development decisions passing through their hands."[15]

Over the past decade, a number of boards have been capable of the sophisticated negotiations with central-city officials and private developers that ensure local input in the use of community space. In fact, most boards have established active land-use review policies, including such methods as the use of standing committees to review development projects, the development of formal community plans for their districts, and the submission of their own proposals for local development. Other boards, however, continue to approach land-use review in an ad hoc fashion, reacting to proposals for community changes with neither a structured process nor a defined notion of their communities' future.

Board success with the technical issues of land-use planning relates to the ability to interact with central-city or private-sector "experts." Boards with access to indigenous sources of expertise — residents with backgrounds in law, architecture, urban planning, or some other skills relevant to land-use issues — have a greater potential to influence their communities' development than their counterparts lacking such expertise. Consequently, lower-income communities remain at a disadvantage in exercising their land-use responsibilities.

A major source of necessary expertise for lower-income boards exists outside their immediate communities in the offices of city agencies, private-sector developers, or advocacy planners. However, two factors militate against the use of these external sources of expertise. First, with the exception of advocacy planners, there would undoubtedly be suspicion in these communities about the motives of either city agencies or private developers. Indeed, without such suspicion, the board system itself would be redundant. And, second, activists from lower-income areas tend to favor more parochial approaches to city politics and have less confidence in city officials than their middle-income counterparts.

Socioeconomic differences aside, board land-use decisions can be reversed by central-city officials. There is little in the way of dependable data, but it appears that when the ULURP process is followed, outright rejection of board decisions rarely occurs. As Norman Fainstein and Susan Fainstein argued: "Even though the community board's decision is not binding, it is very influential with both the CPC and elected officials representing the district."[16] If the boards and city officials disagree on a particular project, the developer may reshape the original development design to tailor it more closely to board desires or incorporate in his or her development costs community public improvements in lieu of desired project changes.

One indication of the boards' increasing influence over land-use planning is recent attempts to limit their responsibilities under ULURP. A number of boards have become adept at trading development projects or specific aspects of these projects, such as expanded size, for local amenities. City officials have proposed limiting negotiations to local amenities directly involving the Environmental Impact Statement (EIS) filed with the proposal. Such a proposal would constrain the boards' range of options in negotiating with developers. The city has also been accused of avoiding ULURP reviews by privatizing some social services like facilities to care for the homeless and by using the Department of General Services to transfer building uses without review. Other participants in the system have accused the Department of City Planning of misusing the ULURP precertification process (getting proposals to the community boards for first-level decisions) to restrict the boards' range of options on development issues.

By opening land-use decision making to public scrutiny, particular problems notwithstanding, the board system has made it more difficult to alter fundamentally the character of city neighborhoods without extensive and public consideration of proposed changes. The board system extended the range of legitimate conflict over land-use issues. Since the implementation of the reforms, a majority of the boards have developed extensive land-use review procedures, and several boards are renowned in the city for their influence on development projects. This is a mark of the success of reform, especially since the charter revisions were not intended to guarantee that the boards would control local development — only that they would have the opportunity to influence land-use planning in their communities.

District Service Cabinets

There are two elements of the community boards' service responsibilities: the district service cabinets and the role of the boards' district managers. For the district service cabinets to function in optimal fashion, two reforms were required — the creation of geographically coterminous community and service-agency districts and the devolution of management responsibility to the district service chiefs, who represent the agencies on the cabinets.

With few exceptions, establishing coterminality of community and agency lines went well. Neighborhood Preservation at Housing Preservation and Development continues to employ districts that cut across community district lines. And the New York City Police Department received a three-year extension from the charter-imposed deadline for the boroughs of Brooklyn, Manhattan, and Staten Island and a second one-year waiver in midtown Manhattan and parts of Staten Island. All other designated agencies and operating divisions developed coterminous districts with the community boards on or close to schedule.

Much of the credit for achieving coterminality more or less on schedule should go to the Koch administration's Community Board Assistance Unit (CBAU), which pushed the designated agencies toward the 1 January 1980 goal. The CBAU was successful because it enjoyed the complete support of the mayor, was staffed with competent professionals, and avoided partisan conflicts by emphasizing its technical assistance role.

The early reports on the district service cabinets were negative. David Lebenstein concluded in 1980 that service delivery represented "the weakest link in the community board chain."[17] In a survey of board members and city officials, the Center for Responsive Government found "a good deal of dissatisfaction" with the district service cabinets.[18] And Madeleine Adler and Jewel Bellush noted that a number of district managers attempted to circumvent the district service cabinets because they found them ineffective.[19]

Observers cite three basic problems. First, the degree of management decentralization within the service-delivery agencies was not sufficient to allow district service chiefs to be responsive to local input. A second problem involved the poor communication between the boards and the agencies as well as a lack of information about agency operations available to the boards. And a third, not unrelated, problem was that because the district managers are appointed by the boards and not by the mayor as they were under the Office of Neighborhood Government program, they are often viewed by agency representatives more as advocates for the community rather than as coordinators of the cabinets.

Not all the early experiences were negative. Although the cabinets were poor coordinators of public services, they did function reasonably well as complaint processors. In 1981, each district service cabinet handled an average of 1,252 complaints from community residents. Furthermore, over 30 percent of the cabinets had developed processes for tracking complaints through the various agencies, and over 50 percent notified complainants of agency actions. One report indicated that 73 percent of complaints referred to the cabinets were resolved.

On an individual level, some boards implemented innovative approaches to their service responsibilities. Community Board 14 in Brooklyn worked with the Department of Sanitation to redesign garbage collection and street-cleaning services for its Flatbush-Midwood district. Community Board 5 in Queens instituted monthly "one-stop service days" so providers of various social services could assemble to answer residents' questions and facilitate assistance. And Community Board 2 in the Bronx developed a plan to deal with illegal dumping in its South Bronx neighborhood. Moreover, several agencies tried their hands at management decentralization. The Parks and Sanitation departments, for example, revised district supervisors' job descriptions and organized training programs at the Urban Academy.

The early district managers tended to view their positions as "launching pads" for managerial careers, and their turnover rate in the late 1970s was roughly 40 percent. Indeed, David Lebenstein, in noting that turnover was a major problem, reported: "At least one-third of the original DMs have left (three years later) and the more competent DMs generally get swooped up by entities (both public and private) that can pay them a lot more."[20]

A number of the early managers complained that their responsibilities were ill-defined by the charter revisions and that the boards placed too many restrictions on their activities. Most acknowledged that they were more effective when dealing with informal contacts in administrative agencies than when working within the district service cabinet structure. Moreover, the managers thought that they lacked the necessary job-related training to be truly effective in their areas of responsibility.

As with the other areas of board responsibility, the community boards' service-monitoring role has increased in importance since the inception of the board system. Coterminality has helped the boards monitor community services by simplifying the process of seeking redress for specific service-delivery problems. Moreover, several boards have adopted the idea of "one-stop service days," which bring agency representatives together to deal with community residents' questions and complaints. Other boards have indicated a willingness and a capacity to respond quickly and decisively to emergency situations in their communities that require immediate agency action. Barbara Gunn, director of the mayor's Office of Operations, contended that the boards function as a check on the office's annual management reports, which include service agency outputs for a fiscal year.

Moreover, some agencies continue to experiment with methods of improving their ties with the community boards. The Human Resources Administration, for example, initiated a program of Human Service Cabinets in five community districts. One report indicates that these cabinets, chaired by the community boards' district managers, made some progress in coordinating services to children, and several have attempted to deal with the housing-abandonment issue in their communities.

Specific innovations notwithstanding, the district service cabinets remain more adept as complaint processors than as coordinators of service delivery within their communities. Two factors, one internal to the boards and the other a function of bureaucratic politics, have produced this limited service role. First, within a community district of between 100,000 and 200,000 persons, service coordination is a complex and time-consuming job, particularly in light of the number of specific service complaints that board district managers must handle. District managers are overwhelmed by the workload and, given the boards' minimal annual operating budgets, the lack of staff support. Moreover, the district managers appointed by the community boards bring little or no central-city backing to their roles. They are expected to coordinate the agency activities of service-delivery professionals without a city political or administrative base.

Diane Morales, director of community services for the borough president of Manhattan, pointed out that these problems are especially intense in poorer communities, where information concerning agency operations is often minimal.[21] Moreover, in these poorer communities, service problems are often critical, and the need for redress is often immediate.

Second, the degree of management decentralization in the service-delivery agencies remains insufficient for accountability to community interests. In fact, several observers have questioned whether there are even "open channels of communication" between district representatives and policymakers in a number of agencies. Indeed, Jane Planken, director of community boards for the borough president of Queens, noted that after some early progress, particularly in the Departments of Sanitation and Parks, there has been a noticeable deterioration in the effort toward management decentralization in recent years.[22]

Management decentralization has not taken place for several reasons. Initially, the demands of agency retrenchment brought on by the fiscal crisis diverted policymakers from the task of administrative decentralization. Indeed, the fiscal crisis produced a need for agency centralization. In recent years, the city administration has appeared hesitant to engage in the political battles necessary to redirect agency management to a more decentralized mode. Edward Rogowsky, director of community boards for Brooklyn, contended that "without a concentrated mayoral effort, meaningful management decentralization will not occur."[23]

The boards' district managers' responsibilities remain vaguely defined, and several have been victimized by internal political battles. District managers' salaries and the funding levels for their offices had not increased sufficiently by 1983 to counter turnovers, and several district managers reported in 1987 that these problems remain unsolved. There are wide pay disparities among district managers as well as controversies over the salary increases given to some managers.

Conclusion

Whether the community-board system in New York City has evolved into an effective mechanism for local influence on policy making depends on how "influence" is defined. The advocates of community control are disappointed by the lack of decision-making power allocated to the boards. From this perspective, the board system does not go far enough. Other observers see the board system as incorporating sufficient decentralization to represent community interests.

From a macroperspective, the community-board system has been institutionalized in New York City politics to a degree that may surprise the cynics and disappoint the true believers. If the board system has not evolved into community control in New York City, neither has it left the precharter status quo undisturbed. The boards are merely advisory bodies, but they have opened the land-use process in New York City to public scrutiny; the boards can neither raise revenues nor allocate resources, but they have influenced the central-city process that does so. And even though the boards have been unable to coordinate service delivery within their communities, district managers serve as local ombudsmen for community residents.

Board capacity, however, is often a function of the socioeconomic characteristics of the districts served. Lower-income communities cannot marshal the resources necessary to deal with the complex issues facing them, and the resulting frustration is having its effects. There are strong indications that these distinctions between boards are having their predictable outcomes; large numbers of minority board members are dissatisfied with the current board system and favor increased community control. It will be ironic indeed if the very communities whose activism is most responsible for the movement toward decentralization in American cities continue to be the communities least well served by the reforms.

NOTES

1. David Lebenstein, "A Report Card," New York Affairs 6 (1980): 12.
2. New York City's Budget Consultation Process: An Analysis of Human Service Budget Request

for Fiscal Year 1981, prepared for Joint Action for Children by New York INTERFACE, Nov. 1980, 1–2.

3. John Mudd, *Neighborhood Services* (New Haven: Yale University Press, 1984), 199.

4. State Charter Revision Commission for New York City, Staff Report, *Community Boards* (New York, 1974).

5. Howard Hallman, *Small and Large Together: Governing the Metropolis* (Beverly Hills: Sage Publications, 1977), 65.

6. Glenn Fowler, "Community Board Wrap-Up," *New York Affairs* 6 (1980): 7.

7. Richard Rich, *Participation and Representation in New York City's Community Board System* (New York: The Center for Responsive Government, 1981), 18.

8. Lebenstein, 11–12.

9. Arthur Zabarkes, "Different Decisions, Different Processes," *New York Affairs* 6 (1980): 29–30.

10. Mimi Ellis, "An Agency Perspective," *New York Affairs* 6 (1980): 32.

11. Carter Wiseman, "Power to the People," *New York*, 5 Oct. 1981, 62.

12. Fowler, 8.

13. *Community Boards: Technical Assistance Needs and Special Projects* (Report prepared for the Fund for the City of New York by New York INTERFACE, May 1979), i.

14. *Special Needs of Community Boards in Poverty Areas*: A Comparative Study of Six Community Boards Representing Middle Class, Lower Middle Class and Poverty Areas (Report prepared for the New York Community Service Society, New York INTERFACE, Dec. 1980), 4.

15. Peter Marcuse, "Neighborhood Policy and the Distribution of Power: New York City's Community Boards" (Paper delivered at the New York State Political Science Association Meeting, New York, N.Y., April 1987).

16. Norman Fainstein and Susan Fainstein, "The Politics of Planning New York as a World City" (Paper prepared for the Fulbright Colloquium, The Center for Community and Educational Policy Studies, Liverpool, Sept. 1986).

17. Lebenstein, 12.

18. Rich, 69.

19. Madeleine Adler and Jewel Bellush, "A Look at the District Manager," *New York Affairs* 6 (1980): 49–53.

20. Lebenstein, 13.

21. Interview with Diane Morales, 2 Sept. 1987.

22. Interview with Jane Planken, 1 Sept. 1987.

23. Interview with Edward Rogowsky, 4 Nov. 1986.

Filling Vacancies in Elective Offices: Popular versus Party Politics

According to a recently completed census, in 1987 there were 38,933 general-purpose local governments in the United States. If conservative assumptions are made about the size of the councils or boards of these governments, and the sex and average ages of their members, it appears likely that about two thousand vacancies occur in local elective offices annually just as the consequence of the death of incumbents.[1] Additionally, of course, vacancies arise because local elected officials resign for personal or professional reasons in the course of their terms, or are removed for cause.

Clearly, although it is a subject that has not received much systematic attention, processes for filling vacancies have considerable aggregate impact on "who governs" America's cities, counties, towns, and villages. Any method for determining when vacancies exist in elective offices, and for filling them, must balance the fundamental need for legitimacy that can arise out of a democratic election with the parallel need to sustain a fully representative and effectively functioning government. In fact, as this study of New York City reveals, the methods used for maintaining and transferring political power outside the normal, scheduled electoral process are a window into the inner politics of the locality.

An examination of these methods thus offers a glimpse of an "insider game" that is most revealing of the values, incentive systems, and power relationships that are defining daily local political life. Since the person chosen to fill a vacancy gains the advantage of incumbency in the next general election, methods for filling vacancies are especially significant. Alterations in these methods therefore have an impact on the incentive system for those ambitious for public office. Ultimately, such changes may lead to significant alterations in the "way things work" in local politics.

Although the New York City charter provisions for filling City Council and borough-presidency vacancies have not been a focal point of public debate, they have been important for political party strength and public careers in the city over the last quarter century. Since 1961, thirty-three people — or more than a fifth of all those who have served during this period — entered the council upon appointment by its members. Eight of the current members (again, more than a fifth) were originally selected to fill vacancies. In fact, if not in form, this process was controlled or heavily influenced by party leaders in several boroughs.

During this same period, seventeen of the twenty-six borough presidents were initially selected to fill vacancies. Over the twenty-seven-year period since 1961, the five borough presidents served a total of 135 years in office. Those first selected to fill vacancies served for a total of 86.62 years, while those who were initially elected served for 48.21 years (see appendix 1). Of the five serving in 1988, only David Dinkins was initially elected as a nonincumbent. Howard Golden (1977), Ralph Lamberti (1984), Claire Shulman (1986), and Fernando Ferrer (1987) were all selected by the City Council, in the years noted, to fill vacancies. Thus, provisions designed for exceptional circumstances, if not the norm, have gained widespread use. Many careers in elective office in New York City were in fact begun or advanced by appointment.

State Constitution and Law

In general, provisions to fill vacancies in local elective offices may involve action by the City Council, the governor, the mayor, the electorate, or a combination of these actors. Such provisions require a means for determining when a vacancy exists, especially in potentially ambiguous circumstances like the partial physical or mental incapacity of public officials or the systematic neglect by such officials of their public duties. They should also include both a time limit for action and a default option to ensure that the vacancy is filled even if local political considerations militate against it. New York State law provides for many of these factors, and the locality is given priority in filling vacated elective offices in most circumstances.

The New York State constitution requires that the state legislature provide a method for filling vacancies in public office and "in the case of elective officers, no person appointed to fill a vacancy shall hold his office by virtue of such appointment longer than the commencement of the political year not succeeding the first annual election of the happening of the vacancy."[2] This and an exception to the requirement that municipal elections be held in odd-numbered years (when vacancies must be filled) make clear the intent of the constitution to minimize the period in which appointed persons serve in elective office. There is, however, a constitutional exception for New York City community school boards, which can forestall filling vacancies until the next scheduled election.

To implement this mandate and at the same time meet the practical requirements of election administration, the state legislature has established a cutoff date of 20 September. An appointed person filling a vacancy occurring before this date serves until the end of the calendar year; a new official elected in November serves the remainder of the unexpired term. Therefore, an appointee wishing to continue to serve must run in the November election. An appointed person filling a vacancy arising after 20 September serves until the end of the following calendar year, and an election is held the following November to choose a successor for the remainder of the term.

New York State law specifies eight circumstances under which elected positions are considered vacant: (1) death of the incumbent; (2) resignation of the incumbent; (3) removal of the incumbent for cause; (4) failure of the incumbent to continue to meet a residency requirement for service; (5) conviction of the incumbent for a felony or violation of the oath of office; (6) judgment of a court declaring the incumbent insane or incompetent; (7) judgment of a court that an election is void or that the office is forfeit; and (8) refusal or neglect by the incumbent to swear the oath of office in a timely manner. In these circumstances, the law and the courts' interpretation of it have given priority to local governments for filling the vacancy, except in the case of constitutional officers, such as district attorneys. If, however, the local government fails to act, the governor may do so.

Special Elections for Congress and the New York State Legislature

For the United States House of Representatives, the Constitution provides that "when vacancies happen in Representation from any State, the Executive Authority thereof shall issue Writs of Election to fill such Vacancies."[3] Although there is no time limit for action and long delays have occasionally occurred, governors are usually prompt in calling special elections. Nominations for these posts are usually determined by hotly contested primary elections.

In 1987, three such elections were held—in California, Connecticut, and Tennessee. The last such special election in New York City was in 1986 for the Sixth Congressional District seat, vacated when Joseph P. Addabbo died. Aldon R. Waldon, Jr., endorsed by Queens Democratic leaders, won the special election in June, despite a legal contest over the validity of the absentee ballot forms used by his principal opponent, Floyd H. Flake. Flake, however, defeated Waldon the following September in the regular Democratic primary and easily won the congressional seat.

Since the adoption of the Seventeenth Amendment, constitutional requirements for the United States Senate have been similar to those for the House, except that "the legislature of any State may empower the executive thereof to make temporary appointments until the people fill the vacancies by election as the legislature may direct."[4] If provided for by state law, special elections for the Senate may be held within a few months after a vacancy occurs, but the pattern in most states is for gubernatorial appointees to serve until a special election can be held in November of the next even-numbered year.

Governors often appoint "seat warmers," persons who pledge not to contest the ensuing election, in order to avoid making political enemies by choosing among the powerful aspirants for a Senate seat. This was the case in New Jersey in 1982, when Governor Thomas H. Kean appointed Nicholas Brady, now secretary of the treasury, to the United States Senate. In contrast, Governor Kay Orr of Nebraska appointed her former campaign manager, David Karnes, to the Senate upon the death of Edward Zorinsky in March 1987 to serve until January 1989. Karnes, who had held no previous elective office, was defeated in 1988 by former Governor J. Robert Kerrey.

In states that regard a Senate seat as more desirable than the governorship, governors have occasionally caused controversy by appointing themselves to the Senate. The last governor to do so was Wendell Anderson, Democrat of Minnesota, in 1976. Like the two governors who appointed themselves before him, Anderson lost the ensuing election for the seat.

Finally, governors are not required to retain partisan continuity when they make appointments to the United States Senate. Nelson A. Rockefeller appointed a fellow Republican, Congressman Charles Goodell, to fill the vacancy created in New York when Robert F. Kennedy, a Democrat, was assassinated in 1968. In the case of the Karnes appointment, Governor Orr, a Republican, altered the party balance of the Senate by appointing her copartisan to replace Zorinsky, a Democrat.

New York statutes provide for special elections called at the discretion of the governor to fill vacancies in the state assembly and senate only if they occur "before the first day of April of the last year of the term of office" or "after such first day of April" if "a special session of the legislature be called to meet between such first day of April and the next general election to be called after September nineteenth in such year."[5] If such an election is proclaimed by the governor, it must be held no less than thirty nor more than forty-five days after the proclamation is issued. Nomination is in accord with party rules.

In 1987, three assembly seats were filled through special election — in Queens, Nassau County, and rural Cattaraugus County. The Queens seat remained Democratic; the Nassau County seat remained Republican. But after a difficult and expensive battle, the Cattaraugus County seat, held by Democratic Majority Leader Daniel B. Walsh, was won by Republican Patricia McGee.

In an especially interesting 1986 case, a Bronx/Westchester senate seat was vacated as a result of the death of John Calandra, a Republican. Democrats had a substantial enrollment edge in the district, and the senate Democratic minority regarded the race as winnable. Governor Mario M. Cuomo, citing two reasons, delayed calling a special election. The first was that under party rules the Democratic nomination was controlled by Stanley Friedman, the Bronx County leader then under investigation by United States Attorney Rudolph W. Giuliani for his involvement in New York City corruption scandals. In addition, Cuomo suggested that Republican party nominating rules had to be cleared by the U.S. Justice Department under the Voting Rights Act. Cuomo's unstated expectation was that the Democratic nominee would do better in this district if the election were held simultaneously with the gubernatorial election scheduled for that November, which Cuomo was expected to win by a landslide.

Republicans, eager for a special election in which they would have a better chance for victory, brought their rules into conformance with those of the Democrats, which had already been cleared in Washington. The governor, no longer able to delay without appearing to deny representation to an entire senate district, called the special election. Guy Velella, a former assemblyman, gained the Republican nomination and the backing of several major labor unions and went on to win handily, retaining the seat for his party.

This special election brought forth suggestions for state legislation requiring primaries for nominations in these circumstances and denying the governor the discretion to delay special elections. No such changes have been made. Events demonstrate that even without a change in the law, the governor is unlikely to delay calling a special election if substantial time is left in a legislative term. The potential political costs of such a course discourage such a strategy.

Charter Provisions in Other Localities

An examination of practices in other large cities and New York State counties reveals a wide range of methods for filling vacancies in councils and local legislatures. In two-thirds of the twenty-one largest cities in the United States, council vacancies are filled by the remaining members of the body. The next most common method is a special election, as in Philadelphia, the District of Columbia, Denver, and Jacksonville. In Philadelphia, the council president calls the election; in the District of Columbia, the Board of Elections; and in Jacksonville, the council itself. In Los Angeles, the council may call a special election if it does not wish to fill the vacancy. The San Francisco charter provides that board vacancies be filled by mayoral appointment. In metropolitan Indianapolis, the selection is made by precinct committee members of the same party from the appropriate district. For at-large seats in Boston, a vacancy is filled by the runner-up in the previous election, who serves the remainder of the term.

Some jurisdictions employ different methods, depending on the time remaining in the term when the vacancy occurs. In Chicago, the mayor appoints a replacement if less than two years remain in the term, and the Board of Elections calls a special election if more time remains. Similarly, in Dallas the council appoints the successor if less than half of the term remains; otherwise a special election is called.

When a council fills vacancies, time constraints are common. In San Jose, for example, the deadline is sixty days; in San Diego, Memphis, and Columbus it is thirty days; and in Atlanta it is twenty days if the general election is less than two years away. In San Diego and San Jose, a default option is included in the charter — that is, a provision for a special election if the vacancy is not filled within the prescribed period to help ensure action. The Columbus charter gives the mayor a vote in filling a vacancy if the council misses the thirty-day deadline. Phoenix gives a tie-breaking vote to the city magistrate. In Washington, D.C., an unusual provision prevents the holding of an election to fill a vacancy until 114 days have passed, presumably to allow enough time for nominations and campaigning.

Another consideration is the number of seats to be filled simultaneously. In cities where the council fills a vacancy, a sufficient number of members must remain for the process to be legitimate. In Dallas, the charter provides that the minimum number of members required to act in this area is four. (Interestingly, this is less than a majority of that eleven-seat body.) For Houston's fifteen-member council, the number of vacancies that may be filled by the charter-prescribed method cannot exceed six. In Baltimore, if there are fewer than eleven council members (one more than a majority) remaining in the body, vacancies are filled by gubernatorial appointment.

In most New York counties, legislators fill vacancies in their bodies by majority vote. Time limits are common, usually requiring action by thirty days (but forty days in Albany County and forty-five days in Schenectady). In Putnam, Rensselaer, and Chemung counties, replacements must be selected from within the district. Partisan continuity in the vacated position is provided for in Herkimer, Chemung, and Monroe counties. Appointed members usually serve until the first of January after the next general election, unless the vacancy occurs so close to election day as to make filling the seat at that time impractical. Counties' use of the same demarcation date as in state law, 20 September, is frequent.

Exceptions to the general practice are found in Herkimer County, where the chairman of the legislature fills vacancies by appointment, and in Oneida County, where the county executive appoints the replacement, with confirmation by the legislature. In Monroe County, the president appoints and the legislature must confirm only if the person chosen to fill the vacancy has no party affiliation.

In Dutchess County, if a vacancy occurs in a district that is wholly within a town or city, the council of that local jurisdiction elects a successor. If the district encompasses more than one town or city, the councils of all the affected local jurisdictions employ weighted voting based on their populations to fill the vacancy. Weighted voting is also used in Schenectady County, where each district representative's vote is determined by the number of votes he or she received in the previous general election.

In Suffolk County, special elections are held within ninety days after a vacancy occurs to chose replacements in the county legislature. The county charter permits appointment only if a seat becomes vacant after an election but before the successor takes office the following January.

Charter Provisions for and Practices in New York City

Throughout this century, the New York City legislature (Board of Aldermen and then City Council) has filled vacancies in its ranks through election by the remaining members. In contrast, vacancies in the office of borough president are filled only by the council members from that borough. Unlike its requirements for the council, the charter makes no provision for partisan continuity in filling borough-presidency vacancies. The mayor convenes the borough's delegation to the council, presides at the election, and votes in case of a tie.

For the council, the 1901 charter indicated that a person "so elected to fill any such vacancy shall serve for the unexpired portion of the term," a provision that contravened the state constitution and has since been deleted. The current charter, like those of 1938 and 1963, includes a residency requirement for a council member selected through vacancy-filling procedures, as well as the provision that the successor be of the same party as the previous member in the seat.

In 1975, the New York Court of Appeals summarily dismissed a challenge to the residency requirement. Although it apparently has not been tested in charter jurisdictions, the requirement for partisan continuity in filling vacancies in the council may be more problematic. In an opinion issued in 1972, the attorney general ruled that the town of Ogden could not require an appointee to have the same party affiliation as the person he followed in office.

The provision for partisan continuity in filling vacancies in New York City was significant when the charter permitted limited nomination and voting, for it kept the Democratic majority from blocking the intent of the electoral system by placing Democrats in vacancies that arose in both district and boroughwide at-large seats held by other parties. Thus, Republicans Theodore Kupferman (1962) and Woodward Kingman of Manhattan (1966), Republican Mildred Rosen of Brooklyn (1966), and Conservative Michael Long of Brooklyn (1980) were appointed to fill vacancies in seats formerly held by members of the same party. The elimination of limited voting and de facto at-large seats reserved for minority parties, along with the overwhelmingly one-party nature of the current council, has made this provision only marginally consequential. It could, however, become important again with changes in the city's electoral system.

As noted above, in the twenty-seven years between 1961 and 1988, a total of thirty-three council members began or advanced their public careers by being appointed to fill vacancies. This number represents 22.7 percent of all those who served. Not all of these members ultimately ran for a full four-year term. Three at-large members saw their positions eliminated, one appointee resigned, one died soon after taking office, and one almost immediately ran for Congress. But of the twenty-six who did seek a full term, all but eight were elected. The exceptions were Woodward Kingman, whom Edward I. Koch defeated in the 1966 general election; Joseph DeMonte, Kenneth Knigin, and Roberto LeBron, who lost in close three-way primaries in 1969; Arlene Stringer and Henry Berger, who lost in primaries to Stanley Michels and Ruth Messinger in 1977; and Nydia Valezquez, who was beaten in a primary by Victor Robles in 1984.

Although it differs distinctly in form from the city charter, the actual procedure for filling council vacancies has been identical to the procedure for filling vacancies in the borough presidencies. In practice, the council defers to the delegation of the borough in which the opening exists. Especially in the Bronx, Brooklyn, and Queens, this practice was a source of power for the county party organization, for the borough delegation in turn took direction from the county leader and the executive committee of the county party.

The strategic objectives pursued by party leaders in filling council vacancies differed, depending on the political context. If a vacancy arose early in the year, the appointment was used to give a chosen candidate the advantage of incumbency so as to strengthen his or her position to fend off intraparty challenges from insurgent groups in November. On some occasions, reformers were replaced by party regulars, altering the balance of power in the council. One example is county leader Pat Cunningham's drive to appoint Barry Salman to replace Lawrence Bernstein in the Bronx in 1970. On other occasions a county leader selected an insurgent for a council seat to compromise differences within the borough party, as Stanley Friedman did in 1979 when he appointed June Eisland in the Bronx. Finally, as occurred with Robert Dryfoos in 1980, a council appointment might simply have been a ratification of the outcome of a primary contest or of another broad-based internal-selection process in the councilmanic district.

Party leaders have often artfully manipulated the occurrence and timing of vacancies in both the council and borough presidencies to advance the interests of their political organizations and to avoid competition. Consider, for example, the manner in which Donald Manes first became the Queens borough president. On 18 September 1971, the incumbent borough president, Sidney Liviss, resigned to accept the nominations of both the Republican and Democratic judicial conventions for a New York State Supreme Court judgeship. The executive committee of the Queens Democratic Party unanimously endorsed Manes for the position. Five days later, the City Council selected him to fill the vacancy. Within six weeks, endorsed by the Democratic, Republican, and Liberal parties, he was elected to serve out the remaining two years of the borough president's term.

Manes entered the borough presidency in accord with state law and the charter provision for this purpose. The vacancy was created prior to the cutoff date in the law, 20 September, though Manes was sworn in after that date. Thus, he was able to run almost immediately with a three-party endorsement, the partial result of an overall deal that involved not only the borough presidency but also cross-endorsements for six newly created New York State Supreme Court judgeships, the filling of a vacancy in the Queens surrogate's office created by the resignation of John T. Clancy in favor of his protégé Louis D. Laurino the day after the primary filing date, and the filling of a vacancy in the Court of Claims created by Laurino's advancement.

To cite another example, Democratic party activist Anthony Mercorella was appointed to represent the Bronx's Fourteenth District in the City Council in 1973. In 1975, Mercorella was nominated for a Civil Court judgeship but waited until after the 9 September primary day to resign from the council. This allowed party leaders to advance Jerry Crispino, unchallenged, for the post. Crispino was selected by the council on 9 October 1975. The vote was unanimous but with nine abstentions, notwithstanding Ted Weiss's objections to the "manipulation" of the process and reformers' assertions that Crispino did not even live in the district.

Alternatives for New York City

Because so many politicians begin their careers in the City Council and rise to the borough presidency through the processes established to fill vacancies, charter provisions affecting these processes are significant. Arguments regarding alternative methods for filling council vacancies, summarized here, in general apply to both offices.

Proponents of the current method argued that despite the manner in which it has been manipulated in the past, election by the remaining members of the City Council remained a reasonable alternative for filling council vacancies as long as gubernatorial appointment was available should the council fail to act. The legislative body itself traditionally judges its members' qualifications, and political authority should flow naturally from that role. Political parties perform important functions, and leaving some influence with party organizations may have some value for the continued vitality of the city's political system. Steps to strengthen the council may give its elected leadership a more substantial role in filling future vacancies — altering the process without changing the charter.

Opponents suggested that the current provision for filling council vacancies has diminished the competitiveness of the city's political system by giving the advantage of incumbency to unelected officials. This advantage inadvertently and inappropriately increases the power of county party leaders. Moreover, if more than one in five city legislators could reach office for the first time without standing for election, fundamental questions emerge about the degree to which the system is democratic. The problem might even increase, in an absolute if not in a proportional sense, if council membership grows. Changing this provision would indicate that the commission intends to make the City Council an effective and accountable legislative body.

Even after the desirability of change was established, experience elsewhere suggested a number of possible approaches. Borough delegations could receive formal power to fill vacancies, giving charter-based status to current practice. This change would recognize the predominantly local interest in this matter while raising the visibility and increasing the accountability of the actual decision process. It would conform the method for filling council vacancies with that used for vacancies in borough presidencies. In order to recognize the importance of the council as an institution in this process, the charter might make the council majority leader an ex-officio participant in the borough delegation's process to fill a vacancy. Under this system, gubernatorial appointment could be retained as a fallback method, in case of delay or inaction by the borough delegation. This approach would preserve the borough role while formally involving the leadership of the council, thereby providing a counterweight to party-leader influence and introducing a broader perspective. It would also preserve a role for the political party and therefore an incentive for aspirants to political office to work for and through parties.

A contrasting view is that such an approach would effect no real change. The process would remain fundamentally undemocratic. Although parties may be valuable in an abstract sense, party organizations have not advanced democracy in one-party New York City but have actually undermined it. Preserving this unintended channel of influence for parties in city government is unnecessary when a better alternative is available — direct reliance on the electorate.

Appointment by the mayor is the method used in San Francisco, in Chicago for vacancies with less than two years remaining in the council member's term, and in some other New York State cities like Yonkers. An analogous process, appointment by the county executive, is used in Oneida County. Its simplicity may make it attractive, but such a process violates the separation-of-powers principle. Moreover, it distances the selection process from the constituency to be served.

In a strong mayoral system, the authority to fill council vacancies gives the chief executive even greater leverage over the legislature. This is especially true if the mayor is permitted to serve an unlimited number of terms and over time gains the opportunity to appoint a substantial number of council members. With a vacancy rate of 1.22 seats a year (the recent historical average) and a thirty-five-member council, a mayor reelected twice would enter his third term having appointed 30 percent of the city's legislature.

In Monroe and Herkimer counties, vacancies are filled by the elected head of the legislature. Unlike mayoral appointments, this method raises no separation-of-powers problems. It would undoubtedly enable the council leader to build a base of personal support over time. And because of the nature of leadership in a legislative body, the selection process would probably be consultative.

An opposing argument suggests that the choice is not linked closely enough to the geographic area to be served by the person selected. Additionally, procedures that centralize power in the legislature may not be desirable. Finally, the majority leader may choose to defer the choice to the borough delegation or to the council as a whole to avoid factional conflict. Such results may reflect a change in charter provisions that does not change actual practice.

Election by committee members of the former member's party in the councilmanic district is the method employed in Indianapolis. A grassroots process that ensures partisan continuity in the post, it strengthens the local political party, provides incentives for party involvement, and places the choice in the hands of some of the people most knowledgeable about the skills and abilities of local leaders. Such a process, however, might effectively return the choice to fill vacancies to a few party leaders or even to the county leader. Strengthening the party organizations in this manner in a largely one-party city might further reduce competitiveness. Moreover, such a process for filling council vacancies is unlikely to result in council participation by local leaders with bases outside the party system.

An alternative possibility is to use special elections for vacancies that occur too late for a candidate to run in the next scheduled general election but a substantial period is left in the term. This practice, common at the national and state levels and used in some other New York cities and Suffolk County, might be combined with appointment by the council or the governor for brief interim periods, or positions might simply be left vacant until the next scheduled election. Nominations could be the same as for general elections. As in some other cities, the date for the election might be fixed by the Board of Elections within limits fixed in the charter.

Special elections would democratize the process of filling vacancies in the council. The power of party leaders, exercised without accountability to the electorate or to party rank and file, would be reduced. Although hampered by low visibility and low turnout, special elections might result in increased competition for council positions from people with community bases outside the regular political process, thus broadening the general base and enhancing the legitimacy of the city's political system.

The contrary view is that special elections to fill vacancies are not the preferred method for local government. Such a practice would undermine a traditional role of the council and weaken it as an institution. One scenario sees party organizations negatively affected by special elections at a time when they ought to be strengthened to make the political system truly competitive. But special elections may give the appearance of democracy without actually being democratic; in fact, nomination and election under this method may well be dominated by established political organizations, because they are organized and familiar with the electoral process. The people who vote will not be typical of the entire electorate. Thus, power would remain with the very people and interests who have always held it. If the reform works, the effects will be more negative than positive for the political system. But there is a substantial chance that it would fail, leaving the real locus of power unchanged.

The 1988 New York City Charter Change

After considering the system in place for filling vacancies and the range of alternatives, the New York City Charter Revision Commission decided to recommend to the voters that vacancies in elective offices be filled by prompt election rather than by succession or appointment. The general election and partisan nominating procedures established in state election law were to be used whenever possible. But if special elections were employed, they were to be opened to a wide field of candidates, not restricted to the choices of party leaders. Finally, to keep campaign expenses for special elections to a minimum, runoffs were not required (see appendix 2).

The commission's recommendations were guided by three basic principles: that it was important that vacancies be filled by election as soon as possible after they occurred; that these elections allow for the maximum feasible competition; and that these allow for the greatest possible voter participation. On election day, 8 November 1988, city voters accepted these recommendations, and the underlying judgments they implied about the need for change in the city's political system, by overwhelming margins.

NOTES

1. United States Bureau of the Census, *Census of Governments, 1987*, 87(1)-1 (Washington, D.C.: GPO, 1988), p. VI; council size is assumed to be six. A survey of cities in the early 1980s revealed an average council size of between six and seven. See Howard T. Sanders, "The Government of American Cities: Continuity and Change in Structures," in *National Municipal Yearbook* (Washington, D.C.: ICMA, 1982), 182. The average for counties is probably close to that for cities. Downward rounding was used on the assumption that villages and towns have smaller boards. Boards were assumed to

be 80 percent male and 20 percent female for the purpose of calculation. This is probably an overestimate of female membership, a conservative assumption because of the longer life expectancy of women. Board members are assumed to be between the ages of thirty-four and sixty-four. This is a conservative assumption because more board members are likely to be older than sixty-four than younger than thirty-four; older people, of course, have higher mortality rates. Mortality rates are from the *Statistical Abstract of the United States* (Washington, D.C.: GPO, 1988), table 118, p. 76.

2. Art. XIII, sec. 3.
3. Art. I, sec. 2.
4. U.S. Constitution, 17th Amendment, sec. 2.
5. Public Officers Law, sec. 42, par. 3-4.

APPENDIX 1

Borough Presidents (BPs): 1 January 1961 to 31 December 1987

Borough	Total BPs	BPs Originally Selected to Fill Vacancies		BPs Originally Elected	
		#	Years Served	#	Year Served
Staten Island	4	3	15.53	1	11.42
Queens	5	5	26.92	0	0.00
Brooklyn	5	4	18.25	1	8.75
Bronx	6	2	9.00	4	18.00
Manhattan	6	3	16.92	3	10.04

Note: Totals do not add to 135, the total number of years served, because of rounding.

APPENDIX 2

Changes in the New York City Charter:
Filling Vacancies in the City Council

Section 24 of the Charter is proposed to be amended as follows:

Section 24. Election; terms; vacancies.

(a) The council members shall be elected at the general election in the year nineteen hundred seventy-seven and every fourth year thereafter. The term of office of each council member shall commence on the first day of January after the election and shall continue for four years thereafter.

(b) Any vacancy which may occur among the council members shall be filled by *popular* election [by a majority of all the council members remaining in office, of a person who must be of the same political party of which the council member whose place has become vacant was the candidate on the ballot if such council member was elected as the candidate of any political party and who must be a resident of the district from which such council member was elected. In the case of a candidate who was listed on the ballot as the candidate for two or more political parties, such candidate shall, for the purposes of this section, be deemed to be the candidate of the party for which he received the highest number of votes.] *as set forth below.*

(1) *Immediately upon the occurrence of a vacancy in the city council, the Majority Leader shall inform the Board of Elections of it, and that board shall publish notice of the date for the election or elections required by this section in the City Record. Once*

the board of elections has set the date for a special election, the board shall publish notice thereof not less than twice each week preceding the date in newspapers distributed within the district, and shall notify by mail all registered voters within the district.

(2) If a vacancy shall occur on or before the last day on which an occurring vacancy may be filled at the general election in the year in which the vacancy occurs with party nominations of candidates for such elections being made at a primary election, then such vacancy shall be filled at such general election and party nominations for such general election shall be made at such primary election. If a vacancy shall occur after such day, it shall be filled at the general election in the following year and party nominations of candidates for such general elections shall be made at a primary election. The vacancy, however, shall not be filled at either such general election if such general election would occur in the last year of the term involved.

(3) Unless a special election to fill such vacancy on an interim basis has been previously held, a person elected to fill a vacancy in the council at such a general election shall take office immediately upon qualification and shall serve until the date on which the term of the council member originally elected to the full term would have expired. If such an interim special election has been held, the person elected at the next following general election shall take office on January first after such general election and shall serve until the date on which the term of the council member originally elected to the full term would have expired.

(4) A special election to fill such a vacancy on an interim basis shall be held if the vacancy occurs

　　(i) at least ninety days before a primary election at which party nominations are to be made for a general election to fill such a vacancy for the remainder of the term involved, or

　　(ii) after the last day referred to in paragraph (2) of this subdivision in the third year of the term involved, but at least ninety days before the primary election in the last year of the term involved.

(5) Such special election shall be held on the first Tuesday at least forty-five days after the occurrence of the vacancy, provided that the Board of Elections may by proclamation schedule such election for another day no more than ten days after such Tuesday and not less than forty days after such proclamation if it determines that such rescheduling is necessary to facilitate maximum voter participation; and further provided that if such special election would otherwise, pursuant to this section, be scheduled for a date which is less than ninety days before or less than thirty days after a regularly scheduled general election or between a primary and a general election, then the special election shall be held concomitantly with such general election.

(6) All nominations in such special elections shall be by independent nominating petition.

(7) A person elected to fill a vacancy in the position of council member at such a special election shall take office immediately upon qualification and shall serve until December thirty-first of the year in which the vacancy is filled at a general election, or, if the vacancy is not filled at a general election, until the date when the term of the council member originally elected would have expired.

Material bracketed [ ] was deleted. Italicized material was added.

Campaign Finance Reform

HERBERT E. ALEXANDER

Public funding was conceived and has been used to help equalize economic resources and to open up the political system to candidates without ready access to personal funds or to wealthy contributors. Government funds, according to advocates, are an alternative funding system designed to enable candidates and parties to avoid obligations, tacit or expressed, that might go along with dependence on large contributors and special interests. Public matching funds are also intended to enhance the role that small donors play in campaigns and, by opening up the nomination process, to make the system more competitive.

Underlying most public-funding systems is the assumption that new or alternative sources of campaign funding are desirable. This is particularly true when state laws limit contributions, as twenty-five now do, or restrict traditional sources, as all but nine do to some degree. The public funds are intended to help provide or—in the presidential general-election period—to supply all the money serious candidates need to present themselves and their ideas to the electorate. The public funds are also meant to diminish or to eliminate the need for money from wealthy donors and interest groups and thereby minimize opportunities for contributors to exert undue influence on officeholders. In the nomination period, public funding is designed to make the contest for the nomination more competitive and to encourage candidates to broaden their bases of support by seeking out large numbers of relatively small, matchable contributions.

The system of public funding of presidential campaigns has operated since 1976, and its consequences have been widely analyzed.[1] Twenty states also have tax-assisted funding of political parties and candidates. Additionally, two cities—Seattle, Washington, and Tucson, Arizona—have enacted public financing, as has Sacramento County, California. Seattle, in fact, twice enacted laws. The first, passed in 1978, operated in the 1979 and 1981 elections and lapsed in 1982 when a sunset provision terminated it. The second was enacted in 1984 and was effective for the 1987 elections.[2] Much can be learned from these experiences with contribution and expenditure limits, public financing of campaigns, and related laws concerning election financing.

The Effectiveness of Contribution Limits

A study by the Seattle Office of Election Administration in 1984 indicated that the city's law limiting campaign contributions in both primary and general elections increased the number of small, individual contributions to closely contested City Council campaigns in 1979 and 1981 while decreasing the numerical and financial participation of individuals and groups making large contributions. The average amounts of contributions to the candidates also decreased. When the law became inoperative in 1982 in accord with its sunset provision, contributions reverted to prelaw patterns. In 1983, both the total number of contributors and the number of individuals contributing to candidates in municipal election campaigns in Seattle fell, while the average contribution as well as the numerical and financial participation of individuals and groups making large contributions rose. In the 1983 campaign, 68 percent of the contributions in closely contested City Council races were $100 or more; in 1979, under the public-financing law, the figure was only 36 percent.[3]

But if Seattle has demonstrated that campaign contribution ceilings can be effective in democratizing the electoral process, there can be problems with limiting contributions as well. In presidential campaigns since 1976, despite public funding and expenditure ceilings as parts of the system, ways have been found to circumvent contribution limits and reintroduce significant amounts of private money into the campaigns.

Political action committees (PACs) were formed by prospective presidential candidates to fund preannouncement political activities. Also, contributions could be made to draft committees, created to persuade an individual to declare a candidacy for the presidential nomination, without affecting individual or PAC contribution limits. Further, under the United States Supreme Court's ruling in *Buckley* v. *Valeo*, individuals and groups are permitted to spend unlimited amounts on communications in behalf of or against candidates so long as the activity is independent of any candidate's campaign. Additionally, federal law imposes no limit on expenditures for internal communications by labor organizations, corporations, and membership groups advocating the election or defeat of a clearly identified candidate.

But perhaps most important, PACs and other organizations are also permitted to spend "soft money" on elections at the federal level, that is, money raised from sources outside the restraints of federal law but spent on activities intended to affect federal election outcomes. For state and local campaigns, "soft money" can also be raised under state laws that may be more permissive than federal law. Thus, despite limits that New York City might adopt, for example, "soft money" could be raised under New York State law, which may have different contribution or other limits. These contributions would free other "hard money" party funds to pay for permissible expenditures on behalf of, say, a candidate for mayor. While designed to promote party goals and benefit all the candidates on the party ticket, such developments would nevertheless raise doubts about the effectiveness of candidate expenditure limits.

The committee of a political party and its allies can also channel "soft money" from willing corporate, union, and individual contributors to not-for-profit organizations that conduct voter registration, turnout drives, or other activities among targeted segments of the population. The money raised and sent to carry on these activities is not subject to federal campaign-law contribution or expenditure limits.

Individual contribution limits have also played a role in replacing the big contributor with the big solicitor — a new political elite on whom candidates have become dependent in the effort to broaden their financial constituencies and raise big money in smaller individual sums. Important fund raisers include direct-mail consultants with access to mailing lists of proven donors to campaigns, entertainment promoters who can persuade their clients to hold benefit concerts for favored candidates, PAC managers who can make contributions, and "elite solicitors" who can tap into networks of individuals capable of contributing up to the maximum allowed.

Many of these tactics could become more prevalent in New York City in publicly funded campaigns, because the contribution limits would force candidates to seek to broaden their financial basis. Additionally, limits, if set too low, might reduce campaign flexibility in New York, as they have elsewhere. Low limits make it difficult or impossible for many candidates to raise the amounts they think they need — perhaps causing them to seek ways of circumventing the limits or deciding not to run for office at all. Low campaign-contribution limits can also prevent candidates from launching campaigns late in the season because of the difficulty of raising sufficient funds in a short time. Contribution limits set too high, on the other hand, may decrease or eliminate the effectiveness of two primary goals of limiting contributions: controlling campaign costs and limiting special-interest influence.

In Tucson, Arizona, the city's campaign financing law has dealt with the problem of "soft money" contributions to building funds and mortgage and maintenance costs as a way of evading contribution limits by including them as contributions in a provision of the law relating to "property-in-kind and things having a monetary value." The charter clearly defines "property-in-kind" and "things having a monetary value." Thus in-kind contributions are counted as contributions subject to the limit, with fair market value placed on in-kind contributions to ensure that they do not exceed the contribution limits.

Loans require special consideration. Federal law defines *contribution* to include a loan or an advance, and so limits apply. Despite the prohibition of corporate contributions, however, certain banks may make loans in accordance with applicable law and in the ordinary course of business, on a basis that will ensure repayment, and with usual and customary interest rates. Candidates for presidential nominations, for example, have borrowed money from banks with anticipated public funds as collateral.

One of the major disadvantages of contribution limitations is that well-known or incumbent candidates are capable of raising money early and quickly, thus giving them an unfair edge over their lesser-known opponents and perhaps keeping some from entering races altogether. It is important, therefore, to consider carefully the optimum timespan within which candidates can accept campaign contributions. Too short a period gives an advantage to better-known or incumbent candidates; too long a contribution period puts pressure on all candidates to establish themselves and obtain contributions earlier than might normally be necesary or desirable. A possible approach might be to provide that nominees or candidates for majority elective offices could accept contributions no earlier than one year before the first day to circulate designating petitions. This limit would be about fifteen months before the primary or election.

Another approach is to seek to prohibit fund raising in a nonelection year or during a legislative session. Several states prohibit fund raising while the legislature meets, both to minimize incumbent advantages and to reduce the incidence of "juice bills"—proposed laws not designed to pass but to attract contributions to sponsors or opponents. While penalizing incumbents, these prohibitions tend to limit potential challengers even more.

Individual and Group Contribution Limits

Before suggesting contribution limits for New York City, it might prove useful to look at the limitations imposed by smaller cities and counties. Seattle, Washington, has set a $350 ceiling on individual contributions to any citywide candidate. Tucson's individual limit was $500, but that amount was superseded by Arizona state law in November 1986, and the limit is now $200. In Sacramento County, California, individual contributions to supervisorial candidates are limited to $250 during each of the off-year elections, $500 during any primary or special election period, and $500 during any general, special, or runoff election period. In contrast, contribution limitations by organizations are $250 and $1,000 in comparable periods.

Because of New York City's vastly larger population, higher cost of living, and sophisticated political culture, contribution limits might be set commensurately higher than in smaller cities. Lower limitations for several of the offices would recognize that they have smaller constituencies and less significance, but an across-the-board figure is easier for potential contributors to understand. An across-the-board limit as high as $4,000 or as low as $1,000 might be considered. Perhaps $2,500 would be a middle ground. Whatever level is chosen, city law cannot conflict with New York State law. Of course, contribution and expenditure limitations would apply only if the candidate voluntarily agrees to participate in public funding. In this sense, limitations are a condition flowing from acceptance of public funds.

An additional factor to be weighed when setting contribution limits is the desirability of building in an inflation index. Under the 1974 amendments to the Federal Election Campaign Act (FECA), for example, an individual contributor was limited to giving no more than $1,000 per candidate for presidential nominations and a maximum of $25,000 annually for all federal election campaigns. Unlike the law's expenditure limits, however, these contribution limits were not indexed to account for inflation. A $1,000 contribution in 1984 had a buying power of about $436 in 1974 dollars.

For purposes of discussion, suggested limits for PACs or other groups in New York City could be either the same as the individual limit or higher. The argument for equal limits is that it is easier to educate the public that a single amount applies alike to individuals, PACs, corporations, labor unions, and other membership organizations. The argument favoring a higher contribution limit for PACs and other organizations is based on the fact that a PAC represents numerous contributors and hence its contribution limit can legitimately be higher than that for an individual. In federal elections the $1,000 contribution limit for individuals corresponds to the $5,000 limit for PACs. Michigan has imposed contribution limits for "special interests" ten times higher than the individual ceiling.

In Seattle, Washington, contributions by groups of "ten or more persons" for citywide offices are limited to $350. Moreover, no person can contribute more than a total of $350 to all political committees that contribute to candidates for citywide offices in any election year. The state of Arizona, as well as the city of Tucson, limits contributions for "most" campaign committees to $200 and donations to "qualified" committees to $1,000. A "qualified" committee is defined as one "which has received funds from 500 or more individuals in amounts of $10 or more in the one year period preceding the last closing reporting date."[4] Donations by organizations to candidates for supervisor in Sacramento County are restricted to $250 for off-year elections and $1,000 during general, special, or special runoff election periods.

One contribution-limit proposal that has been widely discussed is to ban campaign contributions from anyone seeking business with New York City. Specifically, this proposal would disqualify individuals or businesses who gave more than, say, $3,000 in an election from receiving a wide range of discretionary benefits, including contracts without competitive bidding, franchises, revocable consents, and leases or other benefits from land-use transactions.

Under current New York law, individuals may give up to $100,000 to candidates for citywide offices. A study indicated that in 1985, some 175 donors provided half of the campaign financing for the top eight municipal elected offices, including the mayor. Most of these contributors were reportedly individuals or firms that do business with New York City.

The ban proposal, however, has its detractors. Opponents claim that when the concept of "doing business" with New York City is extended to its logical limit, it could affect such a broad range of contributors, including attorneys, architects, public-relations specialists, and lobbyists, that First Amendment rights would be infringed. Once strict contribution limits are in place with an accompanying disclosure system, critics say, it would not be necessary to tell one class of contributors that they cannot exercise their right to contribute as an expression of freedom of speech. Recall that in the *Buckley* case money is equated with speech. Another concern is that a flat ban may increase distortion of the electoral process by encouraging more wealthy candidates to run for office and cause more PACs to be organized to funnel indirect funds into campaigns.

In sum, given the possible consequences of a contribution ban, it seems that public disclosure and media scrutiny of alleged links between contributions and City Council actions may be a preferred course of action.

Another possible action would be to prohibit corporate and labor contributions entirely. The federal system forbids corporations, trade associations, national banks, and labor unions to contribute to campaigns. Some thirty states prohibit corporate contributions, and nine states prohibit labor-union contributions. In these cases, of course, corporations can establish PACs to raise money voluntarily from defined classes of employees, stockholders, and their families. Labor unions can do the same for members of the unions and their families.

There are arguments both for and against permitting corporations and labor unions to contribute. As noted above, giving political money is a form of free speech. On the other hand, public-interest groups complain that wealthy special interests have an undue influence on legislation and close out those who are unable to contribute. Questions are raised about labor unions that would benefit from their own contracts with the city or from contacts with corporations whose employees have organized. Prohibitions seek to equalize the playing field and check groups viewed as having a disporportionate effect on electoral and legislative politics.

Finally, there is the question of contributions by candidates to their own campaigns. Personal expenditure is considered as a personal contribution; included in the definition are the candidate and his or her immediate family. The advantage that wealthy candidates have is obvious. That advantage becomes even more pronounced when opponents, dependent on donations from others, can accept only limited gifts.

The state of Arizona has chosen to deal with this issue by obligating candidates who give more than $10,000 to their own campaigns for a nonstatewide office and $100,000 for a statewide office to notify the city clerk, the secretary of state, and all other candidates for the same office within twenty-four hours. From the time of such notification until they exceed the amount contributed, other candidates for that office are exempted from contribution limits. New Jersey law limits use of personal funds to $25,000 for both the primary and general elections for publicly funded candidates for governor.

Federal law limits a presidential candidate who accepts public financing to expending no more than $50,000 from personal funds. This provision, unlike other limits, has been interpreted to cover campaigns before and after the nomination. Candidates sometimes lend money to their own campaigns in the hope they will be repaid. In presidential campaigns, the $50,000 limit would apply to a loan as well as to contributions or expenditures by the candidate in his or her own behalf.

Under the presidential nomination matching system or the Seattle municipal public-funding program, a candidate first qualifies for public money by raising a threshold amount. Thereafter, the candidate may continue to raise money privately and have a portion of those private contributions matched by public dollars. The candidate is required to accede to certain limitations on the amount of expenditures he or she makes, on the size of his or her family's contribution to or expenditure in behalf of the campaign, and on the timing or uses of the candidate's campaign money. Since these restrictions must be voluntary under the law, they are imposed as a condition for the receipt of public money. The candidate may reject the matching money and ignore the attendant restrictions.

Public matching-fund provisions have indeed increased the importance of contributors of small amounts — both in federal nomination campaigns and in municipal elections. As noted above, a Seattle study showed that the program matching only the first $50 of each contribution resulted in a reduction in the number of people contributing $100 or more, an increase in the number contributing less than $100, and an increase in the total number of contributors to closely contested City Council campaigns. In addition, the average contribution fell from $63 in 1977 to $20 in 1979. When the contribution matching-fund program was removed in the 1983 campaign year, the pattern of campaign financing returned to the one that had existed before the adoption of the matching program.

Most public-funding matching programs require a candidate to raise a minimum amount of money in small contributions before becoming eligible. Under the FECA, for example, candidates seeking the nomination of a political party for the office of president qualify for public matching funds by raising $100,000, with $5,000 coming from each of twenty states, in amounts of $250 or less from individuals. In Seattle and Tucson a mayoral candidate must receive 300 contributions of $10 or more to qualify for public matching funds, while candidates for the other council offices must raise 200 contributions of $10 or more. Additionally, in Tucson only city resident contributions are matched. Finally, in Sacramento County, candidates must demonstrate community support by raising $10,000 in contributions of $250 or less during the election year to become eligible for public funding. Moreover, to ensure that public money is not wasted on noncompetitive races, only candidates with opponents who have raised or spent at least $10,000 are eligible for public matching funds.

Experience suggests that a number of factors should be considered in determining thresholds for public funding in New York City. Care should be taken not to set the threshold requirements so high as to make it unduly difficult for third-party or independent candidates to qualify for public funds. On the other hand, a very low threshold might encourage frivolous candidates. An alternative to matching funds — such as collecting a specified number of signatures from eligible voters — may be appropriate.

The matching ratio set for public funding is an important element in encouraging candidates with less access to wealthy contributors to run for public office. A matching ratio of 1-to-1 or 2-to-1, with the candidate receiving twice the amount in public funds, as in New Jersey's funding of gubernatorial campaigns, is worth considering.

To be eligible for public funds, candidates should be required to "opt in" in a timely fashion and agree to provide necessary information and abide by statutory limits. Concurrently, care should be taken when devising a system to ensure that workable guidelines are provided in a timely way for campaigns that are submitting contributions to be matched. Finally, an inflation index rounded to the nearest $100 or $1,000 may be included.

Obviously, any contribution limits would apply separately on the infrequent occasions when runoff elections are held. Because of time constraints, a candidate qualified for the first primary should be considered to have qualified for the runoff with the same expenditure limits applicable. A flat grant might be provided, say for 50 percent or more of the expenditure limit, without matching funds, if the Political Finance Commission could not process submissions for matching funds and provide money in time to permit candidates to make television and other commitments during the limited period of the runoff.

Similarly, in the relatively short general-election period, 50 percent or more of the expenditure limit might be given as a flat grant to nominated candidates of the major parties. This would ease fund-raising pressures for candidates and would allow them more time for campaigning. It would also permit them to make television commitments. Experience shows that the 100 percent presidential level of funding, with an absolute limit on private funds, simply diverts fund raising to the parties on whose ticket the candidates are running. Therefore, unlike in the federal system, the remaining 50 percent under this proposal might be raised by the candidate's campaign. As in the runoff election, under this alternative for the general election, the same contribution limits would apply and there would be no matching funds.

Finally, New York City needs to provide procedures for minor-party candidates to qualify for matching funds (or flat grants if that alternative is chosen). In principle, a minor-party candidate should be eligible to receive as much public funding in the general-election period as a major-party candidate and should be subject to the same expenditure limits.

Spending Caps and Revenue Sources

Because tax revenues are not unlimited, special caution needs to be exercised in the use of tax dollars for political purposes. Accordingly, a cap on public funding in each phase of the electoral process is suggested. Under federal regulation not more than 50 percent of expenditure limits in nomination campaigns can come from public funds. Similarly, the New Jersey system of publicly funded gubernatorial elections includes caps on the amounts that can be provided to any single campaign in either the primary or general election.

In addition to threshold requirements, most public-funding systems have restrictions that, because they are voluntary, are also constitutionally permissible. Under the 1987 Seattle law, expenditure limits are presented in the form of a campaign contract that candidates must sign in order to qualify for public funds. Similarly, a candidate in Tucson may sign a campaign contract with the city agreeing to abide by limitations on candidates' contributions, limitations on campaign expenditures, and limitations on the use of all contributions as specified in the charter, in exchange for public matching funds. In both Seattle and Tucson a candidate who accepts public financing in the primary must agree to accept it for the general election as well.

With regard to providing the money for public financing in New York City, neither a tax checkoff nor an add-on seems promising as a means to generate sufficient funds. The answer may be to establish a public trust fund similar to that approved in Florida in 1986, setting aside certain amounts on a schedule until payouts are made in the election year. That way, the money can collect interest, and confidence in the system can be established. Candidates would not have to worry about whether the public funds would be appropriated and could plan accordingly.

An advantage of establishing a trust fund in New York City is that appropriations for such a fund can be made by the City Council. A tax checkoff or add-on would require state legislation and state administration. New York City would have to reimburse the state for its revenue loss and costs.

Seattle, without a city income tax, uses appropriations by the City Council based on a checkoff coupon provided in the City Light bills. This $4 checkoff mandates, at no cost to the signer, a transfer from city revenues to the Seattle Campaign Reform Fund. If the coupon is not returned, the $4 remains in the City Council General Fund to be spent at the discretion of the mayor and council. Tucson has enacted a provision somewhat similar to Seattle's; it is for a voluntary add-on to the city's water bills.

Alternatives or Additions to Public Financing

Rather than transferring cash to qualified New York City candidates, in-kind contributions or services might be provided. For example, publicly financed mailings would tend to equalize opportunities for candidates to reach voters. These mailings might be permitted to include requests for campaign contributions. This plan would have the advantage of mandating that public monies be used in direct campaigning with potential constituents. The disadvantage is that this approach would direct spending and not allow candidates to decide for themselves how best to spend public funds. Additionally, though it is difficult to calculate the total costs of such a proposed reform, they would surely be significant.

Another indirect subsidy for candidates' campaigns would be to provide postage and compilation expenses for candidate-information pamphlets. Currently, only Oregon, Washington state, and Seattle provide such pamphlets, which contain a one-page advertisement for each candidate. A copy is sent to each registered voter. A strong case can be made that there is a reason for governments to assume some responsibility for informing the electorate about candidates for public office.

Finally, an additional way to infuse new relevancy into New York City political discourse would be to provide funds to pay for thirty-minute television and radio broadcasts for the major mayoral candidates. These television programs could be shaped by certain reforms. One method would be to require that such programs feature the candidate only (a so-called talking head), a requirement similar to legislation being proposed in the Congress.

A series of the programs could be broadcast on specific issues, such as business development or welfare reform. Opposing candidates' programs would be run back-to-back so that voters could make immediate comparisons. This approach could then be supplemented by an hour-long program, with two or more candidates asking each other questions. As in a debate, the only other participant in the program would be an impartial moderator, not a panel of journalists asking questions.

It would be necessary to establish criteria for making airtime available. Without a significant independent or minor-party candidate, the presumption of such a proposal would be that there were only two major general-election candidates, a Democrat and a Republican. However, a policy of "differential equality of access" could be adopted. Under this policy, if time were purchased for a major-party candidate, it would also be bought on the same station for similar periods for minor-party or independent candidates, but in smaller amounts. This formulation is modeled on the British system of giving minor parties airtime — but less than to major parties.

Judicial, Legislative, and Political Problems

The public seems to believe that campaign costs are too high and campaigns too long and that limiting the amount that can be spent is a convenient way of dealing with both problems. The courts, however, have had to confront the dilemma of expenditure limits. The problem is to balance the First Amendment rights of free speech and free association against the clear power of the legislature to enact laws designed to protect the integrity of the election system. Questions of public discussion and political dialogue are involved, as well as the inherent danger that spending limits will have a chilling effect on free speech and on citizen participation. In the *Buckley* case, the United States Supreme Court concluded that expenditure limits imposed direct and substantial restraints on the amount of political speech but made an exception when candidates accept public funds.

The constitutional problems are compounded by political ones. Legislatures are often reluctant to enact public funding without expenditure limits because of fears of fueling the fires of explosive costs. However, expenditure limits have a great impact on campaigns. If they are too high, they encourage candidates to try to spend up to the limit, forcing them to spend more time soliciting money. If too low, they work to the advantage of candidates who are better known, who have the backing of a superior party organization, or who have the ability to enlist volunteers; incumbents usually have all three of these advantages. Moreover, with low limits, some candidates might decide not to accept the money, preferring not to be held to the limits. This has happened in Wisconsin and Minnesota. If one candidate opts for public funds and expenditure limits and the opponent does not, resulting disparities may jeopardize the system. Candidates also complain that the limits rigidify the system by forcing them to centralize control of spending and to impose strict budgetary restraints, thereby discouraging grass-roots campaigning and the involvement of volunteers in their campaigns.

Limits on independent spending are generally proposed as a corollary to contribution limits. The argument is that contributors should not be able to evade the limits by providng benefits to the candidate above what they could give as a contribution. In recent years, independent spending in federal elections has been carried out by ideological groups whose funds are raised by massive direct mail drives. Some have criticized them for fractionalizing politics and diminishing the roles of the parties. Arguments against controlling independent expenditures, which the United States Supreme Court has reaffirmed, are that such restrictions will limit the amount and particularly the diversity of campaign-related speech.

The Supreme Court held in *Buckley* v. *Valeo* that independent spending was constitutional, so long as the spender does not act in concert or cooperate with the candidate's campaign. In 1982, however, in *Common Cause* v. *Schmitt*, the court divided 4–4 on the validity of a limit on independent spending to support a candidate who accepted public financing. Thus, at least some type of tighter regulation of independent spending may be possible under some circumstances.

At the federal level, efforts to tighten controls on independent expenditures include proposals fully to compensate through public funds a candidate whose opponent has more than $10,000 spent independently for him or her against the candidate to be compensated, strictly to regulate groups that coordinate their independent expenditures, and clearly to identify the individual or group placing independent expenditure advertisements or paying for their use on television and radio and in print.

Federal law exempts both compliance costs and certain fund-raising expenses (up to 20 percent of the expenditure limit) from the spending limits. The compliance costs include not only accounting and legal fees but also such factors as winding-down expenses after an election while a monitoring agency is conducting an audit. The foremost problem with these exemptions is that they require three sets of books — one for compliance, another for expenditures under the limit, and a third for fund raising. An alternative might be to make expenditure limits high enough to include fund raising and compliance costs. New Jersey and several other states, for example, do not exempt compliance costs or make special provisions for fund raising.

Disclosure

Reporting information about political costs rests on the recognition that a contribution to, or expenditure for, a political activity or campaign is a public act for a special public purpose, electing men and women to office. If the people are given full and accurate information on the financing of candidates, political parties, and committees, they will be better able to act according to their best interests when casting their votes.

Disclosure has a unique cleansing power. It tends to reduce the potential influence of financial pressures on elected officials by inhibiting the contributor's expectation of favors and the official's willingness to grant them. Moreover, disclosure provides information concerning the distribution, unequal or otherwise, of financial resources among rival candidates and parties and may help to minimize expenditures somewhat because of the fear that excessive spending will cause the electorate to react adversely. Thus, an effective disclosure system will create financial accountability, increase public confidence in the electoral process, and help to curb excesses and abuses by increasing political risk for those who would undertake sharp practices. Political disclosure laws are now generally accepted in American politics. All fifty states have varying degrees of disclosure requirements, and the federal system places particular emphasis on the need for comprehensive and effective public reporting.

The purposes of disclosure provide the principles on which any reporting system ought to be based. First, the scope of the disclosure law should be broad. Candidates, parties, and other committees must be required to file reports that cover campaigns for nomination as well as for runoff and general elections. Party and political action committees should disclose their finances on a regular basis. In fact, any PAC raising or spending a minimal amount, perhaps $1,000, to influence any election should be required to make a comprehensive dislosure. Second, ample information should be made available before the election, when it can have its greatest effect. Third, effective record keeping and reporting procedures are necessary for the disclosure agency to detect possible violations. Data supplied on prescribed forms should be received by a single, well-staffed agency charged with the duties of auditing, tabulating, summarizing, publishing, and preserving it. Agency officials, responsible for ascertaining and reporting violations and delinquencies to the proper enforcement agencies, should be guided by a set of laws and penalties easily invoked against deliberate violators. Strict compliance should be demanded.

The political problems connected with disclosure arise at three points—first, at the point of responsibility for submitting reports; second, at the point of responsibility for receiving and auditing the reports; and, third, at the point of responsibility for enforcing the law.

At the first point, the problem is to devise a disclosure system compatible with the realities of political, especially campaign, life. Maximum reasonable information should be collected without puting undue burdens on candidates and committees—whose main functions, after all, are not bookkeeping and accounting but campaigning—or on contributors. Reporting requirements should be simple and easily fulfilled. The guiding rule should be to seek the highest commmon denominator of information about political funds that those reporting can be expected to make available, and that the public can be expected to use. A political finance report, while edifying the electorate and satisfying the merely curious, also provides the public and the courts with an official record that can be used against a violator. It is unlikely that a candidate or treasurer will report his or her own violations. The means to overcome this danger are at least partially available, but only within a properly conceived and effectively enforced system.

The second and third loci of responsibility concern those charged with receiving, publishing, and auditing the information and enforcing the law. Disclosure alone is not enough. Not only must political finance data be a matter of public record; they must also be accessible to the public. It is the responsibility of government to perform the indispensable task of compiling and summarizing disclosed data in ways that are useful to the media and the public. The costs of providing such data are minimal, compared with the benefit to the public, but they need to be considered within the overall costs of establishing an agency to monitor the election law and administer public funding if that option is enacted.

The law must clearly define terms within the disclosure system. Among others, definitions of each of the following should be included: candidate; political committee; political party; primary, runoff, and general and special election; contribution (anything of value, including loans); threshold and matchable contributions; expenditure; and independent expenditure. The disclosure information that the agency requires should include — in addition to contribution and expenditure figures — an accounting of cash in hand, receipts, transfers of funds, and debts and obligations. The disclosure agency might be responsible for receiving and making public disclosure reports on independent expenditures, communications costs, "soft money," and any personal ethics or conflict-of-interest statements required of candidates for public office.

Political Parties and Interest Groups

If individual and PAC limits are adopted for New York City campaigns, limits on political party committees also need to be considered. Since political parties are governed by state law, they can serve as vehicles to launder money for city candidate campaigns. For example, a contributor can give up to the limit to a candidate but then give additional money to the party organization, which might transfer this money to the candidate's campaign account. Or the party may pay for advertising in behalf of a candidate who reached the limit of allowable spending. These potential developments highlight just two of the dilemmas facing reformers trying to regulate political party activity when there is an activist party organization working for a candidate on the party ticket.

One way of permitting party committees to work with candidates in their campaigns would be to allow the candidate to designate supporting party committees. Once authorized, the party would have to set up a separate fund for the campaign and agree to accept contributions to that account at the same or a somewhat higher limit as for individual or PAC contributions. It can be argued, however, that there should be no limits at all on individual contributions to parties because they are broadly ideological, are not special interests, and ideally should have the means to play their important roles in a democratic society. The federal limit for individual giving to political party committees is $20,000, compared with $5,000 to PACs and $1,000 to candidates. PAC contributions to party committees are limited to $15,000 under federal law.

When expenditure limits are imposed as a condition for candidates' acceptance of public financing, consideration must be given as to whether political party participation should be restricted separately, beyond the candidates' limits. Distinctions also have to be drawn between candidate campaigning and supplemental or parallel campaigning, consisting of activities such as voter registration and get-out-the-vote drives that might indirectly benefit candidates on the party ticket. Monies for these latter purposes in behalf of the party ticket should be treated differently from monies earmarked for specific candidates. However, these distinctions can be tricky.

In New Jersey, local party organizations can spend $10,000 per county in excess of limits imposed on other contributors, if the money goes to campaigning on behalf of the candidate. For all twenty-one county committees there is an overall ceiling of $100,000 on expenditures benefitting a candidate for governor who accepts public funding.

If a similar formula were applied to New York City campaigns, some might question how realistic it is to assume that five local party organizations could coordinate their activities to conform to such limits. Since there is no citywide party organization in New York City, and since there is a great disparity in the populations of the five counties, another option is to base a limits formula on the federal presidential campaign model for determining party contribution limits, that is, by allowing a fixed sum per voting-age person. Any reforms, of course, would also have to specify how much local clubs could do apart from or in conjunction with the borough party organizations.

A recent United States Supreme Court decision struck down a number of restrictive laws governing political-party activity in California, including prohibitions of preprimary endorsements. This decision reinforces a new trend in court holdings, giving considerable autonomy and latitude to political parties, thus strengthening their role in elections. There is thus some doubt about the possibility of imposing any expenditure limits on the parties. Public disclosure of contributions might be sufficient to inform voters.

Another option is to allow political parties to spend unlimited amounts of money for party registration and get-out-the-vote activities. It is unclear whether such a step would favor the dominant Democratic party, the Republican party, or minor parties in the city. Participation by local parties in New York City elections poses other unique reform challenges. Typically, these minor parties endorse candidates of one of the two major parties, but they also occasionally run their own candidates. When developing reforms like contribution and expenditure limits and public funding, careful thought must be given to ensure that no political parties are frozen out of the electoral process.

One complication arising from the implementation of a party-limitations program, for example, is how to regulate minor-party contributions or parallel campaigning on behalf of endorsed major party candidates. If a minor party endorses a Democrat, should its contributions be included in the aggregate total of money he or she can receive from all political parties? Perhaps a formula allowing local major parties to spend, say, 10 cents per voting-age person, and endorsing minor parties for 5 cents per voting-age person, would allow both major and minor parties to play significant roles in candidate financing, without unduly encouraging extensive minor party activity. There would be a need, however, to enact a prohibition against the establishment of multiple-party committees in each election for the specific purpose of bolstering spending on behalf of a particular candidate.

Under federal law, traditionally powerful interest groups — such as labor unions, corporations, and trade associaitons — are prohibited from contributing directly to campaigns. They can, as noted, establish PACs to raise voluntary funds. But they can also engage in a restricted range of direct campaign activities. Constitutional guarantees have led to the development of the notions of "parallel campaigning" to "defined classes" of employees or members.

If the federal system were adapted to city elections, labor unions, for example, could spend unlimited amounts of money to communicate candidate endorsements to members of the union and their families, a "defined class." Political messages, communicated through house organs, are part of a "parallel campaign" that may be run by the union along with the candidate's campaign.

While this approach has its merits, critics contend that the fine line between parallel and coordinated campaigns can become blurred. One example is a major rally held in a public location at which the mayoral candidate speaks. The general public might not be invited, but the event's impact would no doubt extend beyond the "defined class" of targeted voters because of media coverage. In this case, the communication cost is not reached by a candidate's expenditure limit, causing another exception to the effectiveness of the limit.

Overseeing the Election System

Election commissions, whether federal, state, or municipal, have multiple roles: judge, jury, administrator, prosecutor, enforcer, and magistrate. The potential for tension and conflict among these roles is clear. As serious as is the need for enforcement of the law, actions of the commission should not inhibit free speech or citizen participation. An expansive enforcement policy may produce an unfortunate political climate. Yet weak enforcement policy does not increase confidence in the electoral process.

If public financing is enacted, a nonpartisan commission with an adequate staff is an ideal agency to administer the law. The disclosure system it also administers would enable such a commission better to enforce the law. But the commission's work should be primarily informational and educational, with two overriding goals: to provide information to candidates and reporting entities to assist them in complying; and to make available for public inspection the individual reports filed. The commission should consult about the potential impact of its proposed actions with the political actors affected by its regulations and advisory opinions.

If its educational, administrative, and regulatory functions are well implemented, the agency's enforcement role should be minimal. The commission would ensure that all reports are filed and that those filed are complete and accurate. The agency might initiate enforcement when necessary and would have subpoena power in order to pursue investigations effectively. It could order public hearings and promulgate regulations and advisory opinions.

Epilogue

Burgeoning scandals in recent years once again brought to public attention the influence of private money in New York City politics. Reform efforts at the state level, even when focused on New York City alone, succeeded in the assembly, only to be blocked in the senate. The findings of the State Commission on Government Integrity (the Feerick commission) reinforced fears of reduced competition due to rising costs and the influence of large contributors who do business with the city or depend on favorable public action for their business success.

In this context, the New York City Charter Revision Commission determined that New York State home-rule provisions offered it the lattitude to act, and it prepared to do so.[5] But, stimulated by the commission's interest, the city's corporation counsel made a similar determination, and after considerable negotiation the City Council passed and the mayor signed local legislation to reduce campaign spending, limit the size of contributors, provide matching funds from public sources, and ensure adequate and timely disclosure of campaign finance information.

For the 1989 campaigns, the law capped contributions to participating citywide candidates at $3,000 each for the primary and general election, with the limits for borough president races set at $2,500 and for the City Council at $2,000. Voluntary spending limits were set at $3,000,000 each for the primary and general election for mayor; $1,750,000 for other citywide offices for each race; $525,000 for borough-president candidates; and $60,000 for City Council candidates. For later years, limits will be adjusted in accord with changes in the regional Consumer Price Index. Additionally, expenditures for fund raising, disclosure reporting, and legal challenges to designating positions were excluded from these limits.

If a candidate who accepted limits opposed one who did not, caps and spending limits were removed when the nonparticipating candidate spent more than half the total established in law. Additionally, the participating candidate facing a nonparticipating challenger was given two-for-one matching money, up to half of the established expenditure limit.

For candidates accepting voluntary limits, public funds were available to match private contributions of up to $500 from city residents (or the first $500 of a larger contribution). But to receive matching funds, candidates had to raise "threshold" funding in specified minimum numbers of contributions of between $10 and $500 that were not eligible for matching. For mayor, the threshold level was set at $250,000, including at least 1,000 separate contributions of $100 or more from city residents. Declining levels were set for other offices; for the council, at least 50 contributions of $10 or more from district residents were required. Finally, all candidates receiving public money must disclose considerable information about contributors and "intermediaries" in collecting contributions, a provision designed to address the practice of "bundling" discussed above.

In order to implement and enforce the law a five-member nonpartisan Campaign Finance Board was established, supported by an executive director, a counsel, and a small staff. Two members, not of the same political party, were appointed by the mayor and two by the City Council vice chairman, with the fifth member — the chairperson — selected by the mayor after consultation with the vice chairman. Terms were for staggered five-year periods, with pay on a per diem basis at a rate ($100) later established in the charter.

There was some criticism of the City Council's approach by good government groups. Unsecured loans to candidates were not affected by the local law, nor was the practice of related businesses controlled by a single person or interest giving multiple contributions. The problem of parallel independent campaigns was not addressed. Provisions barring expenditure of public funds to pay campaign employees did not extend to consultants. No disincentive to continuous fund raising by incumbents over the course of four-year terms, a significant source of electoral advantage, was built into the law. Moreover, spending limits — especially for the council — were thought by some to be so low as to be a form of "incumbent protection." Finally, enforcement provisions were relatively weak.

Nevertheless, the council's action gained considerable support as an important step forward. After considerable debate and in light of its recency, the charter commission decided not to seek to alter the outcome of the city's legislative process. Rather, it gave the Campaign Finance Board and its powers a basis in the charter, thus adding to its legitimacy, and sought a public mandate for this action and for full funding of the public-finance provisions for the imminent 1989 elections by presenting it to the electorate as a separate charter-change question. At the same time, the commission incorporated the board and a new voter-assistance program in a newly created Department of Campaign Finance and Voter Assistance and made the board responsible for mailing a multilingual nonpartisan voters' guide on issues and candidates before each city election.

The voters gave campaign and election-reform charter changes overwhelming support at the polls in 1988. Soon after, Rev. Joseph A. O'Hare, a member of the charter commission and president of Fordham University, became the first Campaign Finance Board chairman. The agency began to publicize the law and to prepare detailed guidelines and procedures, as required in the charter, for data collection and for the implementation of spending and contribution limits and public financing.

Early developments quickly revealed problems. Restrictions in spending for the third year in the electoral cycle and the early "opt-in" date for public financing created difficulties for some candidates; changes affecting these and some other provisions were almost immediately enacted by the council. As the 1989 campaign unfolded, Ronald Lauder, a cosmetics heir and a candidate for the Republican mayoral nomination, refused to accept expenditure limits for his primary campaign against Rudolph W. Giuliani, the former United States attorney for the Southern District of New York. But Giuliani also faced opposition for the Liberal party nomination from Donald Harrington, who did accept limits. This raised unanticipated questions concerning the basis for public funding for the Giuliani campaign and its exemption from spending limits in the primary period.

The experiences of these and other candidates at all levels, as the 1989 New York City campaign unfolds, will provide campaign finance reform's first test in New York City. Care has to be taken to distinguish problems of transition unique to 1989 from difficulties inherent in the system. A considerable burden will fall on the Campaign Finance Board as it advises candidates and others on the meaning of the law in concrete circumstances. Clearly, however, the effect of both the local law and charter changes adopted in 1988 will provide the basis for judgments about the viability of the approach taken to campaign finance reform in New York City and of the need for further action.

NOTES

1. See, e.g., Herbert E. Alexander and Brian A. Haggerty, *Financing the 1984 Election* (Lexington, Mass.: Lexington Books, 1987).

2. Alan Miller, "An Analysis of Campaign Contributions in Closely Contested Seattle City Campaigns, 1975–1983," City of Seattle, Office of Election Administration, 5 June 1984, 1–14.

3. Ibid., 7–8.

4. "Impact Summary: Proposition No. 200 and Subchapter A of Chapter XVI of the Tucson Charter," City of Tucson, Campaign Financing Seminar, 2.

5. See Richard Briffault, "Taking Home Rule Seriously: The Case of Campaign Finance Reform," in this vol., 35–52.

From Norms to Rules: Regulating the Outside Interests of Public Officials

PAGE E. BIGELOW

The officials and employees of large cities exercise a great deal of power over extraordinary amounts of money. New York City's direct expenditures, for example, are exceeded only by those of the federal government, New York State, and California. As a result, there is substantial opportunity for the unscrupulous to use official positions for personal financial gain or benefit. Consequently, there is clearly a need to minimize these opportunities and to deter such activities as much as practicable.

Until 1 January 1990, the New York City charter has a chapter entitled "Ethics," the contents of which are actually conflict of interest provisions. Strictly speaking, a "code of ethics" or "code of conduct" of the type found in local or state laws around the country is a collection of general rules of behavior, frequently without any specific penalties. It may deal with behavior, both public and private, and the appearance a public official or employee may present to the public. A code may include some basic conflict of interest principles but comes from an era when it was expected that such hortatory language was sufficient to induce proper behavior. In contrast, conflict of interest provisions in the modern sense are specific, well-defined, fairly technical anticorruption laws aimed at preventing the use of public office or employment for the financial benefit or gain of oneself or another. While the term *ethics* is often used as a kind of shorthand in describing such legislation, conflict of interest laws should not be confused with basically unenforceable codes of ethics.

Sound conflict of interest laws begin with the basic premise that, though other conflicts may exist, the primary ones that can be effectively regulated under law are economic. They arise out of circumstances in which public officials can benefit themselves at the public's expense. A number of essential elements are needed for sound conflict of interest legislation. First, it must define prohibited conduct clearly and provide procedures for recusal from a conflict of interest situation. Second, it must provide for an independent enforcement agency, empowered to administer an effective program of prevention, implementation, and enforcement.

Third, sound financial disclosure requirements are essential. Finally, the statute must have sanctions that will discourage illegal activity by making it impossible to gain financially if caught.

Clear definitions of prohibited conduct help take the pressure of uncertainty off public officials and employees by establishing a distinct line between acceptable and unacceptable activities. It also facilitates compliance because it relieves public servants of the obligation to determine for themselves what conduct is illegal and what may be a matter of questionable judgment or "unethical" in a philosophical sense without being a violation of law. It also generates obstacles to powerful and corrupt officials or employees persuading others to participate in illegal activities. Clear requirements enable public officials and employees to examine their activities in light of their actual or planned personal investments and other interests so as to avoid possible conflicts with their public role or the appearance of such conflicts.

An independent agency should have the power to investigate violations of the conflict of interest provisions and financial disclosure requirements, to issue advisory opinions that prevent problems from arising and protect conscientious public officials and employees, and to initiate enforcement proceedings when violations occur. Financial disclosures make available to the enforcement agency necessary information on the economic life of the public officer or employee that may reveal potential conflicts of interest. Such information may also flag sudden acquisitions of wealth by public officers and employees that warrant further inquiry. A financial disclosure law should require information pertaining to the officer or employee, as well as his or her spouse and other members of the household and require disclosure of assets or obligations within certain set ranges or categories. The strength of the enforcement agency and the design of the financial disclosure requirements should be sufficient to make the probability of detection uncomfortably high. Sanctions for violating the law should range from administrative and civil penalties for filing and compliance violations to criminal prosecution, major penalties, and imprisonment for serious and indictable breaches that result in significant public injury.

There is some difference of opinion as to whether conflict of interest provisions belong in a basic document, a state constitution, or a city charter. As a general rule, state conflict of interest and financial disclosure provisions are not constitutional. Similarly, most city provisions are found either in state statutes or in local administrative codes. In New York City, however, the provisions establishing the Board of Ethics and its powers and providing for conflict of interest prohibitions are in the charter, while the financial disclosure provisions are in the administrative code. In addition, New York State's Ethics in Government Act of 1987 includes some provisions that apply only to New York City as well as those that apply to all local government jurisdictions with populations greater than 50,000.

Board of Ethics

The New York City charter provides for a five-member Board of Ethics consisting of two ex officio members (the corporation counsel and the director of personnel) and three public members, appointed to four-year terms by the mayor. The public members serve without compensation, and one of them is designated chairman by the mayor. The board has been a charter agency since 1975, but it was established by local law in 1959. Although it was intended to be as independent of political influence as practicable, the board's structure, when judged against those in other jurisdictions, does not achieve this because of flaws that prevent real independence.

The board is empowered to appoint counsel and hire staff. The commissioner of investigation investigates at board request and reports the results to it. The commissioner of investigation is also required to forward to the board copies of any written report or statement of finding that may involve a conflict of interest or unethical conduct. The board's major function is to issue advisory opinions on request from the person involved. It must publish these opinions with such deletions as necessary to protect the identity of the party or parties involved. Other board records are confidential. Finally, the board must review the ethics provisions at least once every five years and recommend changes to the City Council.

Two of the board's five members are public officials who are appointed to their public positions by the mayor and serve at his pleasure. Thus they may be more susceptible to strong mayoral influence than the members who do not serve at the mayor's pleasure. There is no general charter provision that would prevent the entire board from being composed of public officials or employees. Most jurisdictions, however, disqualify public officials and employees from membership on such a board (except when it is a legislative committee).

The structure of the board does not prevent domination by a single political party: there is no proscription against a one-party board and no provision for other input, either through appointment or nomination by another official or through City Council advice and consent. The board could be filled with political allies and used to punish political enemies or deal leniently with political friends.

Other jurisdictions generally limit the number of members who can belong to or be associated with one political party, and some provide either for appointments of members on the nomination of another official or actual appointment by another official. Many sharply curtail the political involvement of board members during their term of service by prohibiting personal involvement in political campaigns (either for or against candidates or ballot issues) and by forbidding the holding of political party office or other positions. Requiring legislative advice and consent might allow for public discussion of nominations and could serve to prevent the appointment of unqualified or overly politicized individuals. Such procedures, however, must not be allowed to keep board seats open long enough to render the board inoperative; safeguards might include a requirement for action within a specified period. Finally, to provide for greater independence, some laws provide for the board to elect its own chairman rather than submit to designation by an appointing authority.

Unlike many jurisdictions that mandate overlapping terms to provide for continuity and to ensure that board activities do not lapse for failure to appoint new members, the charter provides for four-year terms that appear to be coterminous; it is unclear whether they coincide with the mayor's. There are potential problems because of the possibility of substantial discontinuity between boards; interpretation of the charter provisions may vary radically from one board to another. An additional problem is that the terms do not run "until a successor has been appointed and qualified." These factors in combination permit two undesirable scenarios: a mayor would simply fail to appoint the board at all or concurrent vacancies would render the board inoperable.

In order to be effective, an independent board of ethics needs to be a working board with an active, rather than a reactive, agenda. The current arrangement for New York City fails to do that in a number of respects: the charter does not mandate regular meetings of the board; neither the powers nor the duties of the board are fully outlined; and the board does not have the authority to investigate. The lack of a mandated meeting schedule suggests that the board's primary responsibility is simply to react to requests or complaints rather than to be actively concerned with the enforcement of the charter provisions.

The board's efficacy is also limited by the lack of a clearly defined mandate. The board can always be questioned about whether a particular positive initiative complies with the intent of the charter. The likely result is a board that chooses a passive, reactive role. Moreover, despite the lack of definitions for many difficult terms the board is not authorized to provide clarification.

The board is not empowered to investigate or to collect evidence but may request the commissioner of investigation to do so. Only the results are reported to it, and the board is not authorized to make any finding or to refer possible violations elsewhere for appropriate action. This practice is not usual, and the result is a board that is perceived as weak and ineffective. Finally, despite the fact that financial disclosure is a key part of the enforcement of conflict of interest provisions, the board is not the filing agency for financial disclosure forms under section 12–110 of the administrative code; its only related role involves decisions on withholding information from public inspection at the request of an official or employee.

Conflict of Interest Provisions

If there is one major criticism to be leveled at the conflict of interest provisions, it is that the style in which they are written is so complicated that, in spite of their broad applicability, they are not easily comprehended by those subject to their restrictions. The complicated structure and style diminish the effectiveness of the provisions by limiting understanding to those with the time and skills to sort out the verbiage.

It may have been expected that the board's advisory opinions would serve as sufficient clarification. This does not appear to have happened. A collection of opinions built up over a period of years but not translated into either clear text or administrative rules is neither readily accessible nor broadly applicable.

Section 2604 of the charter is designed to protect the legislative process and administrative decision making from financial conflicts of interest. A council member with a private interest in proposed legislation must disclose the nature and extent of the interest on the official record of the council; this is fairly standard. The rules of the council appear to require those present to vote, so the provision does not — but probably should — specifically authorize a council member to abstain in a conflict of interest situation. It is not common practice to require a state legislator to refrain from voting (Virginia has been an exception), and it is unusual to bar a council member from doing so, because such a requirement would result in disfranchisement of constituents. But abstention under these circumstances is frequently authorized. Similar disclosure is required from all other city officials and employees.

The charter prohibits a number of activities by members of the Board of Estimate, members of the City Council, and salaried officers and employees of the city when such activities are likely to give rise to conflict of interest situations. Such officers and employees may not: (1) be directly or indirectly interested in business dealings with the city; (2) act on behalf of a person directly or indirectly interested in business dealings with the city; (3) knowingly accept a gift from a person who has a direct or indirect interest in business dealings with the city; (4) represent private interests before a city agency; (5) act as attorney or counsel against the interests of the city in litigation to which the city is party or in an action or proceeding in which the city or a city officer or employee, acting in the course of his official duties is a complainant; or (6) act as a paid expert against the interests of the city in civil litigation brought for private pecuniary gain against the city. An exception is made for officers or employees of the city, except elected officials and specified positions in the Departments of Housing Preservation and Development and General Services with regard to bidding on or purchasing city-owned real property.

There are a number of serious problems besides the complexity of form and language in this section. There is no definition of *interest* or the extent to which the term *indirect* applies. It is therefore difficult to measure the impact that such provisions have on city officials and employees. Moreover, these prohibitions are absolute and make no provision for a city officer or employee to disqualify himself or herself from participation in a matter or from taking action when a conflict of interest exists, even though financial conflicts of interest cannot always be anticipated or avoided. It is not clear whether immediate divestiture of the holding that causes the conflict would remedy the situation. Forced divestiture has long been rejected by those working in the field because of its extreme chilling effect on recruitment of potential public officers and employees. In most other jurisdictions, these options are not considered desirable, and the problem is dealt with by permitting recusal (with the procedures in the law) and allowing the ethics commission to provide specific guidance for individual cases.

Additionally, the prohibition on acting on behalf of a person interested in business dealings is unclear as to where the lines may be drawn. It would not be acceptable to act as an agent for such a person or to make telephone calls or write letters on his or her behalf. Would it be equally unacceptable to provide behind-the-scenes advice and assistance?

If the prohibition of gifts were to be litigated, it could be found void for vagueness because this provision allows the receipt of valuable gifts from lobbyists or other persons not currently doing business with the city but who plan to do so in the future or who have done so in the past. The provision is difficult to administer because it provides insufficient guidance for public officers and employees to determine what employees are under an obligation to know and to what extent they are obliged to inquire.

Finally, the term *private pecuniary gain* is unclear. It may be read to allow an officer to be a paid expert against the city if the federal government or a public interest group is the plaintiff but not if, say, Con Edison is. Similarly, it may prohibit involvement in a case for damages of contract settlement but not in a suit to halt a city action.

A number of other activities are prohibited to members of the Board of Estimate, council members, and all other city officers or employees, whether they are paid or unpaid. Covered persons could not: (1) engage in a business, transaction, or private employment or have a financial or private interest that is in conflict with the proper discharge of official duties; (2) attempt to use an official position to obtain a financial gain, contract, license, privilege, or other private or personal advantage, direct or indirect, for oneself or any person with whom one is "associated"; (3) attempt to influence the course of proposed legislation in the Board of Estimate or City Council without publicly disclosing, on the official record, the nature and extent of any direct or indirect financial or other private interest in the legislation; (4) attempt to coerce by intimidation, threats, or otherwise a city officer or employee to engage in political activities; (5) appear, directly or indirectly, on behalf of a private interest in matters involving the agency in which one serves or before a city agency affecting matters involving the agency in which one serves; or (6) disclose confidential information or use such information to advance any direct or indirect financial or other private interest of oneself or another person.

These provisions cover a much broader category of employees and appointed officials than the prohibitions applying only to elected officials, salaried officers, and employees. As a result, the provisions differ in two ways. Some, such as disclosing confidential information or using one's public position for personal advantage, are the sort of sweeping restrictions that should apply to all public officials and employees. Others, such as the restriction on appearing before one's own agency, are more narrow than the parallel provision that prohibits elected city officials and salaried officers and employees from representing private interests before any city agency. It is appropriate to differentiate between full- and part-time personnel and between paid and unpaid positions, because it is assumed that part-time and unpaid positions require the holders to have some other form of employment. If it is important that such positions be filled, restrictions must not be so rigorous as to prevent large numbers of qualified citizens from filling the positions, as might be the case if all business dealings with all city agencies were prohibited to everyone serving in city government in any capacity.

A city officer or employee is prohibited from using confidential information acquired in the course of his or her official duties, but this prohibition lasts only as long as he or she is with the city. Nothing prohibits the use of such information after leaving government service. In other jurisdictions, it is usual to extend that ban for as much as two years after leaving government service, the theory being that after that the information is likely to have lost much of its value. In 1987, Chicago enacted a provision that sets no time limit on the ban, but whether it will be possible to enforce such a provision is unclear.

It does not appear that either the governing boards or the employees of the thirty-four public benefit corporations operating in New York City — even those covered by the city financial plan and including appointees of the mayor — fall under any of the provisions of sections on prohibited activities. Not-for-profit corporations and local economic development agencies appear to be similarly immune. This is a matter of substantial concern because such institutions have broad powers to spend money, enter into contracts and other financial agreements, market bond issues, and lease city property. These powers provide ample opportunities for conflicts of interest and self-serving financial deals.

Since 1 January 1989, the state Public Officers Law has covered employees of public benefit corporations and commissions of which at least one member or director is appointed by the governor and also members who receive compensation other than on a per diem basis. Most public benefit corporations do have gubernatorial appointees on their boards, but exceptions in the city include the Educational Construction Fund, Health and Hospitals Corporation, Offtrack Betting Corporation, Rehabilitation Mortgage Insurance Corporation, and the Harlem Urban Development Corporation (which has bylaw guidelines permitting members to conduct business with the corporation). But nearly all public benefit corporations compensate board members on a per diem basis or not at all, so coverage extends to only a few public authority board members who receive salaries, such as the chairman and vice-chairman of the Metropolitan Transportation Authority, the three board members of the Thruway Authority, and the chairman of the Housing Finance Agency.

Public benefit corporations and commissions not covered by the Public Officers Law are covered under the amendments to the Municipal Government Law, which will take effect on 1 January 1991, but the applicable provisions of that law deal only with financial disclosure provisions. It will not prohibit members from doing business with the entity, whether that involves selling goods or services to it, buying property from it, or marketing bond issues on its behalf.

A major omission in the charter is any provision prohibiting city officers and employees from accepting contingent compensation for aiding or representing a person in a matter before a city agency. Because contingent compensation is based on achieving a desired result, it can provide a particularly strong temptation for someone to engage in influence peddling or trading favors. This provision is standard in most conflict of interest laws, and even the weak ethics provisions of the old New York State law prohibited such activity.

Finally, there is the question of other members of an official's or employee's household contracting with the city or appearing before city agencies. There are no circumstances under which this is prohibited — not even contracting with the same agency that employs or is directed by another member of the household. This problem is complicated by the dramatic increase in two-career households. Clearly, it would not be advisable to make restrictions so broad as to interfere unreasonably with the employment, career, or livelihood of another member of the household because of the difficulties it would likely cause in attracting and retaining qualified city officials and employees. However, it does seem wise to prohibit doing business with an agency in which a member of the household holds a position of responsibility.

The charter allows seven exceptions to the prohibitions described above. Council members may appear without compensation before a city agency on behalf of constituents or "in the performance of public official or civic obligations." It is unclear why this is permissible only for council members and not other elected officials like borough presidents. The usual practice in other jurisdictions is to prohibit appearances for compensation with a caveat that nothing in it shall be construed to prevent an elected official from making uncompensated appearances on behalf of constituents and as part of his or her public duties or civic obligations. The right to appear on behalf of constituents is usually limited to elected officials because they are directly chosen by the voters and are seen as acting on their behalf, as opposed to appointed officials who are responsible to the appointing authority.

Other exceptions allow city officials and employees to receive any benefit or facility available to citizens, residents, or classes of citizens or residents and to hold "insubstantial" investments and interest as long as the investment or interest does not create a conflict with official duties. It is unclear from this section what an "insubstantial" investment is, and there is an implication that substantial investments that do not conflict with one's official duties would be as unacceptable as those that do present a conflict.

City officials and employees may be affiliated with, employed by, or represent a person whose business dealings with the city form "an insubstantial and unimportant part of its total business" if he or she has no direct or indirect interest in such business dealings and receives no direct or indirect compensation or other benefit in connection with them. There is no definition of how extensive a financial holding must be before it becomes "an interest," what "an insubstantial and unimportant part of its total business" means, or whether a quarterly dividend on stock shares, for example, constitutes "indirect compensation" from the proceeds. Questions may arise as to whether it is a great problem that a member of the Historic Preservation Commission holds $1,000 or even $100,000 worth of shares in the company that produces bullet-resistant vests for the police so long as the contracting process was equitable. This section appears to raise more problems than it solves. One final problem is that this subdivision can be subject to manipulation in which a given partner would not receive his or her share of the profits from work with the city, but have the foregone income made up through internal transfers of funds from other sources. There are also exceptions for payments for noncity services provided by physicians on the city payroll and for police officers holding jobs in the private security field.

Under certain circumstances an officer or employee, other than an elected official, may act as attorney, agent, broker, employee, officer, director, or consultant for a not-for-profit corporation, association, or other such entity interested in business dealings with the city, but the head of the city agency involved, the commissioner of investigation, and the Board of Ethics must determine that the proposed activity would further the purposes and interests of the city and would not constitute a conflict of interest. This section is clearly designed to recognize the important role that charitable organizations play in New York City and the importance of wide participation in their activities, but it has been criticized for requiring too many approvals before such activities are permitted. Two factors suggest that these approvals may be warranted. The first is that "not-for-profit" is simply a type of corporate structure and not all not-for-profit corporations are charitable organizations. The second is that allowing a city official or employee to be an employee of a not-for-profit corporation implies that the bar on compensation applies only to compensation for city-related activities of the corporation. This means situations could occur that would merit extensive and careful scrutiny and finely drawn permissions.

For three years after the termination of service, the charter prohibits a member of the Board of Estimate or City Council, or an officer or employee of the city, whether paid or unpaid, from appearing before any city agency or receiving compensation for services rendered on behalf of a private person, in relation to any matter with which the member was directly concerned during his or her period of service. That ban is extended to eight years for action on behalf of a private person that is against the interest of the city. This prohibition may be waived when such employment or action would further the purposes and interests of the city—if, after written approval from the head of the city agency, the corporation counsel and the commissioner of investigation, the Board or Ethics finds that the employment or action does not involve a conflict. A city officer or employee, whether paid or unpaid, is also prohibited from soliciting, negotiating for, or accepting employment involving any activity from which, after leaving the city service, he would be disqualified by the postemployment restrictions.

The charter's postemployment (or "revolving door") provisions are more stringent than those of most jurisdictions, which have a limit of up to two years and no special limit when one is appearing against the interests of the state or city. The provision for extending a waiver is probably wise. A caveat worth adding would be that the section is not to be construed to prohibit acceptance of employment with the city and appearances before city agencies on its behalf.

While the postemployment restrictions specify what one may do with regard to employment following government service, there is no prohibition on seeking or offering employment that would pose a conflict of interest when such employment is concurrent with city service. Many city positions are not full-time or not compensated, and those who hold them must be otherwise employed. While engaging in conflicting employment is prohibited, this deals with the situation only after it occurs. Many public officials and employees are screened before assuming their post, and the appointing authority may be assured that their current employment provides no conflict of interest. The lack of clear and direct guidance on the undertaking of new employment can result in misunderstanding and inadvertent violation of the charter at the same time that it is legal for a person to offer a city official or employee a job that, if accepted, would result in a violation. Dealing with the problem more directly might be preferable.

In 1986 the state legislature added more postemployment restrictions to the charter for members of the Board of Estimate, officers and employees of the city who are appointed by the mayor and employed full-time, and officers and employees of the city who are employed in policy-making positions. None of these people may solicit, negotiate for, or accept employment from or contract services with any person while personally participating, directly concerned with, or actively considering any matter concerning that person on behalf of the city. The flaw in this language is that it could serve to prevent one city agency from hiring or contracting with a departing employee from another agency if the employee is personally participating in, directly concerned with, or actively considering any matter affecting that agency. This problem could be easily corrected by exempting city agencies from such restrictions.

Violation of these provisions constitutes cause for fine, suspension, or removal from office or employment; in addition, violation may, at the option of the comptroller, render the contract or transaction forfeit and void. Knowing and intentional violation of a provision of the section is a misdemeanor that, on conviction, leads to automatic forfeiture of office. In addition, a council member or other officer or employee who willfully violates or evades a provision of the law relating to his or her office or employment, or who commits a fraud upon the city, or who converts public property to his or her own use, allows another to do so, or through gross or culpable neglect of duty allows that to happen, will be deemed guilty of a misdemeanor. Additional penalties for a violation include forfeiture of office or employment and being forever barred from receiving or holding any office or employment under the city.

There are a number of problems with the penalties section. First, it is unclear how the law is to be enforced. If the Board of Ethics finds a violation or, more commonly, finds "reasonable cause" to believe that a violation has occurred, does it refer the matter to the prosecutor? Is this purely a prosecutorial function with no real role for the board or its findings? Where does the department of investigation fit in? There are no ethics commissions that have the power to find a criminal violation, much less impose penalties for it.

Additionally, the charter does not provide for civil penalties for violations. Many laws elsewhere provide for a commission or board to institute a civil action to collect penalties. In addition, boards or commissions that are also the filing agencies for financial disclosure forms are frequently empowered to impose administrative fines for failure to file and for late filing. Actions against those who refuse to file are, again, taken through the court system.

Disparate factors are involved in voiding contracts. Who is responsible for finding violations? Which is the appropriate authority to void a contract? The comptroller? The mayor? The Board of Ethics? The Law Department? Because of these uncertainties, voiding is not required but permitted. Assuming that a violation has occurred, the first consideration is clearly the interest of the public. Another factor is possible damage to innocent third parties. These are policy decisions rather than "ethics" decisions and suggest that a practical solution may be to place the power to void with the mayor or an executive agency that already deals with policy questions. An argument could also be made for conferring that power on the Law Department, which can ensure that appropriate language in the contracts will represent the city in litigation regarding such voiding.

Serious questions can be raised as to whether the penalties for knowing and intentional violation of section 2604 are adequate. It is unusual for someone convicted of a conflict of interest to be sentenced to jail. For an unspecified misdemeanor, the maximum fine is $1,000. The financial benefit from acting in a conflict of interest can be many times the $1,000 maximum fine. Thus there is only a limited deterrent. The penalties would be more effective if they guaranteed that fines would always exceed profits. Penalties for action that cannot be shown to be knowing or willful should at least enable the city to collect whatever financial damage it suffered as a result of the violation.

Finally, the financial disclosure provisions covering city elected officials, officers, and employees are contained in section 12–110 of the administrative code rather than in the city charter. Financial disclosure provisions are an essential element in the capability to enforce conflict of interest laws. Since one measure of the effectiveness of a conflict of interest law is its enforceability, the financial disclosure provisions should be designed so as to signal actual and possible conflicts of interest. The lack of enforcement provisions in the financial disclosure law means that, for all intents and purposes, this tool is not available for enforcement of the charter's conflict of interest provisions.

The New Charter Provisions

The preceding text was adapted from a paper written for the New York City Charter Revision Commission (CRC) to aid in its study of the conflict of interest provisions. New York voters approved the Charter Revision Commission's proposal for the revision of these provisions in the November 1988 election. The new provisions will go into effect on 1 January 1990. Many of the comments and criticisms of the current provisions were clearly taken into account in the design of the CRC proposal.

Under the new charter provisions, the Board of Ethics will be reconstituted as a three-member Conflicts of Interest Board, with appointments by the mayor with the advice and consent of the City Council; the mayor will designate the chair. The members may not hold public office, public employment, or political party office; in addition, they may not appear as lobbyists before the city. They will hold three-year overlapping terms (not to end until a successor has been appointed and qualified), receive per diem compensation, and, after written notice and opportunity to reply, can be removed for substantial neglect of duty, gross misconduct in office, inability to discharge the powers or duties of the office, or violation of the conflicts of interest section. The board may appoint counsel and employ staff; the counsel's authority is to be defined in writing and may not extend to issuing advisory opinions, promulgating rules, issuing subpoenas, issuing final determinations of violations, making final recommendations, or imposing penalties. The board may, however, delegate to the chairman the ability to issue advisory opinions. This particular delegation is unusual and probably ought to be approached with caution.

The board will meet monthly, promulgate rules, and adjust the threshold amounts for determining an "ownership interest" based on the Consumer Price Index every four years. It is responsible for providing initial and ongoing education and training about the conflict of interest provisions for city officials and employees; each incoming public servant will be required to file a statement with the board within ten days of beginning service that attests to having read the conflict of interest provisions and pledges to conform to them in the future. Advisory opinions issued by the board will be binding, and procedures for considering and reconsidering them are provided for. Publication of advisory opinions with deletions to protect privacy is also required.

The board will become the filing agency for all financial disclosure forms and will be responsible for examining them for compliance with the financial disclosure law and for possible violations of the conflict of interest provisions. This provision is particularly significant because it brings the institutional arrangements surrounding financial disclosure into compliance with the Ethics in Government Act of 1986. The Charter Revision Commission did not deal with the financial disclosure provisions in the administrative code. It is therefore up to the City Council to bring them into compliance with the equal or greater stringency requirement of the state law.

The board will be able to instruct the commissioner of investigation to conduct an investigation, and he or she is required to submit a confidential written report of factual findings to the board. The commissioner is also required to report on other investigations that may involve the conflict of interest provisions, whether or not such investigation was initiated by the board. While this provision does not give the board investigatory powers, it is a distinct improvement over the board's current authority to request an investigation and have results (but not necessarily factual findings) reported to it and gives the commissioner the prerogative not to inform the board about other investigations that involve its area of jurisdiction.

The Conflicts of Interest Board will receive complaints, decide whether there is probable cause to believe a violation has occurred, hold hearings regarding the possible violation, and determine whether a violation did occur. Violations are misdemeanors and carry a fine of up to $10,000, forfeiture of office or employment, the possibility of voidance of the action in violation of the law, and other disciplinary action. The ability of the board to find probable cause and to find a violation — particularly given that a violation is a misdemeanor — is troubling. Questions arise regarding due process, the standard of evidence, representation and procedures, and whether it is appropriate to have a nonjudicial body determining guilt or innocence in a criminal matter. These provisions could easily become a subject of litigation.

The Conflicts of Interest Board has the potential to be a significantly more effective enforcement body than the Board of Ethics. Much will depend on the initial appointees. While the charter requires appointment of a counsel, unlike most state laws it does not specifically provide for an executive director. This could be taken to mean that the board was intended to concern itself more with the formal legalistic aspects of the law (e.g., advisory opinions and review of complaints) than with the sound administration of it (e.g., checking financial disclosure forms for completeness and to ensure that there are no actual or potential conflicts of interest, continuing outreach and education efforts both in city government and to the public, ensuring that appropriate information is readily accessible to the public). With this ambiguous tone in the charter language, the first board will likely set the pattern for the board's future.

This pattern will also be influenced by the budget allocation for the board's operation. This is a stringent law — sufficiently so to raise serious questions about the city's ability to recruit and retain high quality personnel in the future. But to make the law work, enforcement must be active and rigorous. In other words, the probability of detection of violations must be high enough to make compliance prudent and desirable. The very severity of the law, which includes some lifetime prohibitions, is likely to make serious enforcement complicated, extensive, and expensive. Inadequate funding could reduce enforcement to responding to complaints rather than ongoing monitoring and random checks. Were this to occur, the probability of detection of violations could drop far enough to make compliance more optional than mandatory.

The addition of some much-needed definitions to the conflicts of interest chapter adds substantial clarity. At the same time a number of important terms that are not defined provide ample opportunity for the Conflicts of Interest Board to exercise its rule-making power. It is unclear whether the county district attorneys are covered under these provisions.

In sum, this complicated law will not be readily understood by many of those subject to it. It will therefore be necessary for the board immediately to produce superior educational and training materials, to be updated regularly as rules and advisory opinions change the shape of the law. Unless such materials are developed, the statement to be signed about having read and being committed to the conflict of interest provisions may be literally true but for many could not be taken to indicate a clear understanding of what has been read.

As under the current provisions, public servants are required to disclose publicly in the official record of the legislative body the nature of any interest in proposed legislation if they attempt to influence its course.

The new provisions prohibit any public servant (broadly defined and excluding only unpaid members of advisory committees) from having an interest in a firm if he or she knows it is engaged in business dealings with his agency. An interest in a firm includes any position with that firm as well as an "ownership interest" held by the public servant, his or her spouse, or an unemancipated child that exceeds $25,000 (in cash or other commitment) or 5 percent of the firm (whichever is less) or the same amounts with regard to its total indebtedness or any lesser interest when the public servant, spouse, or unemancipated child exercises managerial control of or responsibility for the firm. Pension plans, deferred compensation plans, mutual funds, and blind trusts are excluded. The lack of any definition of *managerial control* or *responsibility* raises questions about where the line is to be drawn. If the spouse of a public servant is a partner with Price Waterhouse, for example, does that mean that there is a conflict of interest if Price Waterhouse has a contract with the agency — or only if the spouse is a managing partner?

In addition, public servants who hold a prohibited "ownership interest" before becoming subject to these charter provisions, who did not know of a business dealing that would cause such an interest to be prohibited, or who has the interest and enters into a business dealing that causes it to be prohibited, must either divest the interest or disclose to the board and comply with its order. The board may order whatever action (including divestiture) it deems necessary to mitigate a conflict of interest; it shall, however, take into account the financial burden of any decision on the public servant. The matter of forced divestiture is a troubling one, and it is unusual to find conflict of interest provisions that give a board the authority to order it; the more usual route is to provide for methods by which the public servant may disqualify himself or herself from participation or action when such a conflict exists. The way in which the Conflicts of Interest Board handles the matter of forced divestiture could materially affect the ability of New York City to recruit and retain quality personnel. An error could have a severe effect, causing talented personnel to leave and making it difficult to fill vital positions; this could inflict near-fatal damage to the credibility of the conflict of interest provisions.

In addition, the interpretation of when a person exercises managerial control or responsibility regarding the firm and when that will result in a judgment that a prohibited interest exists will be important, as will be the solutions the board will find to resolve such a situation. The matter of how to handle the problems of two-career families is one that faces all such commissions around the country — without any general consensus on the best way to approach the matter. It is unlikely that forced divestiture of a spouse or a requirement that a spouse find another line of work would be considered acceptable options. The term *agency* as used in this section is broadly defined for high-level officials.

Public servants who have an acceptable interest in a firm may not take any action affecting it with three exceptions: (1) elected officials may take action but must disclose the interest to the board and on the record of the City Council or Board of Estimate if it involves those bodies; (2) appointed community board members may take action except that they may not vote on any issue that might result in a personal and direct economic gain to the member or any person with whom the member is associated; and (3) if the interest is less than $10,000, such action is not prohibited but the conflict must be reported to the board.

Public servants are prohibited from engaging in any business transaction or private employment or having any financial or other private interest (direct or indirect) in conflict with the proper discharge of official duties. They may not use or attempt to use their official position for financial gain or for a number of other benefits or privileges for themselves or any person with whom they are associated. A public servant is prohibited from disclosing confidential information obtained through official duties or from using such information for personal benefit or gain for himself or another; this ban continues even after leaving public service and thus may be unenforceable. The acceptance of valuable gifts (as defined by the board) is prohibited, although officials are specifically permitted to accept gifts when customary on family and social occasions. Public servants may not represent clients against the interests of the city, but provision is made for the possibility that elected officials and the executive branch may be on different sides of some litigation; this ban does not apply to those situations. Similarly, public servants are prohibited from acting as paid experts against city interests in civil litigation.

The new provisions substantially change the postemployment restrictions. Public servants may not appear before their former agency for one year; *appear* is defined as communication for compensation. Elected officials and other specified appointed officials are prohibited for one year from such appearances before any agency in the branch in which they serve. No former public servant may appear, whether for compensation or not, before the city in relation to any matter involving the same party or parties with respect to a particular matter in which the former public servant had participated personally and substantially during his period of public service. There is no termination date to this prohibition. Public servants are still prohibited from soliciting, negotiating for, or accepting positions prohibited under the postemployment restrictions.

An exception to all these prohibitions is made for positions with or representation on behalf of any local, state, or federal agency. Similarly, a former public servant is not prohibited from association with a firm that appears before a city agency or from acting in a ministerial matter regarding business dealings with the city. As in the current charter, an additional exception to the prohibitions is provided when the acceptance of a prohibited position would not be in conflict with the purposes and interests of the city if such an action is approved in writing by the Conflicts of Interest Board after approval by the head of the agency or agencies involved.

Finally, an interesting new provision prohibits a public servant from entering into a business or financial relationship with another public servant who is his or her superior or subordinate. While this prohibition is clearly aimed at instances when a public servant might use his position to persuade a direct subordinate to lend him money or enter into some kind of business enterprise, it also appears to prohibit marriage, which is also a financial relationship. The lack of definition of how direct a superior or subordinate relationship must be to be prohibited could raise some interesting questions. It is likely that the Conflicts of Interest Board will need to provide additional guidance.

Conclusion

The new conflict of interest provisions of the city charter provide some significant improvements over the old ones. The new Conflicts of Interest Board has been given both power and responsibility for enforcing the law, educating public servants about their responsibilities under it, and providing further guidance and definition through advisory opinions and regulations in areas where the charter is ambiguous or unclear. This grant of power would clearly allow the board to have a far greater impact on the conduct of public servants and the awareness of the ethical standards expected of them than it was possible for the Board of Ethics to have. The provisions that empower the board to find probable cause that a violation has occurred and then decide whether it did occur are a matter of considerable concern, particularly since a violation is a misdemeanor and carries additional penalties involving the person's ability to hold public office or employment. It will probably be necessary for the commission to look outside the field of government ethics for guidance in adopting procedures that will properly protect the rights of the accused.

The new provisions with regard to financial interests and prohibited dealings with the city are more restrictive than those they will replace and, on their face, almost as ambiguous. While the rule-making powers of the Conflicts of Interest Board should be able to alleviate the ambiguity, the degree to which unnecessary restrictions may be made on the activities of public servants raises concerns about the ability of the city to attract and retain high-quality public servants. This problem could be exacerbated by frequent use of forced divestment to solve conflict of interest situations rather than providing for methods of recusal from conflicting situations.

As of 15 May 1989, there were no answers to the most important of the questions. The names of those chosen to serve on the Conflicts of Interest Board had not been sent to the City Council for confirmation. The actions of the first board and the tone of its work will materially affect the success or failure of the law. Too much rigidity, particularly in dealing with situations where conflicts of interest are unexpected and unintentional, could make it difficult to attract quality personnel. Were this to happen, the resulting pressure to amend the charter could result in such weakening of the conflict of interest provisions that it could render them ineffective. On the other hand, too much leniency and flexibility could make the law meaningless and simply add to public cynicism about government integrity. The task will be complicated by the problems of dealing with two-career households, which the cost of living in New York City makes a virtual necessity for most families.

There is also the question of what will happen with the financial disclosure provisions. The state Ethics in Government Act requires that the city's provisions be of equal or greater stringency than the state requirements. If the city fails to adopt provisions of sufficient stringency, it will be required to use the state form. However, the state requirements as reflected in the state form are unduly complicated, unwieldy, and intrusive. They are not well designed as an enforcement tool, and such things as a desk audit for superficial completeness and to detect actual or potential conflicts of interest will be time consuming and labor intensive. A full audit will be even more so. And yet both the desk audit and the full audit are important tools in ensuring compliance with the financial disclosure provisions; in turn the financial disclosures are important tools in enforcing the conflict of interest law. It is still unclear how much money will be necessary to administer the conflict of interest provisions and how much will be available, given the budget deficits at the federal, state, and local levels and the ever-increasing needs in the areas of health, social services, and criminal justice.

The new charter provisions were approved by the electorate with the clear expectation that they would materially improve the ethical atmosphere in government and somehow put an end to many of the problems of corruption. They have great potential for encouraging ethical conduct on the part of public servants and for making it easier for them to understand what is expected of them. There are areas of potential difficulty in the administration of the provisions, but many of those pitfalls can be avoided. Whether they can weather the almost inevitable disappointment that will come when it is clear that they are no panacea and deal with only a small part of the problem of corruption is a question that can only be answered with hindsight.

Toward Fairness and Openness in City Administrative Procedures

RICHARD A. GIVENS

On 8 November 1988, the voters of New York City enacted a new Chapter 45 of the New York City charter, creating an innovative City Adminstrative Procedure Act (CAPA). The question had been submitted by the Charter Revision Commission. By placing this initiative before the voters, who approved it by an almost four-to-one margin, New York City gave the CAPA a magisterial dignity that is difficult for city agencies to ignore; its electoral success could gain nationwide attention.

The CAPA makes several landmark changes that should improve the city's administrative operations in ways that may be relevant in other metropolitan areas. One impetus for its development was a pattern of city agencies' adopting what amounted to binding rules without public notice. Another was the existence in many agencies of unfair combinations of prosecutorial and judicial functions. At the same time, the Charter Revision Commission was interested in establishing standards of fairness and effectiveness in city administration appropriate for the twenty-first century. A third source of some of the innovations was a series of recommendations by the New York State Bar Association's Task Force on Simplification of the Law, which included suggestions for simplification at the municipal level.

The Right to Know What Regulations Must Be Obeyed

The single most salient change adopted by CAPA may be its recommendation (also made by the task force) that city regulations purporting to be binding on outside parties must be published in a single place, indexed by subject, and kept up to date. Otherwise, such laws would be unenforceable. The objective is to create a compilation comparable to the Code of Federal Regulations (CFR) at the city level. A former provision of the charter already required publication of such a compilation, but it had never been consistently carried out.

Such a directive is of crucial importance to those who must comply with municipal regulations throughout the country. The provision seeks to end the predicament of a party who acts as properly as possible, only to be faced by an obscure regulation, such as Local Ordinance No. 4,017, contained in the City Record of 7 December 1931, which provides a penalty of $1,000 with compound interest for each day that Form 5.4(C)(ii) has not been on file.

The requirement of notice is so basic, of course, that courts would be justified in holding a regulation unenforceable even without a specific provision, unless some reasonable form of notice — industry publications, press, or textbook coverage — exists, even if such coverage is not an officially indexed publication. Some agency personnel claimed that indexing all their regulations was impossible. Large numbers of regulations were so difficult to find that the agencies themselves were unsure how many existed or what they covered. In recognition of this problem, the charter allows a reasonable period for agencies to publish regulations as well as a procedure for reviving old ones not found at first — but only after they are properly published.

In this case, as in other municipal legislation, the public generally got what it demanded. A bureaucracy will grow lax, inefficient, and unfair, if citizens and municipal leaders allow it. But an event such as New York City voters' enactment of CAPA may encourage similar action in other cities by proving that reform is possible in such situations.

In providing for a compilation, CAPA does not seek to emulate the Internal Revenue Code by dealing with minute details of procedure, which the legal historian Karl Llewellyn predicted would end in a multivolume encyclopedia "or plain exhaustion."[1] Instead, CAPA omits many of the provisions of federal and some state administrative procedures, which the commission may have thought amounted to "overregulating the regulators."[2]

One reason for this choice was to avoid forcing voters to choose between due process and, say, better trash collection or police protection. Another reason was that many commissioners thought that the detailed regulation of regulation could be counterproductive and could produce more paperwork, cost, error, and delay. Extreme skepticism may be justified concerning quantitative analyses that require or rely on unavailable or questionable underlying data. For instance, disadvantaged people tend to complain the least; quantitative information will therefore understate their problems. The cost of getting quantitative estimates to show that an action is cost-effective may itself prevent a necessary action from being cost-effective.

For these and other reasons, CAPA includes none of the following: sunset provisions, often the basis for adding to regulations rather than eliminating them; formal cost-benefit or impact analyses; paperwork-reduction reports, which create more paperwork; formal regulatory flexibility analyses; on-the-record rule making; legislative vetoes; and executive or budget office reviews of agency rules. Instead, the crucial changes made by CAPA aim at openness and fairness to the citizen.

Rule Making

New York City agencies can no longer announce policies binding on the private sector — profit or not-for-profit — without publishing a proposed rule and seeking public comment. This provision makes general the principle applied in *Association of Messenger Services* v. *City of New York*, which overturned a ban on bicycles in some parts of the city that had been enacted without prior notice. Narrow exceptions to this legislation exempt purely internal regulations, temporary emergency rules, and some traffic rules.

A regulatory agenda must be prepared by New York City rule-making agencies informing the public of expected rule changes, taking into account overlapping state and federal requirements. The goal is not to ban municipal rules covering subjects dealt with at higher levels of government but to make sure that they are necessary and that compliance requirements are appropriately consistent. Where workable, this procedure would permit municipal authorities to enforce existing requirements if state or federal resources are inadequate but without adding to the burden on those who must comply. In some instances, state-federal-local coordinating committees have been useful in developing common strategies and cross-designations of personnel to act for other agencies as well as their own.

Furthermore, every rule shall be simply written, using ordinary language where possible. This requirement ensures that city rules are comprehensible to those who must comply; it permits technical terms only where necessary. As mentioned, all rules must be published in a compilation indexed by subject to be enforceable.

Additionally, Statements of Basis and Purpose must be issued and submitted to the New York City Council for its information for all but temporary emergency rules. The Statement of Basis and Purpose, similar to that used in federal practice, will provide the public with an explanation of the objectives of a rule and aid in its interpretation, as well as in the formulation of public comments. Prior notification to the council allows it to act as it sees fit — but neither permits a legislative veto of a rule except through ordinary legislation nor requires legislative approval of rules.

Adjudication

The adjudication provisions of CAPA were written against a background of profound skepticism about the fairness of permitting the same agency both to initiate and to judge the same cases. Such an action creates a combination of prosecutor and judge reminiscent of fabled instances of "command influence" in court martials. For this reason, CAPA created a cadre of hearing officers not tied to any particular agency, who are supervised by a separate Office of Administrative Trials and Hearings (OATH).

Other procedural safeguards were also established. First, uniform standards were established where current law requires a hearing on the record. For the first time, overall requirements beyond those of the state and federal constitutions have been established for city administrative adjudication when a hearing on the record is required by constitutional interpretations, statutes, or rules. As pointed out in the commission's section-by-section analysis, agency practice as well as written authority is relevant to whether such a requirement exists.

Second, agency hearing officers must be assigned solely to adjudicative duties. To promote impartiality, agency hearing officers can no longer be assigned to other duties. They will issue recommended decisions, which must be provided to all parties unless a statute or agency rule allows them to make final decisions.

Third, ex parte communications, including internal agency directives not published as rules that may relate to the merits of a case, are banned. Thus, agencies' issuance of internal staff guidelines or legal opinions, not formally adopted as rules under CAPA procedures but furnished to agency adjudicators or hearing officers without being available to private parties, is prohibited. It will no longer be acceptable to inform a party that a separate Freedom of Information request must be filed to obtain such ex parte communications, which even then may or may not be made available.

Finally, recommendations as well as final decisions must be furnished to all parties. Some agencies' former practice of treating hearing officers' reports as confidential internal documents, furnished only to the agency that makes the final decision — arguably violating due process — is now specifically prohibited.

Further Challenges

CAPA represents great progress for New York City and possibly for other political subdivisions that may adapt parts of it to their needs. But it leaves many problems unaddressed. For example, there remains the deeper question of whether administrative adjudication can ever be entirely fair. When agencies judge their own cases, the suspicion of partial rulings may never be entirely extirpated. Administrative adjudication, at least in the first instance, is undeniably essential to large-scale grant programs and initial tax administration. But for cases in which the government acts in a sovereign, coercive capacity, perhaps only the neutral judicial resolution of disputes can provide impartiality. Thus the Task Force on Simplification of the Law recommended that administrative adjudication be phased out to the fullest extent possible.

At the least, full judicial review might be provided — and indeed deemed required by due process — in such instances. But the combination of agency adjudication and judicial review may take more rather than less time in some instances as compared with judicial action alone (if court procedures can be speeded up). The task force also made recommendations in the field of judicial review.[3]

Another question that must be addressed is how the public sector can act more efficiently, fairly, and effectively with the available resources. If a job cannot be done effectively, the details of procedural safeguards become relatively unimportant. CAPA or similar codes of fair procedure can provide the skeletal structure, but only citizen commitment and creative leadership can ensure results.

This means, above all, focusing on the true goals and objectives. Only then can means be developed to further the goals defined, but care must be constantly taken that the means not be converted into ends. Unfortunately, this common trend often results in means becoming counterproductive and defeating the theoretical goal they were designed to serve.

Requiring agencies to define their priority objectives is but one method to prevent this outcome. The true key to dealing with the problem is understanding the inherent tendencies of bureaucracy and how they can be counteracted — issues surfacing during the great emergencies that confront nations, municipalities, and other organizations. Without this, the inevitably necessary management of appearances tends to replace rather than assist emphasis on real results. Nickle-and-dime enforcement emphasizing statistics replaces a focus on important cases — as when a broken light bulb in an apartment hallway and a leaking roof causing rotten floorboards are treated identically and each leads to a routine $50 fine.

Bureaucratic structures may be only what one makes of them, but they can focus attention on the need to deal with challenges. The task force recommended several changes in its Interim Report number 1, "Internal Bureaucratic Structure of Agencies" (1986) and elsewhere.

First, it recommended encouraging anonymous reports of inefficiency as well as impropriety. Those inside an agency often know of counterproductive bureaucratic waste that can readily be justified to outsiders. Those likely to understand such inefficiency also appreciate that in many organizations, speaking up in a way that threatens some co-workers means future conflicts that will block their careers. To overcome this problem, the task force recommended that all audits and program reviews include anonymous interviews with working-level employees and middle managers. These interviews would deal with bureaucratic error, delay, and expense rather than mere impropriety. Obviously, such reports may be malicious, unfounded, or simply wrong, and hence should be neither credited nor acted on unless independently corroborated after all affected were able to provide information on the subject.

The second recommendation was for charts of all steps routinely involved in performing an agency's important duties. Most organization charts reflect structure from the top down. A different kind would document each step at which the most important functions of the agency are performed. Such a view can be used to focus on and eliminate excessive bureaucratic paperwork and layers of review. The key to the usefulness of such a chart would be that it describes the bureaucratic process at the level of each individual point at which a record would be created. For example, approval by the commissioner of a teenager's application for a work permit might in some agencies involve preliminary review of file and approval by clerk as to form of papers, approval by supervisor, recommendation for commissioner's action by assistant to the commissioner, signature by the commissioner, logging of file, forwarding of file to mailing division, and record of mailing to applicant.

The task force's third recommendation was for protection of whistle-blowers who report inefficiency as well as impropriety. Employees who report bureaucratic inefficiency could be protected from adverse action as well as those who report impropriety — even when not done anonymously. But merely being a whistle-blower need never protect an employee from adverse action that would have been justified anyway. It should be made clear that whistle-blower protection does not create any legitimate expectations justifying damage suits but authorizes equitable relief, such as reinstatement of the employee solely for the benefit of the public.

The fourth recommendation by the task force called for the cross-designation of personnel. During the price-control emergencies of World War II and the 1970s, local personnel were often cross-designated as federal price-control inspectors. This practice occurs locally in other contexts as well and can be used more widely to reduce costs and increase effectiveness.

The fifth recommendation was for coordinating committees involving multiple agencies at multiple levels of government. Coordinating committees representing agencies concerned with similar problems at all levels of government, including regional offices of federal agencies, have often been effective in developing joint law enforcement, legislation, and other initiatives to increase the effectiveness of governmental efforts.

The task forces's sixth recommendation was to assure employees that increases in productivity will lead to their redeployment in more crucial tasks without loss of compensation or benefits. Such a promise is crucial to securing enthusiastic support rather than resistance to steps that would increase efficiency.

The seventh recommendation was for a deliberate policy of decentralization of decisions properly capable of delegation. As documented by C.N. Parkinson, organizations tend to gather individual decisions at the top and to add bureaucratic layers of review.[4] This restricts communication in the organization and prevents central managers from reviewing crucial choices, planning ahead, or effectively monitoring the organization as a whole. The result is, of course, increased delay, error, and expense. This problem is usually successfully attributed to inadequate rather than excessive formal internal bureaucratic controls. Bureaucracies are most effective when seeking to protect their own turf — for example, by convincing outside reviewers that what is needed is more central control, management information systems, statistical reports, policy planning divorced from the carrying on of the activity to be planned, signatures reflecting approval by multiple levels of review of every action, and so on.

These tendencies are successfully counteracted in small organizations or whenever there is sufficient external pressure for results, as in a prosecutor's office where courts dismiss cases for unnecessary delay or in successful wartime military or industrial organizations. If managers, auditors, reviewers, legislative-oversight staff, private securities analysts, and others can be brought to recognize the crucial importance of overcoming the gravitational tendency, it could be done.

The eighth recommendation of the task force called for a balance of rules and goals. The prevalence of what Justice Oliver Wendell Holmes once called "delusive exactness" seems to drive people to search for certainty through ever more elaborate rules — often disregarding the likelihood that such requirements will not be comprehended, much less obeyed. Greater use of common sense and establishment of goals rather than precise recipes for reaching the goals could be a powerful ingredient for making the public sector more effective. This concept can be enlivened by defining goals based on public comment and internal input from the bottom up as well as from the top down, followed by instructing all existing agencies to use their existing powers to promote those goals.

Finally, the task force called for leadership with enthusiasm. If the top managers of an organization are enthusiastic about reaching important and obviously worthwhile goals and can protect employees from the fear of losing jobs if they succeed, such leadership can be contagious. It can often serve as a substitute for the kind of stifling, detailed prescriptions as to how a job is done that never foresee the actual conditions under which the instructions must be carried out.

The army has been described as a machine designed by geniuses to be operated by idiots. This kind of thinking guarantees failure in both the armed forces and government enterprises; if people work in an atmosphere encouraging idiocy, they will perform as idiots. Fortunately, results can be changed by changing expectations.

To the extent that the United States reaches for its highest goals, the feeling of opportunity to contribute to something of historic importance will be felt throughout the public and private sectors. A lean, effective, and fair public sector at all levels of government that works with all other levels can do its part to promote these goals. This objective can be furthered by the proper skeletal structure, toward which CAPA represents one contribution. It can be furthered even more by setting proper goals and by focusing all possible effort on them with such means as the human resources waiting to be tapped in every organization.

Many other initiatives are possible, such as the elimination of duplicate forms required by multiple agencies and multiple levels of government. Authority for mayors, governors, and other higher officials to compel action over the inertia of agencies protecting bureaucratic turf may be necessary in such instances. The task force recommended a single income-tax form for filings at all levels of government, with payments allocated for state and local filings, as in New York State. Similarly, one-stop service is possible in many instances, permitting one lead agency to act for others — even at different levels of government — in providing routine approvals, for example.

Institutional Protection

CAPA seeks to enhance the opportunities of citizens to contribute to the functioning of the public sector and to secure fairness. But attention must also be devoted to protecting the institutions of the public sector itself. Particularly in a society with ever more powerful techniques for implementing actions, powerful institutions at both public and private levels are absolutely necessary and extraordinarily dangerous. American municipalities and states, as well as the federal government, large businesses, and many not-for-profit entities, are definitely in such a situation. The budgets of some United States cities exceed those of many nations.

The institutional sector must seek to deal fairly and responsibly with the ordinary citizen. But it also naturally needs protection itself. The dangers increase if an institution's survival or functioning are threatened, in which case the public will demand even harsher measures to ensure the continuation of the functions of the endangered institution. Thus, in addition to the fairness and effectiveness of municipal and state governments in performing their functions, the ability of institutions to defend themselves must be considered. One threat is the increasing numbers of lawsuits, which are dangerous to the purses of municipalities that cannot claim sovereign immunity. However contradictory the doctrine may be to the notion of a government of laws, sovereign immunity does serve to limit some, but far from all, kinds of raids on the deep pockets of governmental units possessing the power of taxation. Short of a total rethinking of how such matters should be handled, what can be done?

Whatever solution may be chosen, it must protect employees and officers as well as governmental entities from unwarranted fear of liability. Fear on the part of those who perform crucial duties is even more dangerous to the functioning of government than the mere monetary liability of the entity.

One limited measure that may sometimes be effective is to include in city charters and other enactments of all kinds standards that provide a proper, exclusive means of obtaining recompense for wrongs (presumably through a nonjury procedure). Further, where no monetary recompense for violations of a newly extended provision of some kind, such as one dealing with whistle-blower reinstatement, is intended, a provision may be devised such as "nothing in this [provision] shall create any legitimate expectation that its requirements will be fulfilled, create any property or liberty right or right to sue any entity, agency, or person, or be used to support any claim of any kind of damages for violation. The sole remedies for violation shall be limited to the validity or invalidity of action taken, rescission of transactions, reinstatement, or similar equitable relief."

Employees, contractors, or others doing business with the entity, who might seek any benefit in connection with a provision not intended to create damage remedies could similarly be asked to sign a waiver: "I agree that I cannot sue [the entity] or any employee or officer of it for money damages or legal fees under any source of law because of violations of [the provisions involved]. I recognize that I have no legitimate expectation that [provision] will be followed, since it was enacted to protect the public. I understand that my opportunity to seek whatever redress other than damages is available is granted for the public's protection and not as a matter of vested right. Thus I have no property or liberty right which can be protected by monetary redress for any violation of [charter or law involved]."

Such waivers should not, of course, be sought from claims for compensation, benefits, retirement pay, wages earned through work performed, rights under antidiscrimination provisions, or the like. The net effect of institutional protection should be greater citizen protection. The fear that protection of whistle-blowers from dismissal may mean multimillion dollar lawsuits by disgruntled employees, for example, will be minimized.

Dynamics of Change

Will these kinds of changes occur? The process will probably always be incomplete. However, some of these kinds of innovations must occur, and when they are successful they will give a comparative — and at times competitive — advantage. This relative edge will in turn encourage, induce, and sometimes force others to pick up the innovations that are effective.

This push toward greater effectiveness will be supplemented by citizen pressure for both fair and effective performance in the public sector. One of the most significant aspects of CAPA is that it was drafted not by ongoing governmental machinery but by a citizen Charter Revision Commission, none of whose members or staff then worked for the municipal government or were even on loan from it (although consultation with New York City agencies and the fund of experience of the members of the commission were so effective that the city administration urged voters to approve all five of the charter initiatives on the ballot 8 November 1988).

Wider public consultation may be one of the keys to many of the challenges confronting the United States at all levels. The preamble to the Constitution states th. t "We the People" created the document — suggesting that not merely public servants but all citizens can and must exercise leadership in developing approaches to ever-changing problems. If differing interest groups can agree on "non–zero sum" solutions creating gains for all instead of some, public servants will usually be delighted to compete for credit for implementing them.

With this benefit in mind, the Task Force on Simplification of the Law included laymen in its cadre and is working on its proposed "Introduction to Federalist Papers for the Twenty-First Century" with the hope that others will join them in seeking to formulate modern applications of the basic ideas of the original Federalist Papers — that each part of the overall structure must do its own part while allowing the other segments to do likewise. This seemingly obvious and simple yet powerful idea would mean decentralization within as well as between institutions, while compelling those at the top to do their part to create an environment in which all can succeed in their own tasks. It would mean closer supervision in the case of truly hazardous and long-term decisions that demand the highest level of attention. It would mean respecting the citizen's role in the process, thus providing the kind of fairness and openness that CAPA seeks to promote, while recognizing that much more remains to be accomplished.

NOTES

1. Karl Llewellyn, "Meet Negotiable Instruments," 44 *Columbia Law Review* (1944): 298, 322.
2. *New York Times*, 3 June 1981.
3. Task Force on Simplification of the Law, "Goals for Legal Simplification for the Twenty-First Century — Part One: Legal Procedures" (March 1988).
4. C. Northcote Parkinson, *Parkinson's Law and Other Studies in Administration* (New York: Ballantine, 1975).

Strategic Planning and Large-City Governance

ROBERT W. BAILEY

Most academic analysts who speculated over the governability of large American cities in the late 1960s and early 1970s concluded that the more heterogeneous a city became the more ungovernable it would be.[1] Indeed, there was a sense that large American cities, particularly New York City, were becoming dominated by an unruly alliance of interest groups, professional service providers, and mobilized clients, all operating in an environment where veto points within the policy process were proliferating uncontrollably. In this environment the "gatekeepers" were failing in their political responsibility to assess the integrity of policy demands, and small but earnest groups seeking large and expensive entitlements were not met with countervailing, "aggregative" political forces. In short, the local policy process was itself a significant source of America's urban crisis.

Today, the central concern is not "governability" but representation. The key question is how and to what degree essentially administrative enterprises can meet the constitutional, statutory, and court-applied test of fair and effective representation. In New York City the challenge is a direct legal one, since the Board of Estimate's apportionment was held unconstitutional by the United States Supreme Court on 22 March 1989. In other cities — such as Boston and San Francisco — concern over issues of representation are reflected in an ongoing debate over whether their city councils should be chosen by citywide elections, on a ward or community basis, or by some other form of apportionment. In Cleveland, Ohio, groups successfully reduced the size of the council, thereby increasing the representational basis of each councilmanic district. And yet this new crisis, one of "representation" and institutional structure, is also a crisis in governability — a sense among the governed that community and legitimacy exist in their city.

This essay deals with the issues of governance and representation as they pertain to public-sector strategic planning on the local level, particularly in New York City. It proceeds with an understanding of two critical issues. First, strategic planning is essentially a management approach — or style — derived from private-sector organizations. As such, its applicability to public-sector management is problematic and exciting. Second, since local government is essentially a service organization that gives rise to conflict on issues of hierarchical control within a city government and the separation of powers at the top political level of government, debates over institutional change are ultimately arguments over the relationship between executive and legislative authorizations.

It is not a contrivance to link the issues of governance, representation, and planning in discussing the use of strategic planning by large American cities. Indeed, in Europe and Japan this relationship attracts sophisticated political discourse. As many American cities and states introduce strategic plans for economic and social development, the linkage of these issues has become increasingly important. In Indianapolis, New York City, and the state of Delaware, for example, various modifications of corporate strategic planning approaches have been applied in public-sector settings. And these changes have in turn created new issues. How do policymakers — in the broad sense — relate information generated by economists and analysts to the needs of their jurisdictions? How do policymakers, ever seeking new subsidies for potential or contemporary investors, balance the marginal incentives of the market with the social needs of residents? How does a political system seeking "growth" find the resources to deal with the negative effects of such growth? At a minimum, strategic planning provides a framework within which these issues can be discussed.

Aspects of Strategic Planning

Commentators have generally identified six basic steps in the strategic-planning process. While all do not agree on the relative importance of the steps, the order in which they should come, or their complete adaptability to the public sector, there is a consensus on the questions that should be asked at each stage.

The first step is to set the goals of the organization. Obviously, in private-sector management this task is easier than it is in the public sector. Making a profit is the primary, unifying goal of business management. Despite both analytical and judgmental differences in assessing the calculus of profitability, this common denominator greatly aids the private-sector strategic planner. In corporate management, a unifying base value means that strategic debate revolves around a second set of issues: issues of product history, corporate image, long-term versus short-term investment, capital inventory, new products versus old, and so on. The planner first asks how changes in the larger environment will affect each of these variables and then chooses the organizational goals in order to adapt to change.

Public-sector policy making lacks a unifying criterion in goal setting like profitability in the corporate sector. Indeed, the absence of such a definitive goal focuses the debate on other criteria — such as power, votes, press attention, policy analysis, and cost-benefit analysis. For middle management the absence of a unifying criterion creates problems. With no internal pricing system, even senior managers often have difficulty choosing among competing goals. Setting such goals in a diverse political environment is one of the critical aspects of strategic planning for policymakers and public managers alike and is closely related to the issue of representation.

The second stage is to scan the environment. The planner, policy analyst, economist, and demographer — public and private alike — join to predict the trends and changes that are important to a wide variety of organizations. The public-sector planner will be concerned with such factors as changes in population groups and developments in sectors and subsectors of the economy. Planning concerns range from the impact of changes in international trade to the availability of water, power, and natural resources.

Although this part of the process might seem to be the least problematic of the six stages of planning, it has at least two vulnerable aspects. First, the political agenda underlying data collection substantially limits planning. The explicit needs of the business community help the forecaster to collect data that answer questions typical of business planning. The lack of unifying values allows the public planner to choose the questions to be answered or to be influenced by political factors. For all its benefits, public-sector strategic planning may elevate "nondecision making" to its most explicit level. Second, there are technical issues of data collection and forecasting. Public-sector strategic planners, like their counterparts in the private sector, depend on the data-collection systems of third parties: federal and state agencies, the regional Federal Reserve Banks, the Bureau of the Census, or private consultants who rely on econometric models. These third parties collect data at varying levels of sophistication for their own purposes, not specifically to meet the planner's needs. With scarce data-collection resources of his or her own, the public-sector planner will be tempted to use surrogate variables to meet planning needs, and each decision to do so introduces uncertainties.

The third stage is an internal assessment of the assets of the organization. Assets in the private sector include the physical plant, inventory, the quality of human resources, brand-name recognition and loyalty, and cash assets. For the public-sector planner, many of these dimensions may seem irrelevant. And yet the quality of human resources is often the most underestimated potential source of productivity enhancement in government, and public planners usually ignore the public analogue to product loyalty — a sense of political legitimacy.

The fourth stage is to adapt the organization's structure to the plan itself. A standard issue in public management — indeed in all organizational theory — is the degree to which structure conditions policy or to which policy dictates structure. In fact, the two have a symbiotic relationship. On a scale of organizational malleability, business institutions have more structural mutability than do public-sector organizations. Urban government can be subjected to some institutional alterations, but because change can distort established or traditional political relationships it is difficult to alter the local institutional setting on a regular basis.

The diversification of corporations in the 1960s and 1970s indicates the degree to which strategic planning influenced corporate arrangements. In the public sector, issues of decentralization and accountability frequently arise, as do the differences in financial structure and policy options between general-purpose local governments and public authorities. But the analogy between corporate organizations and local government quickly breaks down. As an administrative unit, local government should be able to change its structure so that it can take advantage of a changing environment. As a representative organization, however, it is also required to have channels that check executive and bureaucratic abuses of power. But in a politicized bureaucracy political and bureaucratic careers are often buttressed by established and familiar situations; the clientele relationships sustaining those situations thus create further barriers to change.

The fifth stage is implementation. William Anthony, in his analysis of strategic planning for line managers, identified five steps in making operative a strategic plan and planning process: developing operational objectives, specifying "action steps," scheduling action steps, integrating the strategic plan with line budgets, and creating goals and standards that can be linked to the organization's management information systems.[2] Each of these steps can be directly applied to public-sector planning.

The most difficult political issue in implementing a public strategy concerns the degree to which the planners wish to influence private actors. Implementation cannot be reduced to operational guidelines but becomes a political process. To what degree does the local government use its potential incentives to influence private decision makers? (Indeed, to what degree do local governments have incentives to influence private actors?) When either direct public expenditure or indirect tax expenditures will be used to create incentives indicated by the plan, implementation becomes political.

The sixth stage is feedback, the reflection and assessment of the plan's impact on the environment and potential modification of the plan. Since a strategic plan should be broadly written, its full impact must be assessed in broad terms — almost a societal audit. What is its effect — if any — on economic trends, morbidity and mortality, and the movement of people? If the plan's goals are not being met, how should it be changed to meet them?

These six stages largely define the process of strategic planning but do not exhaust all its aspects. They simply represent a near consensus among those who engage in such planning and write about it.

Coercive, Indicative, and Informational Planning

The division of executive and legislative powers characteristic of large-scale government in the United States almost requires a peculiarly American strategic-planning process. Although applying private-sector strategic planning to public-sector activities will provide some of the benefits available to private management, there must be limits. The very nature of the United States political system requires that any type of economic or social planning be open at both the formulation stage and the implementation stage.

The comparative question between public and private planning centers on the degree to which the plan is to be coercive, indicative, or informational. These questions, in turn, tend to depend on the linkage between the strategic-planning process, the capital plan, and the budgetary process. In the private sector, strategic planning can be immediately implemented by senior executives and stockholders' trustees — marshaling withheld earnings, credit capacity, or other resources to implement the plan. But in the public sector there is a disposition against such a direct link of the annual operating and capital budgets to a strategic plan, if only because many would perceive such a procedure as undemocratic.

It should first be stated what a strategic plan in the public would not be. Coercive plans, allowing the public sector to direct the investment decisions of the private sector, are clearly unacceptable. Not only would such plans be contrary to the American civic culture but also to the legal authorizations of local government. Even if such issues could be resolved, the very openness of the urban economy — what Norton Long called the "unwalled city"[3] — would foreclose any direction of private capital. Only a city-state like Singapore could approach such a planning system, and then incentives would help more than coercion.

An indicative planning process, as in France, might serve as a better model for United States urban strategic planning, but it also has limits. Public-sector indicative planning does not rest on sanctions as in a coercive plan, but on incentives to encourage private investment in areas that government finds beneficial to the polity as a whole. Access to capital at lower than market rates, infrastructure investment, tax expenditures, and subsidized research and development — all combined with the capital planning process of state-owned enterprises — are some of the characteristic policy instruments in an indicative planning process. At the core of this process is the willingness of government to dedicate at least some slack resources to implement the plan.

Providing such incentives is common in the United States. The federal government through its tax codes indirectly influences capital flows; and on the state and local levels infrastructure investment, industrial-development authorities, and other instruments similarly attempt to create an environment conducive to business investment. Examples are now legion. California, to take one case, has created its own pool of research funds to spur high-growth enterprises. New York State, to cite another, has attempted to assist in the development of high technology "seed" enterprises. What separates all these programs from the indicative planning processes common in Europe is their disparate nature. The United States provides subsidies without planning.

Since a coercive planning process at the local level would be unacceptable to most Americans and impractical to the legal and planning communities and since only some aspects of an indicative planning process are feasible, the most promising public-sector strategic planning is an informational plan. In a shifting political environment, strategic planning can focus the attention of changing political leaders onto continuing issues relevant to economic and social development. In addition, it can provide information to groups whose policy preferences may differ from those of the executive or legislative leadership. Thus a strategic plan does not dictate policy but organizes the policy process, pointing to the options available, but leaving to elected political leaders the choice they are to follow. Deciding between trade-offs is a political responsibility. Understanding that trade-offs exist is the responsibility of the planning process.

Strategic Planning and Urban Governance

How would such an informational and indicative planning process work for a large American city? Two perspectives suggest themselves. First, there is the "city" in its narrow, legal sense: the various legislative, executive, and subsidiary agencies and semiautonomous organizations that are directly part of any city's public sector — in short, the municipal corporation. A plan according to this perspective would integrate a city and its public enterprises' policy and social goals with their financial plans, capital plans, cash-flow plans, credit potential, and executive budget. Though not a coercive plan because of its scope, surely this could be an indicative plan to the degree that urban government could generate slack resources or persuade the public authorities outside its direct control to participate in the planning process.

Second, the city is an integrated political economy, physical environment, and political body in which public and private organizations operate in an interdependent social environment — in short, a socioeconomic region. The manner in which strategic planning can be applied to any city's public sector largely rests on which of these two perspectives one adopts.

Taking these perspectives into account, it is clear that strategic planning as an indicative plan can be applied — in a limited way — to the overall management of a city's public sector. Many state and local agencies have intraagency and interagency planning mechanisms that resemble strategic planning systems. In New York City this effort goes back at least to the administration of John V. Lindsay, when modified notions of cost-benefit analysis were introduced by Rand Corporation consultants. The city's 1975 financial crisis led to the institutionalization of many managerial reforms, including Edward I. Koch's establishment of the mayor's Office of Operations to perform interagency planning and coordination functions.

But can strategic planning be applied to a city as a whole? Can some formal or informal public instrument be established to coordinate all the intended and unintended policy impacts of public activity on private activity so as to spur social and economic development? This is a more subtle and complex question, and it generates issues of practicality and democratic legitimacy.

A strategic plan for urban government must consider both an indicative and an informational perspective — for the city as a municipal corporation and for the city as a regional economy. Each perspective will condition different characteristics of a plan and the planning process. Thus, a strategic plan for cities, at its best, would be the synthesis of an indicative plan within city government and an informational plan for the region as a whole.

Several benefits of this kind of "synthesis planning process" can be identified: enhanced coordination of capital planning; integration of capital planning, financial planning, and budgeting; overcoming "particularistic interests"; assessment of unintended policy consequences; generating a potential solution to the ongoing conflict between community and regional planning; establishing an independent source of information for business groups; and creating a channel for policy feedback.

Enhanced coordination of capital planning. Capital planning in many cities is now divided. Part of the process is accomplished traditionally by local government; but, increasingly, capital-planning decisions are made by public authorities and public-benefit corporations. In the 1960s the burden of public-sector capital investment in New York City, for example, was financed by general-obligation bonds issued by the city's municipal corporation, overseen by the City Planning Commission, with the Board of Estimate serving as the central political authority in decision making. Today, in contrast, much of the capital investment in New York City is by public authorities, e.g., the Port Authority of New York and New Jersey, the Metropolitan Transportation Authority, the New York State Urban Development Corporation, the new Municipal Water Finance Authority.

The current system has the advantage of overcoming the "pork barrel" capital planning process characteristic of the Board of Estimate when it dominated the annual capital-budget process and a school building in the Bronx, for example, could come only at the cost of a firehouse in Brooklyn. The intervention of public-benefit corporations and authorities allows for longer-term capital plans in different service areas. Nevertheless, the lack of formal and central capital planning undermines coordination among the different service areas, casts doubt on political accountability, and clouds the trade-offs inherent in limited credit potential. A strategic planning process should assist in focusing public-sector capital investment into higher-yield activities, systemizing the understanding of trade-offs in capital investment as the region stretches its ability to bear debt.

Integration of capital planning, financial planning, and budgeting into a strategic plan. For state and local governments on the scale of New York City, a strategic planning process would help to coordinate capital planning, financial planning, and annual budgeting as it does in the private sector. New York City is a $26 billion public corporation with numerous operating agencies and authorities. Regional authorities bring the public sector well over $30 billion a year in operating expenses. Integrating the city's budget and understanding the incidence of the city's taxing policy, the cost-benefit impacts of its operating agencies, the investment strategies of its public-benefit corporations, and the policy intents of all cross-subsidizations that occur in the financing of the city's service delivery agencies would contribute to a better comprehension of the overall impact of the city's activities on its economy and the quality of life of its inhabitants. Most states and many large cities could similarly benefit.

Overcoming "particularistic interests." The economic and social diversity of most large cities — especially New York City's — generates a panoply of interests and needs peculiar to different groups and neighborhoods. In New York City, Manhattan often focuses on finance and international business, while Brooklyn, the Bronx, and Queens see light manufacturing, regional service jobs, affordable housing, and community development as critical issues. One benefit of a strategic planning process might be to provide an additional avenue to overcome group and neighborhood conflicts in the city.

A strategic plan, both as a series of individual community strategic plans and as a citywide planning process, could help considerably toward overcoming what is now called the NIMBY (Not-In-My-Backyard) problem. In a sense, strategic planning runs counter to some of the worst political trends of the political process, without undermining any advantages. The political process has a short attention span and deals in discrete, incremental policy adjustments. Strategic planning provides a longer-term perspective that considers many additional factors.

Unintended policy consequences. A strategic plan would force policymakers to take into account the accumulated secondary impacts of policies. These unintended effects may undermine primary intentions or policy goals. The necessary reflection on long-term goals, on how to achieve them, and on trade-offs among various policy options forces policymakers to think about issues they might have ignored. As in a system of management by objectives or other goal-directed planning processes, public-sector strategic planning would force the executive branch, the legislature, budget directors, and directors of regional public-benefit corporations to consider the impact of policy suggestions on the long-term economic and social development of the region.

Community planning and strategic planning. Many community activists in New York City fear that a strategic-planning process might undermine the system of community boards or the present land-use process, called ULURP—the Uniform Land Use Review Procedure—both of which give neighborhoods some voice in influencing development policy. A coercive plan or even an exclusively indicative plan would be realistic grounds for such a fear.

Nevertheless, the most significant obstacle to effective community planning in New York or elsewhere in the country is the lack of objective information and professional analysts to interpret the available data. Strategic planning—as an informational plan—would allow local community groups to obtain the kind of independent data that would be useful in formulating neighborhood positions on citywide development plans. A strategic planning staff should monitor long-term demographic, social, economic, and even epidemiological trends. This information should inform the policy process, giving skeptical neighborhood groups a basis for more serious policy debate. As an informational plan, the strategic plan in a democratic environment must always be advisory in intent, presenting information to all, not directions from a few to the many.

Information for business groups. As an informational plan, a strategic plan would help all groups and organizations in a city to make wise strategic decisions of their own. The investment decisions of any large corporation will likely outlast the term of any council member or mayor. Forcing a city to articulate long-term goals, to make choices among competing social policies and development strategies, to consider environmental and natural-resource limits, to rationalize its borrowing patterns, and to understand the accumulated secondary impacts of its tax policies will help corporations to plan better on their own. A good strategic plan would indicate which sectors of the private economy a state or city should encourage while leaving others alone.

Policy feedback. Planning also has the advantage of allowing planners to examine why the plan as designed may not fulfill expectations. Plans are constructed. Whenever they fail to predict events or when suggested policies approved by the planning mechanism do not produce the intended results, this negative feedback forces all involved to reconsider the policies themselves, the data base on which the policy suggestions were made, or the planning process itself. As in economic modeling, failures in the strategic-planning models will lead to their improvement. Thus a strategic plan is also a planning process. Indeed, in some ways the actual plan is not as important as the process that formulates it.

Ultimately, the politics of strategic planning will reflect the civic culture in which it is adopted. In a city dominated by corporate elites, strategic planning will likely become an indicative plan focusing on downtown development and leaving the negative effects of growth to other political arenas. That has been the experience of Indianapolis. In a more open civic culture, strategic planning as an informational plan may actually benefit community groups, finally providing them with objective information on the impacts of economic and social policies.

A strategic plan is ultimately a discussion document. In developing and effecting it, executive and legislative branches may seek a consensus on how government might inform public and private decision makers of ongoing trends and how central-city authorities intend to deal with these forecasts. Thus, while the plan and the planning process may produce a particular set of goals for a city's economic, social, and environmental development, the political persuasiveness of the plan should determine its ultimate success. No plan that favored business or labor or a section of the city or any particular group could become a guide toward building consensus for citywide economic and social development. Instead, it would necessarily become a source of conflict.

The Institutional Setting for Strategic Planning: The New York City Example

The eventual institutional placement of a strategic planning process will necessarily have an impact on the primary characteristics of planning. The fundamental issue is the relationship between power, resources, and the planning process. Stress on the indicative aspects of strategic planning will emphasize power, administrative competence, and resource allocation. Stress on the informational aspects will emphasize analytical skills, the quality of data, political independence, and the communication of information to as wide an audience as possible.

Strategic planning and the executive. Perhaps the most obvious institutional locus for strategic planning is with a city's chief executive. In New York City, the strong-mayor–council form of government presents an executive with legal authorizations among the most powerful in the United States.[4] In these circumstances, placing a strategic-planning process within the executive has several advantages. First, the annual executive budget could easily be related to the strategic plan — and vice versa. Second, social and development incentives under executive control can be used to implement the plan, thus enhancing the "indicative" aspects of strategic planning. Finally, the executive staff of any mayor or governor usually far exceeds that of other public-sector actors; that is an obvious advantage of an executive-dominated planning process.

There are, however, drawbacks in a mayoral-dominated process. First, the strategic plan would be identified with a mayor's political agenda, which is obviously contentious, since it represents a particular coalition of constituencies supporting a particular mayor at a specific time. The basic concept of strategic planning — providing information to all groups in the city and identifying objective trends — might be colored, as the current mayor's Management Plan and Reporting System often is, by short-term political needs and past political commitments.

A second drawback is that the executive is tied to the daily policy crises of governing a large city. Inevitably, there will be pressure to draw long-term planners into fighting the daily fires facing an executive.

Strategic planning and the legislature. The second major possibility is to integrate strategic planning into the city's primary legislative process. The advantage here is that the legislature, apportioned on a district basis, might provide a more effective channel for the representation of community interests. Nevertheless, given the part-time nature of most city and county councils, their staff limitations, and the political constraints facing many members, a council — even New York City's — lacks the resources and political backing that a strategic planning process requires.

The current alliance of party leadership and councilmanic staff in New York would give the city a different kind of strategic plan, possibly turning what should be an independent planning process into a mechanism for institutional confrontation with the mayoralty. Indeed, with the legislature already disadvantaged vis-à-vis the executive, the danger that a planning staff would be diverted to short-term work would be even greater as budget, community, and borough interests arose.

Strategic planning and the Board of Estimate. This institutional option is unique to New York. The Board of Estimate, composed of borough and citywide elected officials, dominates the city's capital planning process, influences land-use control, and affirms all contractural relations between the city and any vendors. It has a special relationship with the City Planning Commission and the Bureau of Franchises. Having all these special powers — particularly in the capital planning process — the Board of Estimate is an obvious locus for a strategic planning process, which again would enhance the indicative aspects of a strategic plan. The board also has the advantage of better representing citywide interests than does the City Council.

Although the capital planning history of the board is often one of borough parochialism, it does offer an arena of citywide debate — even if the debate is often episodic and operates behind the scenes. The board does have executive functions within city government, but its history as an "administrative" unit has not been laudable. Recently, for example, as overseer of the city's franchise system, the Board of Estimate has been associated with corruption and slow decision making. And besides, the board is at the center of the current legal challenge to New York City's system of representation, making it uncertain whether in the future it could serve as any focus for strategic planning.

The MAC/FCB/OSDC complex. New York City's 1975–78 financial crisis left a complex of institutions that changed the manner in which public policy was made. Although the initial power of the Municipal Assistance Corporation (MAC), the Financial Control Board (FCB), and the Office of the Special Deputy Comptroller (OSDC) for New York City has ebbed, they remain important financing and monitoring agents for the city's public sector.

The advantage of using the MAC/FCB/OSDC complex as the center of a strategic planning process is that the new plan could be easily linked to both the financial planning process, which is now overseen by the Financial Control Board and to the financing and refinancing potential of the Municipal Assistance Corporation. The MAC/FCB/OSDC complex also has an advantage because it is the nexus between the city as public borrower and the investment community as private investor and because it oversees the city's public sector as a whole. Again, these characteristics would aid greatly in implementing planning — that is, enhancing the indicative aspects of a strategic plan — and possibly provide the most effective institutional locus for the plan.

Nevertheless, there are drawbacks. The most significant may be the fact that neither the MAC board nor the Financial Control Board is elected. Both are identified with business and corporate interests in New York and are largely viewed with suspicion by labor and community interests. While the MAC/FCB/OSDC complex may offer the most effective route toward implementing a strategic plan, it also brings into bold relief the legitimacy problems that strategic planning presents in a democracy.

The City Planning Commission (CPC). A fifth option is to have the City Planning Commission oversee a strategic planning process. The Planning Commission in New York City has a long history and represents the city's institutional memory regarding land use and capital planning. At different times in the city's history, the commission has drafted master development plans, such as the 1967 plan sponsored by the Lindsay administration, which heavily influenced development patterns. Specific innovations like amenity planning and ULURP leave the clear impression that the City Planning Commission could administer a strategic planning process. The commission has the additional advantage of reporting to the mayor through the Department of Planning and is the statutory adviser to several other city agencies and institutions, including the Board of Estimate. This advisory capacity could assist in adapting the executive budget and the capital plan to the strategic plan.

The advantage to Planning Commission involvement in strategic planning is also its great disadvantage — the historical identification of the commission with normally defined planning in the past. The emphasis of strategic planning is not so much on land use or capital planning, the CPC's traditional concerns, but on the relationship between long-term changes in an organization's environment and how the organization can adapt to those trends to minimize its vulnerability and maximize its gains. It is clear that any strategic planning process would have to cooperate with the Planning Commission and the Planning Department. Nevertheless, it may be true that because the commission has been so identified with other kinds of planning in the past that a new perspective is needed.

A separate institution. The final option is the creation of a separate institution to develop a strategic plan and oversee a planning process. The great advantage of a new institution is that the process itself would have few political constraints, since the institution would be independent. The Regional Planning Association's 1927 outline for arterial highways in and around New York shows how the persuasiveness of a plan may outweigh real political power. But by having such independence, a separate strategic planning mechanism builds no constituency, nor has one — except for the trained professionals who will offer it. Nor would there by any enforcement powers beyond the plan's persuasiveness. Without the direct backing of the executive, without being part of the political processes of the City Council or the Board of Estimate, an independent agency would be designing a purely informational plan with few "indicative" aspects.

Conclusion

The crisis facing New York City today is different from the one of 1975, and yet some of today's problems find their base in the solutions to the problems of the mid-1970s. The financial crisis precipitated structural changes in public policies designed to encourage economic development and to deal with fiscal scarcity. These changes, in turn, created wealth for some and hardship for others. The distribution of that new wealth and new hardship is at the center of today's political discourse in New York City and in much of urban America.

In the midst of such economic and social conflict, New York City also faces a legal crisis of representation. The evolution of case law on local institutions has always centered on a dialogue between two poles: whether local governments are essentially instruments of public choice for the local citizenry or an administrative convenience for higher levels for government. Whatever direction circuit and Supreme Court decisions take in the future — beyond the present *Morris* case — New York City itself must prepare a remedy to the social finding that one of its central institutional arrangements is proportionally skewed against the interests of the poorest of the five boroughs.

Strategic planning offers both an opportunity and a threat to any solution on the overriding issue of representation. As an informational plan, strategic planning would allow the numerous groups in New York City access to the kind of information available now only to the corporate sector and the mayoralty. As an informational plan, strategic planning could end the monopoly over economic and social data currently held by the most powerful groups in the city and provide a firmer base on which to debate the implications of various development policies. And yet a purely informational plan — even if it assisted advocates for the poor in the political debate — could not effect its own recommendations.

On the other hand, strategic planning as an indicative planning system — coordinating incentives and disincentives to influence private decision making — might be a mechanism to alter the balance of power among those whose gain in economic revitalization is obvious and those whose losses are hidden. Or, because of political access and understanding of corporate-sector strategic planning among some, an indicative plan might further imbalance community influence in their challenge to economic and political elites.

Stragetic planning will come. New York City, like most other large American cities, will adopt some type of strategic planning process, if only out of competitive necessity. In this process the balance between informational planning and indicative planning will largely be determined by the local institutional setting and the matrix of power relationships in each city. The issue that must necessarily be faced in urban governance is whether strategic planning advances the integrity of the political discourse or becomes a convenience for reinforcing the influence of economic elites.

NOTES

1. See, e.g., the last chapter of Wallace Sayre and Herbert Kaufman's *Governing New York City: Politics in the Metropolis* (New York: W.W. Norton, 1965); Demetrios Caraley, "Is the Large City Becoming Ungovernable?" in *Governing the City: Challenges and Options for New York City*, ed. Robert H. Connery and Demetrios Caraley (New York: Academy of Political Science, 1969); and Douglas Yates, *The Ungovernable City: The Politics of Urban Problems and Policy Making* (Cambridge, Mass.: M.I.T. Press, 1978).

2. William P. Anthony, *Practical Strategic Planning: A Guide and Manual for Line Managers* (Westport, Conn.: Quorum Books, 1985), pt. II.

3. Norton Long, *The Unwalled City* (New York: Basic Books, 1972).

4. Much of the literature on New York's mayoralty before the 1975 financial crisis recognized this, though analysts argued that political constraints actually rendered much of the legal power ineffective. See Yates; and Jewel Bellush, "Mayor-Board-Council: The Real World of New York City Government," a report to the Executive Director of the Citizens Union, mimeographed, 1973. The financial crisis redressed much of this political and managerial weakness by providing the mayor with a new array of financial and managerial tools to counter much of the tendency toward devolution of power within the city's public sector. See Robert W. Bailey, *The Crisis Regime: The MAC, the EFCB and the Political Impact of the New York City Financial Crisis* (Albany, N.Y.: State University of New York Press, 1984), chap. 6.

Holding Government Officials Accountable for Infrastructure Maintenance

EDWARD V. REGAN

"Maintenance is perhaps the single most important element of government's stewardship obligation. It is also the element that is easiest to defer, and the one most likely to be cut from the current expense budget."[1]

National Council on Public Works Improvement,
Final Report to the President and Congress,
February 1988

The collapse of New York City's West Side Highway in 1974 was a historic event. It demonstrated that public facilities essential to our lives and economy could fall victim to simple neglect. The collapse occurred because for years the city had failed to maintain the reinforced concrete roadway or to paint the steel structure that held it up. Unprotected from the elements, the highway lost the capacity to carry traffic — as was vividly shown when a truck plunged through its weakened deck.

Unfortunately, the West Side Highway incident was only the first in a series of major infrastructure failures in the New York metropolitan region. By the mid-1970s, for example, it became widely acknowledged that billions of dollars of new investment would be required to forestall the total breakdown of the city's world-renowned subway system. The collapse of a bridge over Connecticut's Mianus River was further evidence of the fragility of the public infrastructure. Crumbling walls and leaky roofs in many New York City school buildings created poor learning conditions and probably aggravated the already high student dropout rate. Finally, in the spring of 1988, New York City announced that the Williamsburg Bridge, a vital East River thoroughfare, was unsafe and would have to be closed, pending an assessment of costly repair and replacement options. Thus dramatized, issues that had begun to attract the attention of experts in the late 1970s now entered the public's awareness. Concern rose to a peak, and the "infrastructure crisis" could not be denied.

A sound capital plant is essential to the economic vitality and overall well-being of any city or region. Roads, bridges, schools, water lines, and sewerage systems are some of the things that people consider before deciding where to live or work or locate their businesses. Moreover, the failure of a major system could have catastrophic consequences. In New York City, for example, almost 2 million people a day depend on the public transportation network to get to and from work; even limited breakdowns inconvenience commuters and hurt businesses. The inability to move goods and services over the roads, bridges, and highways could cripple the economy of the entire region. Failures in other critical areas, such as the water delivery and sewerage systems, waste-treatment facilities, and water-pollution-control plants, would quickly jeopardize the economy and the health and safety of the city's population.

If maintained adequately, in conjunction with a sound capital replacement program, these important systems and facilities would perform almost indefinitely. Yet maintenance budgets are routinely starved by governments at all levels. Neglect, not age, is the root cause of most infrastructure failures in this country. Simply put, deferring maintenance is a handy expedient for public officials faced with problems in balancing their budgets. In fact, for many politicians, the term *deferred maintenance* is not even viewed as pejorative; it sounds like a government program!

But deferring maintenance is an unwise policy that usually leads to great cost and considerable disruption. Such has been the case in New York City, where a significant portion of the city's current $57 billion ten-year capital program is now being dedicated to rebuilding facilities to make up for past neglect.

This essay explores two principal problems that keep public officials from carrying out effective maintenance programs. It points out the need for countervailing measures, such as disclosure and planning requirements, to create a disincentive for public officials to defer maintenance. Using New York City as a case study, the essay then goes on to discuss changes in the city charter approved in 1988 that are designed to provide a counterweight to the forces that work against sound maintenance planning and budgeting.

The first problem, which can be called the "cut the ribbon and run" phenomenon, consists of a series of factors that tend to distort the rational decision-making process when it comes to appropriating funds for maintenance. The second problem can be called "seat of the pants" planning: since governments have yet to develop the systems and expertise to assess their maintenance requirements accurately, planning is minimal while action is heavily constrained by external budgetary factors.

"Cut the Ribbon and Run"

The expenditure of money to maintain facilities in good working condition is affected by the fact that many cities have not one but two annual budgets: an expense budget for current operating purposes, funded with current taxpayer dollars; and a capital budget for major capital improvements and replacement, financed largely with funds borrowed through bond issues and repaid over many years.

It is in the expense budget that municipal officials face the hard political choices they are compelled to make among competing demands for services like police protection, education, health care, fire, and child welfare, all of which have strong and vocal constituencies. In addition, cities must fund state- and federally-mandated items. In the case of New York City, such mandates, which include income maintenance (welfare), medical assistance (Medicaid), and special education, consume a large portion of the expense budget.

Expense budget dollars are scarce, and public officials tend to reserve them for the most visible and compelling activities. The cost of painting a bridge or repairing a road must also be paid from the expense budget. But maintenance activities, while undeniably in the public interest, tend to be regarded as having low visibility and correspondingly low political payoff. A television news editor, for example, is unlikely to be interested in bridge maintenance. Moreover, the consequences of the failure to scrape and paint a bridge in a particular year are not evident at the time. People do not think that the bridge might collapse in the next year or even in a decade or two.

If a bridge does collapse or require major rehabilitation from lack of maintenance, two things happen. First, it must be rebuilt. But now, instead of being charged to the expense budget, the new bridge can be financed out of the capital budget — with bond proceeds. Repayment of the principal and interest on the borrowed funds is stretched out over many years, and the only cost that needs to be funded through the expense budget, with current tax dollars, is the debt service charge on the borrowed funds. Thus the cumulative cost of years of neglect is transferred from one generation to the next. It would have made more sense to scrape and paint the bridge in the first place and prolong its life.

The second thing that happens is that when the bridge is rebuilt, or the road reopened or the school building rehabilitated, there is the opportunity for an "event" marked by a ribbon cutting, with press coverage and high visibility for all concerned. This is one reason why public officials like capital-spending programs. Regular maintenance, on the other hand, is simply not newsworthy.

Thus, there are significant fiscal and political incentives for public officials to defer maintenance — in good times as well as bad. These benefits lead them to overlook basic common sense and responsible management. Any homeowner knows that a leaky roof needs to be repaired before the house starts to fall down. Only in government is it viewed as more desirable to let the house fall down and rebuild it later and then to allow the rebuilt house to deteriorate all over again. This "cut the ribbon and run" mentality pervades the governmental decision-making process and has a devastating impact on the condition of a city's capital plant.

"Seat of the Pants" Planning

A 1984 Urban Institute study of maintenance strategies for capital facilities looked at ten American cities, including New York. Among other things, the study found that: "The primary factor determining total capital or operating budget maintenance allocations for an agency seemed to be the amount determined to be centrally available for the year. The numbers were heavily affected by the previous year's funding level and projections of the next year's revenues. *We did not find any local government in which a services funding level was determined by a formal, systematic examination of needs*, such as providing evidence that added funds could be applied to significantly increase service quality."[2]

These findings, as they pertain to New York City, confirm the observations of my staff over a ten-year period. Agency officials entrusted with the care and protection of our most valued public assets have not developed or even sought out information that could form the basis of rational maintenance planning. Instead, they take a "seat of the pants" approach heavily constrained by budgetary considerations.

Accompanying this approach is a woefully inadequate level of public disclosure. In the absence of reliable estimates of maintenance requirements, there is no yardstick against which to evaluate the adequacy of budgetary allocations. To complicate matters, municipal budgets are not typically organized in a way that facilitates a review of the amounts actually provided for maintenance. This is certainly the case in New York City. A citizen concerned about maintenance expenditures, for example, or a City Council member faced with difficult choices in voting on the budget may want to know how much the mayor's budget proposes to spend for maintenance and how much is really required. But this information does not exist, certainly not in a form suitable to promote informed decision making.

Decision makers ought to know, based on sound evidence and rigorous analysis, what maintenance requirements are — and what the costs of neglecting maintenance are likely to be. Such information could then be considered in the light of available resources when determining maintenance budgets. A local council member may well focus on whether the grass is being cut regularly in a park within his district, but not on whether a bridge there is being scraped and painted; he can see the grass getting longer but not the bridge rusting. As long as the public remains uninformed about the extent to which public assets are not being safeguarded, public officials will be encouraged to continue the prevailing pattern of neglect.

Charter Reform

As New York State comptroller, responsible among other things for bond issues, I have long been concerned about the lack of scheduled maintenance requirements for major capital projects, and I have proposed legislation to impose such requirements. Unfortunately, these proposals have languished in the state legislature. The establishment of the New York City Charter Revision Commission in 1986 presented a unique opportunity to tackle the issue of deferred maintenance at the city level, where many of the worst problems have arisen. Therefore, in May 1988, I sent then-Chairman Richard Ravitch a letter urging that the commission act to strengthen the charter's capital-maintenance requirements and enclosed draft legislative language that formed the basis of the ballot proposals.

In formulating an approach to counter the considerable forces that impede the implementation of adequate infrastructure maintenance programs, a basic question needed to be considered: whether to impose a specific legal mandate to provide the necessary maintenance. Such an approach might require that budgetary appropriations for maintenance be set at levels deemed sufficient to prevent the premature deterioration of capital facilities.

Rigorous requirements of this kind have been applied to public authorities that issue revenue bonds. The bonds whose proceeds rebuild the subway trackbed, for instance, also require the trackbed to be maintained. The premise behind such requirements is that bondholders have a legitimate concern about the condition of the facilities that they rely on to generate the revenues necessary to pay debt service on their bonds. Examples of entities subject to such requirements include New York City Transit Authority and the New York City Municipal Water Finance Authority created in 1985.

The New York City Transit Authority is required, under certain bond covenants, to engage an outside engineer to render an independent opinion as to the adequacy of its inspection, maintenance, and repair programs. The threshold test under the bond covenants is whether these programs are sufficient to ensure the continued operation of the transit system. Maintenance costs must be logically derived, reasonably estimated, and provided for in the Transit Authority's operating budget. Similarly, the city's Water Authority is obligated to retain an independent engineer for the purpose of certifying the reasonableness of the amounts required to operate and maintain the city's water and sewerage systems.

Where, as in New York City, capital facilities are funded by general obligation bonds rather than revenue bonds, the arguments in favor of required maintenance are different. Governments, through their capital budgets, borrow large sums of money to pay for capital improvements. These bonds are secured not by a specific revenue stream but by the "full faith and credit" of the issuing entity. Principal and interest payments on these borrowed funds are stretched out over many years, the costs to be borne largely by future taxpayers. This plan makes sense in theory, since future taxpayers also realize the social and economic benefits of facilities that are financed with the borrowed funds. But for practical purposes, these future gains require that newly constructed facilities be maintained in sound condition. Otherwise, as has turned out all too often to be the case, future taxpayers will pay twice: once to build the facility and again to rebuild it prematurely because it was neglected.

This system hardly seems fair. It is therefore appropriate to argue that, when governments obtain long-term loans to fund capital improvements, a covenant is implicit in that transaction to maintain them properly so that those who will pay the bills in the future are assured of receiving the benefits as well. Since governments have failed to recognize and live up to that covenant, there are grounds for arguing further that it should be made explicit.

The major benefit of this approach, however, can also be seen as a major weakness. Nondiscretionary spending requirements constrain the budgetary choices available to public officials, and this in turn diminishes their accountability. New York City's budget already contains significant nondiscretionary spending requirements. For example, like many other cities, New York is required to make actuarially determined annual contributions to its pension systems and to pay set levels of annual debt service on its borrowings. In addition, New York State requires its localities, including New York City, to pay a share of the state's $12 billion Medicaid and public assistance expenses. The city's elected officials have much less direct control over these expenses than they do, for example, over staffing levels or equipment purchases.

If public officials are to be held accountable for their performance, they must have the authority to make tough choices in their budgetary deliberations. Less discretion means less accountability. From this perspective, adding new spending requirements may not be the best policy. A preferable approach, therefore, is to level the playing field so that maintenance can compete on a more even basis with other budgetary priorities. This approach has been adopted in the revisions to New York City's charter. While leaving the determination of the amounts to be spent on capital-plant maintenance in any given year in the hands of public officials, where it belongs, the charter now contains provisions requiring full and timely disclosure of budgetary choices. The new charter provisions do not provide absolute assurance that neglect of the infrastructure will be curtailed once and for all. Before such neglect comes about through a failure to appropriate funds, however, legislative bodies and the public would have to recognize and consent to this to a much greater degree than ever before.

The charter revisions specifically require the city to inventory the capital plant, assess its condition, and develop a four-year plan setting forth the budgetary requirements for maintaining the capital plant in a state of good repair. The estimates contained in this plan must be certified as to their reasonableness by professional engineers or architects, who may be either in-house or independent, as the city chooses. The responsibility for the maintenance of each component of the city's capital plant must also be assigned to a particular agency or department, thereby establishing clear lines of accountability at the appropriate managerial level.

The new charter provisions require the mayor, when submitting his executive budget, to set forth the amounts provided for maintenance of the city's capital plant and explain any differences between these amounts and the levels certified as being needed for this purpose. The mayor must also report on the actual expenditures for maintenance in the previous and current years and explain any variances between planned and actual expenditures. This requirement is intended to promote ongoing vigilance over maintenance appropriations both during the budget-adoption process and throughout the budget year.

To keep the process manageable, only facilities that have a minimum capital cost of $10 million and a useful life of at least ten years must be included in the plan. Of course, the mayor may find it useful to expand the report to cover facilities and projects that do not fall within these criteria, and the new charter provisions do not preclude him from doing so.

Conclusion

Failure to provide adequate maintenance ultimately inflicts great harm on a municipality's physical and financial condition. It inevitably results in a deteriorating physical plant, disruption of services, and heavy costs in both the capital and expense budgets to repair and replace neglected facilities.

In November 1988, New York City's voters overwhelmingly endorsed proposals for improving infrastructure maintenance. The vote in favor of these proposals was the largest given to any of the five charter questions on the ballot (over 88 percent). It seems clear that when asked the attentive electorate will support the broad public interest in adequate maintenance programs.

The new charter provisions are a measured and appropriate response to the formidable impediments to the development of adequate maintenance policies that are inherent in the political process. A formal systematic evaluation of maintenance needs will provide a sound basis for budgetary and operational planning that is currently lacking. Expanded and timely public disclosure of the city's maintenance policies will make it politically more difficult to neglect maintenance.

Of course, accomplishing constructive change entails more than just passing a law. In implementing these provisions, New York City will be breaking new ground, and in so doing it will undoubtedly confront problems that were not envisioned in drafting the charter amendments. The diligence and creativity that will be required during the implementation phase will be central to the overall effectiveness of the process in the future. The city administration has adopted a positive approach to implementation of the new provisions. The city's Office of Management and Budget has been designated to coordinate a citywide effort, and each capital facility-using agency has designated a representative to represent it on all related matters. Also, the city is in the process of letting a contract for consulting assistance by seeking outside expertise. This seems like a good start.

The reasons for neglecting maintenance go beyond the failings of any one city administration. They are virtually inherent in the budget process. The measures that have been adopted in New York City, through the process of charter revision, show great promise as a means of counterbalancing these considerable forces. The experience in New York City should be monitored closely by other jurisdictions with similar problems.

NOTES

1. National Council on Public Works Improvement, *Foundations: A Report on America's Public Works; Final Report to the President and Congress* (Washington, D.C., 1988), 21.

2. Harry P. Hatry and Bruce G. Steinthal, *Guide to Selecting Maintenance Strategies for Capital Facilities* (Washington, D.C.: The Urban Institute Press, 1984), 72. (Emphasis added.)

Toward Charter Change for Better Land Governance

RONALD H. SILVERMAN

The future of New York City depends in important ways on the use and abuse of local real estate. Even if the federal courts had not required a revision of the New York City charter, the great development wars of the 1980s would have drawn public and professional attention to a variety of fundamental quality-of-life issues. In more generalized terms: At what point does development become overdevelopment, even in densely populated New York City? When does a residential development for profit unjustifiably depreciate neighborhood values? How are the city's growing needs for homeless shelters, jail barges, waste disposal, and other public facilities to be reconciled with the competing interests of vulnerable neighborhoods? In more specific terms: How are we to mitigate the undesirable spillover effects of megaprojects like the redevelopment of the Times Square area and the substantial Metrotech office park project in Brooklyn? Is public access to the East River to be forever barred by a wall of luxury buildings and expanding hospitals? Should private houses in quiet middle-class areas of Queens and Brooklyn be leased or purchased by the city for the care of abandoned infants?

To resolve such contentious quality-of-life issues, the New York City charter has long provided the cornerstone for an ambitious and complicated decision-making system that allows the city to engage in a wide variety of planning, zoning, and other regulatory actions. Because this land-governance system is both difficult to understand and often imperfect in its operations, it has become a special subject of interest for those most concerned with the revision of the current New York City charter.[1]

Describing the System

A comprehensive introduction to the current New York City land-governance system invites historical, "formal," and "functional" descriptive efforts. Even the briefest historical overview identifies a long history of debate and collective ambivalence over fundamental process questions that are still important. Since the inception of the system just before the city's first and pioneering zoning resolution of 1916, for example, concerned citizens and city officials have debated whether a more centralized or more decentralized land-governance system was preferable. Basic policy debates through the years also raised a second large and perhaps even more important question: What shall be the respective land-governance roles for professionals, elected officials, and the public at large?

The extended debate over such essentially "political" questions, as well as numerous process issues of a more technical character, may be organized with reference to successive historical periods, each commencing with a certain noteworthy event: the zoning resolution of 1916; the Thacher charter revision (1936); the replacement zoning resolution of 1960 and the Cahill charter revision (1961); the Goodman charter revision (1975); and the Ravitch/Schwarz charter revision (1988–89).

The New York City Zoning Resolution, ultimately approved by the Board of Estimate and Apportionment in July 1916, generated and influenced widespread national enthusiasm for comprehensive municipal zoning. The administration of the new zoning resolution, however, was quickly captured by certain local and special interests. During the 1920s and early 1930s, members of the Board of Estimate controlled the application of and amendments to the city's zoning resolution, often in response to aggressive special-interest groups and self-serving property owners seeking particular localized development advantages. Requests for permission to develop were typically funneled through borough party organizations and the borough president's offices to the Board of Estimate. Land-use deliberations by the Board of Estimate, then dominated by the borough presidents, were apparently much influenced by the custom of "borough courtesy." When a borough president advised a vote for or against a development proposal in his borough, the other members were much inclined to defer, fully expecting similar deference with regard to their own land-use problems.

Such a localized and heavily politicized land-governance system also invited a certain conspicuous degree of corruption, particularly in and around agencies like the city's Board of Standards and Appeals. By the late 1920s, and extending into the early 1930s, concerns over partisan politics, corruption, and the lack of centralized administration and planning helped to shape a new reform agenda, inevitably influenced by the Great Depression and the New Deal.

In early 1935, Mayor Fiorello H. LaGuardia appointed a particularly important charter revision commisison, chaired by Judge Thomas Thacher. The Thacher commission was especially responsive to suggestions that the land-governance system be centralized in a new city planning commission. The final report of the Thacher commission noted that the new agency was to be: "a responsible, independent [city planning] commission concerned with the welfare of the whole city to advise and report upon all questions affecting the growth of the city, including the expenditure of capital funds, changes in zoning and changes in the city map."[2] In the judgment of many critics and reformers, Mayor LaGuardia among them, the Board of Estimate "was too partisan and too borough-conscious to have a free hand over planning matters."[3] As a result, the land-governance powers of the Board of Estimate were to be sharply reduced, with the Thacher charter incorporating the most extreme set of restrictions on Board of Estimate zoning and planning powers in the city's history.

Nonetheless, this determined reaction to the land-use related excesses of the Board of Estimate hardly ensured the success of the new central City Planning Commission (CPC). Despite the importance that the Thacher commission placed on centralized planning and the preparation of a master plan for the entire city, the new City Planning Commission failed to produce either an official master plan or a comprehensive revision of the original 1916 zoning resolution. In fact, the CPC's "nonpolitical voice promoting the general interest" appeared to be a poor match for self-serving local interests and assorted borough warriors during much of the 1938–45 period and beyond.

While a comprehensive replacement zoning resolution, incorporating various regulatory innovations, was finally approved by the Board of Estimate in December 1960 after considerable reform efforts during the late 1950s, public and professional skepticism continued to grow both about the effectiveness of the CPC and about the prospects for comprehensive planning. Disappointment over the CPC's efforts to implement its ambitious six-volume "Plan for New York," published in the late 1960s, contributed to the formal rejection in 1975 of the master plan requirement earlier incorporated into the Thacher charter.

The relatively modest changes in the land-governance system wrought by the 1961 Cahill charter revision did little more than to strengthen mayoral land-use powers. The 1961 charter, despite certain formal provisions for enhanced community participation in the system, seemed inadequate to the challenges of the later 1960s and early 1970s. Whether or not the social problems and civil unrest of that turbulent period truly reflected fundamental social changes, the final report of the 1975 Goodman Charter Revision Commission was particularly concerned with the "deep citizen disaffection with municipal government, as presently structured." While the Goodman commission's final "planning" proposals were unhappily constrained by the city's fiscal crisis of the mid-1970s, they included a number of seemingly important changes, appropriately described in the words of the commission's final report:

(1) The Planning Commission shall have at least *one member from each borough.*

(2) The *Master Plan* shall be *eliminated* and replaced with flexible requirements for Citywide and local plans for the development and improvement of the City. Plans may be initiated by the Mayor, City Planning Commission, borough boards and community boards. All plans shall be reviewed by the City Planning Commission and approved by the Board of Estimate.

(3) *Advance notification* of all preliminary and final plans of public agencies, public benefit corporations and private agencies and developers for the use of City land shall be provided to the affected community boards and borough presidents.

(4) A *uniform procedure* shall be established for the review of land use subject to City

regulation. The procedure shall apply to changes in the city map, designations of zoning districts, housing and urban renewal projects and plans, site selection, franchises and revocable consents, special permits and such other matters specified by the Board of Estimate and the City Planning Commission. The uniform procedure shall involve initial review by the affected community board, discretionary review by any borough board if a matter involves two or more districts, and central review by the City Planning Commission and Board of Estimate.[4]

The new system, formally effective as of 1977, was to incorporate a newly specified and systematic process for multiple agency reviews, with new provisions for both public participation and a newly clarified and enhanced role for the Board of Estimate as the central political agency of last resort, even with respect to hardship variance and special permit decisions of the Board of Standards and Appeals. Despite the formal charter declaration that the New York City Council "shall be vested with the legislative power of the city," the 1975 Goodman charter revision continued to exclude the council almost entirely from the land-governance process, just as the previous Thacher and Cahill charters had done.

While the scope of this essay precludes detailed formal description of the current system's many component agencies and their duties, relationships, and distinctive procedures, it is appropriate to emphasize certain especially noteworthy formal features. First, the formal land-governance system, provided for by the Goodman charter of 1975, is very complex. No fewer than eleven city agencies, departments, and official actors play important roles in the current system: (1) Board of Estimate, (2) mayor, (3) borough presidents, (4) City Planning Commission, (5) City Planning Commission chairman/director of City Planning, (6) Department of City Planning, (7) Community Boards, (8) Department of Buildings, (9) Board of Standards and Appeals, (10) Landmarks Preservation Commission, and (11) Department of Environmental Protection. Several other charter agencies, such as the Borough Boards, the Art Commission, the Department of Housing Preservation and Development, the Department of Parks and Recreation, and the Department of Ports, International Trade and Commerce, play less important or more occasional roles in the total land-governance system.

In addition to this large number of agencies and actors, the New York City charter specifies certain decisional procedures and regulatory processes in great detail. The much discussed Uniform Land Use Review Procedure (ULURP), for example, receives extended charter treatment. This process, regarded by the Goodman charter commission as "perhaps the most striking innovation of the new [1977] charter" was especially designed to convert community involvement from "a haphazard ad hoc basis" to an assured and systematic role in multiagency deliberations over various discretionary land-use matters. ULURP was conceived of as an especially useful arrangement for the disposition of not only controversial zoning changes and applications for special permits but also for reviewing the sale or lease of real estate by or to the city, as well as site selections for various capital and infrastructure projects. While the process was predictably time consuming, it was to be strictly conducted in accordance with a charter-specified timetable at every stage, as illustrated by figure 1.[5]

FIGURE 1

Uniform Land use Review Procedures—Section 197c, New York City Charter

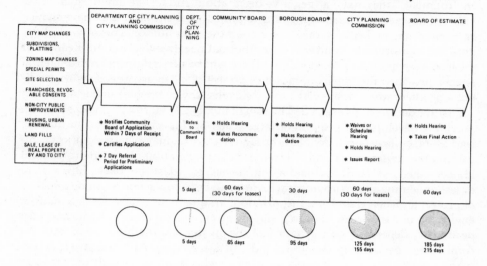

* Items which involve more than one Community Board are referred to the Borough Board.

The formal complexity of the total land-governance system, moreover, is also related to the limitations of the charter text itself. However detailed its ULURP provisions, the current charter is also strikingly incomplete in providing for the total land-governance system. Other formal legal instruments, external to the charter itself, provide important components of the total system. The city's administrative code, executive orders, agency rules and regulations, and even state and local laws providing various property-tax policies all include instrumental parts of an exceedingly complex system. The New York City Zoning Resolution itself both implements and supplements the charter and provides an especially important land-use policy and operational cornerstone.

The costly and controversial City Environmental Quality Review (CEQR) process is mentioned nowhere in the current charter. Rather, a mayoral executive order, issued in 1977 and designed to implement controlling state legislation, provides guiding detail. Under Executive Order 91, the Department of City Planning and the Department of Environmental Protection have been designated as the "co-lead agencies" for most environmental reviews. While recent litigation may require changes in this administrative arrangement, the current CEQR process begins with the submission of a "project data statement" to the co-lead agencies by any applicant who seeks a discretionary land-use action from the city (e.g., special permit or site-specific amendment to the New York City Zoning Resolution). In cases where the lead agencies determine that a project has "no significant effects on the environment," they issue a "negative declaration" ending the environmental review. If, however, the lead agencies determine that the project may have significant environmental effects, they may issue either a "conditional negative declaration" or a "positive declaration." A conditional negative declaration means that the lead agencies have concluded that there will be no significant environmental effects, provided the applicant modifies project plans in accordance with conditions or alternatives designed to avoid adverse environmental impacts.

Positive declarations are issued in a small number of more extreme cases, often involving development projects of large scale. Such declarations mean that the lead agencies have concluded that the land-use action may have a significant impact on the environment and will require the preparation of an "environmental impact statement" (EIS). Depending on the negotiated "scope" of the EIS, a more or less wide-ranging environmental review will be conducted to examine a variety of project impacts related to transportation, air quality, waste disposal, and other environmental concerns. Certain planning, economic, and social factors may also be studied, depending on the nature of the project and the outcome of "scoping conferences" between the developer and lead agency staff. After a draft EIS is prepared, and the mandatory public hearing is held, lead agency staff may require supplements to and modifications in the draft EIS. A revised draft EIS will be declared a final EIS by the lead agencies provided that they conclude that the project's adverse environmental effects have been sufficiently minimized or avoided. Once the EIS is certified as final, the project sponsors can proceed to any further review stage, like ULURP, that may be required.

Even the barest sketch of the numerous charter and noncharter components of the larger land-governance system, therefore, suggests an extended and exceedingly complex process, with important implications for charter revision efforts. Most important, excessive formal complexity unhappily works to make the land-governance system largely inaccessible to the understanding of most citizens. While well-informed voters may influence the evolving structure and operations of the system, it is also clear that more is required to hold it accountable than a conventional exercise of the local franchise. This specialized system requires a design that provides for the responsible and restraining oversight of different monitoring agencies.

There is, however, still another useful way to describe New York City's land-governance system. In addition to historical and formal modes of description, the system also invites a simplified but deeper description in certain "functional" terms. While there are scientific and practical limits to our ability to describe the system in terms of its real functions, effects, or consequences, even an imperfect descriptive effort of this kind enhances understanding and reveals something closer to the important realities of the system.

In fact, it is misleading to describe this system as a "planning" process. The use of such ambiguous terminology, so freighted with historical failure and debatable policy preferences, often works to obscure more fundamentally important or core characteristics. Whatever else New York City's land-governance system may be, it is actually a system:

(1) for the very ambitious regulation of land;

(2) that reduces and increases land-related wealth, often distributing and redistributing land-related "goods" and "bads" in controversial ways;

(3) that reflects numerous, complex, and sometimes inconsistent goals and policies; and

(4) that engages or aspires to engage in increasingly sophisticated forms of impact analysis, despite certain limited empirical methods and scarce technical resources.

These key real-world characteristics are especially interesting for their "linked" implications. Certain other important characteristics are linked to, implied by, or even compelled by these core features. Conflict, for example, is the predictable result of any system that seeks ambitiously to regulate land use and development in a variety of important wealth-affecting ways. Clearly, a system that distributes and redistributes land-related wealth, or advantages and disadvantages, in questionable ways is bound to generate its fair share of controversy.

For much the same reasons, the city system has been and is likely to remain highly political in character. Any such system that affects the income, wealth, and welfare of numerous and diverse people, in a large variety of tangible and intangible ways, is bound to attract the devoted attention of elected officials. Though the system aspires to be more data-based and even scientific in certain ways, it can hardly avoid the need to accommodate sharply competing interests and complex land-governance goals that are sometimes incompatible or in a state of policy tension.

The land-governance system is just as predictably discretionary in character. It has relied and will continue to rely on various forms of selective or differential decision making in response to a complex and changing city environment. The ambitious New York City system needs a certain discretionary latitude to make different decisions in different circumstances. Indeed, the growing capacity for impact and data-based analysis encourages discretionary determinations that are more responsive to unique or distinguishing development characteristics.

In turn, a highly discretionary system will incorporate a certain degree of land-use bargaining. Whether or not we approve, city officials, private developers, community boards, and neighborhood organizations all have powerful reasons to bargain with one another over land-use matters. To the extent that bargaining serves to advance certain important fiscal objectives, city officials can hardly be expected to resist the temptation.

A highly discretionary land-governance system that frequently involves bargaining is also likely to be costly. In fact, all the core characteristics predict noteworthy administrative costs. The very complexity of the city's ambitious regulatory system almost inevitably creates certain delays, as well as other direct and indirect costs. The land-governance system now needs and will need the costly efforts of numerous city officials, private developers, and their even more numerous professional employees and agents. Moreover, the system engages the serious interest of numerous citizens and community organizations. Public participation, of course, is hardly cost-free.

Finally, corruption is not only the occasional product of corrupt officials and others but is perhaps a durable if not permanent feature of New York City's land-governance system. This depressing conclusion is linked to many of the real-world characteristics identified above — discretion, bargaining, and seemingly high administrative costs. The high dollar stakes for private developers, in particular, create certain undeniable incentives for a variety of more or less subtle behaviors of questionable honesty. The complex land-governance system also provides numerous opportunities for corrupt behavior in many different forms at many different stages of the total process.

Evaluating the System

Evaluating the current land-governance system is even more difficult than describing it. Efforts at result-oriented analysis are particularly likely to be unsuccessful. It is simply too difficult to assess the net effects of either the land-governance system as a whole or its component parts in cost-benefit terms.

Fortunately, we can respectively employ certain process standards or values. "Process values" are prized for two reasons. First, they are likely to produce desirable process results or effects, even if such net results cannot be independently verified. Second, such values are worthy features in and of themselves. It somehow seems intuitively right that the city's land-governance system be both "rational" and "honest" in character.

Together, certain important process values constitute a set of workable standards. Most thoughtful observers agree that the New York City system for land governance will be a better system if it:

(1) is *rational*,

(2) with reasonable administrative costs;

(3) allows for the reasonable *participation* of competing interests;

(4) has appropriate *flexibility* in responding to new and changing needs and demands;

(5) is reasonably *predictable*, in terms of both its decisional outcomes and procedures; and

(6) has a developed capacity for *peaceful resolutions* of trouble cases,

(7) in substantially *honest* ways,

(8) so that the process itself is widely regarded as *legitimate* in character and broadly worthy of respect among both winners and losers.

Even such compelling standards, however, have their limitations. An attempt to specify the meaning of a general term like *participation* reveals a deeply ambiguous concept that needs clarification and requires careful usage. Moreover, there are certain tensions, if not inconsistencies, between and among certain process standards. A "rational" system, which engages in careful fact-finding and a comprehensive assessment of all relevant policies, may also be a system much delayed in making final land-use determinations. Similarly, a "flexible" system, truly responsive to changing needs and circumstances, may be less predictable and invite certain forms of dishonesty.

In short, most efforts to assess the success or failure of the city system, in whole or by parts, are likely to be imperfect. Even if we agree that result-oriented or cost-benefit type evaluations are impractical, we are still forced to employ a set of initially appealing but very complex if not inconsistent process standards or values.

Efforts to apply such process standards to the current land-governance system, however, do help identify certain important and sometimes even curable problems. The current system, for example, aspires to be an increasingly rational process. Indeed, in certain impressive ways, it has improved its capacity for important kinds of data collection and impact analysis. Nonetheless, the very same system still suffers from certain prominent deficiencies. Rational impact analysis is still sometimes superficial or substantially avoided. When a project complies with existing zoning, for example, it proceeds "as of right" without a particularized staff study of environmental and other specific project consequences.

Even when the system attempts serious impact analysis, usually connected to the City Environmental Quality Review process, it is often criticized. Some critics charge that the administration of the CEQR process suffers from excessive delays and uncertainties, as well as from a lack of standards to guide staff discretion at certain key points. Finally, critics have argued that in most cases neither the community boards nor the Board of Estimate has the resources to exercise truly rational oversight.

The system is also arguably flawed when measured against a second process standard: administrative costs. The charter-specified Uniform Land Use Review Procedure (ULURP) may needlessly delay certain minor projects that do not require extended review at several different agency levels. Conversely, ULURP may not apply to certain much more important land-use actions. Such exclusions from ULURP may contribute to costly controversy surrounding certain discretionary land-use actions.

The problem of costly delay is especially related to the so-called precertification stage, prior to ULURP itself. While the charter text does not use the word *precertification* or specify relevant detail, the period after an application has been filed for discretionary land-use action but before ULURP commences is a key and troublesome stage in the total process. Before a project application is sent to the relevant community board for review, as the first stage in ULURP, the staff of the Department of City Planning must certify the application as complete and ready for ULURP. Such certification not only depends on the submission of certain data but on completion of a significant portion of the CEQR process. CEQR, ultimately required by state law, will be more or less complicated and extended, depending on the nature of the project and its environmental impacts. Particularly when a comprehensive environmental impact statement is required, the environmental review process may extend the precertification stage prior to ULURP for months, if not years.

Nonetheless, while developers commonly complain about costly administrative delays and staff indecision, the significance of such delays and other dollar administrative costs may depend on a number of project, market, and other circumstances. While it is arguable that both private developments and public projects are affected by processing delays and other costs, such costs may be relatively less significant for high-profit projects. At the same time, information, processing, and delay-related costs may be particularly significant for smaller private developers and with respect to certain public or publicly assisted projects having only minimal or no profit margins available to absorb administrative costs.

The success of the land-governance system may also be measured against a third important standard. Is the system "appropriately participatory" in character? That is, does it permit just the right degree of public or community participation without submitting complex land-use issues to an uninformed, even impassioned process of group decision making?

While *participation* is virtually synonymous for some with the term *democracy*, it is also a very complex concept that means different things to different persons involved in the land-governance system. Nonetheless, a notable common thread runs through much of the debate and controversy over the participatory character of the city's current land-governance system. Many proponents and opponents of more public and community participation agree that its participatory elements are generally unsatisfactory.

Many community board members and certain City Council members and borough presidents argue that:

• Discretionary decision making should be decentralized, especially through the establishment of borough-level agencies, connected perhaps to the offices of the borough presidents.

• The community boards lack influence over staff input during, and decisions at, the precertification stage, particularly with respect to certain aspects of CEQR.

• The community boards lack access to and influence over City Planning Commission deliberations.

• The community boards lack access to important land-use data.

• The community boards lack professional staff assistance and other technical resources.

• Too many important land-use matters, with significant community impacts, are excluded from the scope of ULURP and, therefore, receive inadequate community review.

• Too many legislative-type hearings, particularly Board of Estimate hearings, are merely empty and futile exercises in late-night speechmaking.

There has also been sharp criticism at the other extreme. Some critics of the current system complain that the community boards have too much rather than too litle power. Particularly in the underdeveloped outer boroughs, some community boards have been criticized for their obstructionist if not exclusionary activities. Certain community boards have also been criticized for bargaining with private developers. In some cases, community boards and certain neighborhood groups have exchanged their approvals of particular projects for a variety of developer concessions in kind or in cash. Mayor Edward I. Koch, the chair of the City Planning Commission, and others have criticized this form of bargaining and have proposed restrictive new guidelines.

In short, the current land-governance system has been faulted both for being insufficiently participatory and for allowing excessive power, especially bargaining power, to the community boards. Whether or not complaints about participation are justified, no aspect of the system has attracted quite the same passionate attention. Clearly, numerous New Yorkers care deeply about the democratic qualities of their land-governance system.

A fourth standard for evaluating the system is reflected in the following question: Is the current land-governance system "appropriately flexible"? Critics of very different persuasions have charged either that the system is too inflexible or that it is much too flexible insofar as it permits numerous discretionary determinations and frequent land-use bargains. In fact, both of these competing criticisms are worthy of serious consideration. The Uniform Land Use Review Procedure appears too rigid in treating relatively minor matters in much the same way as it provides for the disposition of more important ones. The formal ULURP schedule, specified in detail in the charter itself, permits too little opportunity for expedited decision making even where it would be clearly appropriate.

The system, however, has more often been criticized for its excessive flexibility. Land-use deal making is seen as unfair when there is a disparity in bargaining position and resources. Developers complain that they are often coerced into making certain concessions, either in kind or in cash, that have little or nothing to do with the mitigation of adverse development impacts or the environmental effects of their projects. Conversely, some community groups and elected officials object to deal making in principle because they fear that city agencies are likely to be distracted if not overwhelmed by the expertise and superior resources of private developers.

City officials are also faulted for being too preoccupied with the revenue and fiscal implications of new private development, often at the sacrifice of other more important planning values. If New York City agencies regularly exchange additional development densities for cash or contributions in kind like subway-station improvements, other worthy goals like the provision of adequate light, air, and open space may well be submerged in the process.

In addition, too much land-use bargaining will burden and distract both staff professionals and members of agencies like the City Planning Commission. Deal making, therefore, may make an already high-cost governance system even more costly to administer. For many critics, land-use deals are only likely to encourage various forms of dishonesty. At a minimum, the excessive use of regulatory descretion, in exchange for certain attractive considerations, threatens to produce the appearance if not the fact of corruption.

Nonetheless, criticism of the system as excessively flexible may fail to take into account certain important real world factors. New York City, with its complex and quickly changing environment, poses a special challenge to land-use regulators. While a much less discretionary system, with land-use bargaining severely restricted, is appealing for a number of reasons, it is also unlikely as a practical matter. The city's land-governance system can hardly dispense with the need to differentiate numerous projects and to exchange development and regulatory concessions. While a system providing more opportunities for as-of-right development seems tempting, public criticism of such a deregulation strategy is also predictable.

In addition, a more cooperative system for accommodating competing land-use interests may be more consistent with a spirit of local democracy. In short, it is arguable, all factors considered, that discretionary bargaining is the better way to successful land governance, provided it can be channeled and confined in responsible ways.

While perfect predictability may be an elusive if not impossible goal in a dynamic and complex real estate economy, we continue to seek both process and outcome predictability. Despite the current charter specifications controlling ULURP, many critics have noted the lack of guiding detail with respect to the precertification stage. Staff review of a developer's application, prior to the formal commencement of ULURP, may continue for an extended and unpredictable period. Similarly, the City Environmental Quality Review process has been criticized for its subjective decisional standards. In short, the land-governance system has been characterized as unpredictable because it lacks certain important time limits and clarified decision-making standards.

In addition, the prospects for a predictable process and predictable decisional outcomes are sure to be adversely affected by staff turnover, inexperience, and other staff and agency limitations, especially in the context of a system that regularly incorporates new zoning and other regulatory innovations. Political considerations also count. Political agencies like the Board of Estimate are virtually certain to produce a number of creative and unpredicted compromises. Finally, the constant threat of litigation contributes to the system's reputation for unpredictability.

The litigation-related uncertainties surrounding the city's land-governance system also raise an important question: Is the system too conflict-ridden? The answer is obvious. Virtually all major private-sector projects, and many smaller ones, are sooner or later embroiled in controversy, if not actual litigation. Even seemingly worthy projects proposed by the most respected not-for-profit institutions like universities, museums, and hospitals are often met by intense neighborhood and public criticism. City agencies, in particular, have regularly provoked sharp community opposition to a variety of proposals related to the location of infrastructure and community service facilities like shelters for the homeless.

The costs of such conflict are both tangible and intangible in character. In addition to extended delays, compelled project changes, and the dollar costs of litigation, relations between and among private developers, city officials, and community groups are regularly compromised if not permanently impaired.

The dispute settlement capacity of the system has also been faulted for its lack of neutral or independent decision making. Many critics charge that the professional staff of the Department of City Planning and most members of the City Planning Commission are "players" with a point of view dictated by the mayor rather than neutral umpires exercising independent judgment and oversight. Despite a recent show of independence by some borough presidents, various critics regard the Board of Estimate as little more than a feeble check against unwise mayoral land-use decisions. As a result, litigation is all the more inevitable, as opponents of certain discretionary land-use actions and determinations seek more independent and impartial forums.

The final standard used to evaluate the land-governance system is a particularly compelling one. To the extent that the system is less than honestly managed, it will forfeit an important measure of popular and professional respect. While there has been little or no recent evidence of raw bribery in the zoning and land-governance system, there is a long history of corruption in the Department of Buildings and, more generally, in the city's construction industry.

Moreover, the system's reputation for honesty depends in part on important appearances. The first and in some ways the most serious integrity problem relates to campaign contributions. In a word, many private developers have contributed large amounts of money to many members of and candidates for the Board of Estimate, in particular. Whether or not generous campaign contributions have influenced discretionary land-use determinations by elected officials, the land-governance system has clearly been compromised by this practice. Whatever the reality, the system *looks* as if regulatory favors are for sale. In response to this situation, the last three years have seen major changes, in the rules governing campaign contributions to city officials and candidates for city office adopted by the State Legislature, the City Council, and the city's voters in response to a charter commission ballot proposal.[6]

The system has also been compromised in other ways by various conflict-of-interest problems, some related to the "revolving door" between city agencies and private-sector development firms. While the problem is a complex one, some public officials have occasionally seemed less devoted to public service than to the pursuit of lucrative future private-sector employment. In 1988, the Charter Revision Commission proposed and the voters adopted a comprehensive new conflicts-of-interest chapter, which included strong postemployment restrictions.[7]

The land-governance system also suffers, in fact and in reputation, from the dishonest or negligent evasions of certain unprincipled developers. In recent years, too many developers have been caught in a pattern of deliberate noncompliance with various zoning rules and land-use regulations. Clearly, there is a need for improved enforcement mechanisms.

On balance, this general effort to evaluate the city's land-governance system produces a mixed judgment, though one to the negative side. In terms of the seven complex categories of evaluative or process standards, it seems fair to characterize the current system as increasingly committed to both more rational and more appropriately flexible forms of decision making—though not, of course, without certain important qualifications. At the same time, the current system is more flawed with respect to most of the other criteria. In the degree of public participation, predictability and integrity, the system seems more deficient than not. It is particularly noteworthy that it is conflict-ridden in the extreme. While the system may not suffer quite as much from delay and other "unreasonable" administrative costs as conventional wisdom suggests, it still inflicts seemingly high costs in both absolute dollar and other terms.

Such risky and somewhat subjective net judgments, of course, remain open to good-faith disagreements and continuing debate. What is less open to question, however, is the existence of an important set of negative public and professional attitudes. Even if the land-governance system were found to be less rather than more flawed, there is no denying the unpopularity of the current system.

In fact, the city's land-governance system may have lost its legitimacy. While the term is often used casually and imprecisely, legitimacy simply relates to the capacity of the current system to command popular and professional respect, from losers as well as winners. In this "legitimacy" sense, it is quite clear that the system is failing. Many New Yorkers, including some very well-informed ones, no longer believe that the status quo will do. Numerous critics, fairly or unfairly, appear to be firmly if not passionately convinced that the city's land-governance system must be changed in important if not fundamental ways.

Changing the Charter

Rational revision of the land-use portions of the current city charter, therefore, requires careful attention to a long agenda of problems. It also requires a secure but venturesome technical capacity to use a large inventory of concrete change devices, in different combinations, and in new structural arrangements.

It may or may not be appropriate to eliminate or to modify the powers of important existing agencies like the City Planning Commission, the Board of Standards and Appeals, and the Landmarks Preservation Commission. A logical catalog of interesting strategies and models for charter change, ranging from a minimal change model to near radical revisions, all require the careful consideration of agency procedures, membership and leadership options, available staff and technical resources, and the feasibility of distinguishing administrative from policy-making or legislative functions. A creative and combined use of new hearings options, supermajority voting rules, second-look procedures, and other process specifics may well lead to a promising new charter foundation for a usefully modified land-governance system.

At the same time, it is important to note a very important speculative element in even the most technically competent efforts to change the city's land-governance system. Whatever decisions are ultimately made about the roles of key agencies like the Board of Estimate, the City Council, the borough presidents, and the City Planning Commission, and however cautiously we estimate the effects of both major structural and more modest procedureal changes, we are inescapably engaged in a certain degree of guesswork. The real effects of substituting City Council oversight for final Board of Estimate reviews, for example, are difficult to predict, particularly over the longer term. Allowing borough presidents and community boards enhanced powers over private and public projects may or may not contribute, on balance, to the city's welfare. Given New York City's irrepressibly diverse and rapidly changing environment, there are obvious risks in securely predicting the effects of most charter changes.

In the final analysis, this cautionary note invites an important perspective on charter change as it bears on the regulation of local land uses and land-governance in general. It may be useful for certain purposes, especially for public relations, to conceive of charter revision as a local form of profoundly important constitutional change. At the same time, the wisest charter changes in the land-governance system may be more incremental than dramatic in character. It is also useful to consult the relevant history of previous charter revisions. With respect to land governance, the very same fundamental and perplexing issues have resisted durable resolutions. This in turn suggests that, however creative the charter changes of 1989, they are unlikely to be for all time.

NOTES

1. This essay is derived from a two-volume study, *Land Governance and the New York City Charter,* prepared by the author as a consultant to the New York City Charter Revision Commission. Neither that report nor this essay is intended as a reflection of the commission's views or positions, but both represent the conclusions of the author.

2. *Report of the New York City Charter Revision Commission* (17 August 1936) [Thacher Commission Report] in L. Tanzer, "The New York City Charter, Adopted November 3, 1936; with Source Notes, A History of the Charter and an Analysis and Summary . . ." (Clark Boardman Co., 1937), 473, 483. Among other reasons for proposing a new City Planning Commission, the Thacher commission hoped that the new agency would "publicly" confront elected officials "with the interests of the public at large. Too often such interest finds no advocacy because the local political or special interest is organized and the general interest is not," idem.

3. S.J. Makielski, Jr., *The Politics of Zoning: The New York City Experience* (Columbia University Press, 1966), 53.

4. *Final Report of the State Charter Revision [Goodman] Commission for New York City* (1975), 11. Emphasis in the original.

5. Department of City Planning, *Uniform Land Use Review Procedure: A Guide for Community Boards,* Jan. 1977, NYC DCP 77-04.

6. For more informaiton on this subject, see Page E. Bigelow, "From Norms to Rules: Regulating the Outside Interests of Public Officials," in this vol., 141–57.

7. For more information on this subject, see Herbert E. Alexander, "Campaign Finance Reform," in this vol., 123–40.

Index